Helping Male Survivors of
Sexual Violation to Recover

of related interest

Enhancing Sexual Health, Self-Identity and Well-being among Men who have Sex with Men
A Guide for Practitioners
Rusi Jaspal
ISBN 978 1 78592 322 7
eISBN 978 1 78450 636 0

Working with the Trauma of Rape and Sexual Violence
A Guide for Professionals
Sue J. Daniels
Foreword by Ivan Tyrrell
ISBN 978 1 78592 111 7
eISBN 978 1 78450 375 8

Helping Children to Tell About Sexual Abuse
Guidance for Helpers
Rosaleen McElvaney
ISBN 978 1 84905 712 7
eISBN 978 1 78450 235 5

Counselling Skills for Working with Shame
Christiane Sanderson
ISBN 978 1 84905 562 8
eISBN 978 1 78450 001 6

Counselling Skills for Working with Trauma
Healing From Child Sexual Abuse, Sexual Violence and Domestic Abuse
Christiane Sanderson
ISBN 978 1 84905 326 6
eISBN 978 0 85700 743 8

Introduction to Counselling Survivors of Interpersonal Trauma
Christiane Sanderson
ISBN 978 1 84985 693 5
eISBN 978 0 85700 213 6

Narrative Approaches to Working with Adult Male Survivors of Child Sexual Abuse
The Clients', the Counsellor's and the Researcher's Story
Kim Etherington
ISBN 978 1 85302 818 2
eISBN 978 0 85700 145 0

Helping Male Survivors of Sexual Violation to Recover

An Integrative Approach –
Stories from Therapy

SARAH VAN GOGH

Jessica Kingsley *Publishers*
London and Philadelphia

First published in 2018
by Jessica Kingsley Publishers
73 Collier Street
London N1 9BE, UK
and
400 Market Street, Suite 400
Philadelphia, PA 19106, USA

www.jkp.com

Library of Congress Cataloging in Publication Data
A CIP catalog record for this book is available from the Library of Congress

British Library Cataloguing in Publication Data
A CIP catalogue record for this book is available from the British Library

ISBN 978 1 78592 363 0
eISBN 978 1 78450 715 2

Printed and bound in Great Britain

Appreciations to all in the community of Re.Vision Centre for Counselling & Psychotherapy, and all colleagues and clients at Survivors UK, London, past and present. Thanks for help and support with my writing to: Beth Acheson, Sally Anderson, Antonia Boll, Roz Carroll, Catherine Culbert, Penny Culliford, Bridget Davey, Mary Eleftheriou, Brett Kahr, Sissy Lykou, Nicky Marshall, Thomas Moore, Sophia Neville, Alan Robertson, Chris Robertson and Ewa Robertson. Thanks to Greg Richards for help with the diagrams. Thanks to Elaine, Graham, Mark, Jacob and Michael for family support.

In memory of Dr Alan Corbett, an inspiring supervisor, and my father, Andrew Dudman, who both embodied the fact that teaching can be an act of love.

CONTENTS

Introduction   9

1   Containing and Working with a Male Survivor's Rage   15
    Sam

2   The Therapeutic Use of Music to Help with Dissociation   47
    Jay

3   The Need to Both Respect and Dismantle Defences   70
    George

4   Using the Imagination to Help Reconnection
    with a Transitional Object from Childhood   96
    Dami

5   Dissolving the Illusion that Abuse Was Love   119
    VJ

6   Chronic, Complex Trauma: The Legacy of Surviving
    Organised Child Sexual Abuse   148
    Stu

7   Time-Limited Work with a Male Survivor Experiencing
    Post-Traumatic Shock Disorder   180
    Neil

REFERENCES   220

FURTHER READING   222

INDEX   226

INTRODUCTION

THE SEXUAL VIOLATION OF MALES

Men who have experienced sexual violation often have a kind of invisibility in the world. They are not prominent in literature about therapy, in research about sexual violation, or even generally in the public awareness, although this has begun to change recently in the aftermath of the revelations about high-profile predatory figures in the media world and the abuse of young males in football and other sports. But, on the whole, the idea of a man or a male child being raped, sexually abused, manipulated or used by another is still a deep taboo for many people.

If we cannot face this taboo, we are collectively failing to look into the reason behind an enormous amount of suffering and even of death.

In an article in *Therapy Today*, Phil Mitchell, himself a male survivor of sexual violation and a specialist clinician in this field, makes the point that 'Of the 6,188 suicides registered in the UK in 2015, three quarters were males. It could be argued that, for some males, especially those who have been sexually exploited, death can be seen as preferable to being seen as less of a man' (Mitchell 2017).

Sadly, even some in the caring professions continue to feel that there is something so grotesquely awful and unthinkable, so incomprehensible – or even downright unbelievable – about a man or boy being sexually hurt or objectified, that they fear they do not have what it takes to be able to work with this issue or do not wish to even attempt it. In a systematic review of research published online in the *International Journal of Mental Health Nursing*, only 22 per cent of people using statutory mental health services are ever asked by mental health staff about previous experiences of abuse. Of those who were asked, women patients were far more likely to be asked than male patients (Read *et al.* 2017).

In nearly 20 years of working with male clients who have experienced sexual violation, I have seen a common factor in all the work I did with this client group which enabled them to feel less in pain, less alone, more hopeful, and better able to look after themselves and heal from their trauma. This common factor was that the person coming for help was offered a combination of three things. First, warmth and care from whoever worked with them. Second, the opportunity to think rigorously about whatever they are bringing into the consulting space. Third, that the work can happen in the context of a boundaried relationship with a person whom they trust and by whom they feel respected.

I have written this book to encourage and embolden those in the helping professions who think they might not have the capacity or skill to support this client group, to trust that they certainly can be of use to them, whenever they offer this combination of warmth and rigorous thinking within the context of a secure therapeutic relationship.

What follows is an account of some integrative therapy work, with men who have been sexually violated, in the form of seven fictionalised accounts. I have, in effect, written the type of book that I would have liked to read myself, before I worked with my first male client who had been sexually violated, to help get a sense of what sort of things I would hear from them, how it might feel to work with them, and what would probably be helpful and not so helpful for them.

Whenever I read books about a certain area of therapeutic work in order to inform myself better, I know that the parts which tend to catch and hold my attention and then stay in my memory as a resource are the case studies, the vignettes and the transcriptions of verbatim exchanges from a session. These give the flavour of who actually said what to whom, and they most clearly demonstrate why the therapist took the approach that they did, and, crucially, they show what happened as a result, both within the room, and in the client's life beyond the room.

It is certainly of great use for my 'left brain' thinking-self to read about theories and research findings. Yet my 'right brain', deeper, slower, more relational, intuitive-self needs to be shown how it actually *feels* in the room with the client, when those useful theories inform clinical practice. So I have made up the stories I am about to tell, in order to try and illustrate what it looks, sounds and feels like when a therapist works, in an integrative way, with different men who have experienced a variety of sexual violating experiences. To do so I have drawn on the nature of the real experiences and the real suffering of a wide variety of men I have worked with in different settings over the last 17 years, in an attempt to give a flavour of what it was like to witness their trauma, their courage and their will to recover. I have, as the saying goes, told small lies to tell a big truth.

The chapters that follow are fictional accounts of work that describe short- and long-term therapeutic work with men of varying backgrounds, ages and sexualities, who each experienced different kinds of sexual violation, some in childhood, some as adults. I have used the word 'therapist' to indicate anyone working explicitly with the emotional and psychological wellbeing of another. I have used the word 'client' to indicate an individual who comes for emotional and psychological support in any setting where such support is offered professionally. I have included in these fictional accounts one that tells the story of a piece of therapeutic work that, in some ways, was *not* effective enough. This is intended to reflect the reality of any therapist's work, and in particular, therapy with men who have suffered profound, prolonged and complex trauma and abuse. Such men need much more than weekly therapy sessions in order to heal, and our society still, unfortunately, often fails to adequately support many who have this painful history.

I hope that the format I have chosen, i.e. fictional accounts of a therapeutic process, reflects a basic truth that clinicians are forever discovering in their work and then attempting to disseminate in different ways: that effective therapy is not only about knowing and skilfully applying important ideas and techniques but is, ultimately, about forming a meaningful and feeling connection with the client, whether that lasts a few hours or several years.

I decided not to interrupt the narrative flow of each chapter with many explicit references and links to the theoretical frameworks that inform my interventions. However, I also did not want to be too much like the apocryphal old sailor who replies to a curious traveller who asks how he knows what to do in a storm, 'I don't rightly know, but when the storm comes, I just does it.'

I have, therefore, included below an outline and brief description of the theoretical models that can each contribute to an integrative approach to the therapy. Each chapter begins with a brief overview of the work, to help clarify the part played by a number of different therapeutic perspectives.

AN INTEGRATIVE THERAPY APPROACH

An integrative therapy approach could be said to bring the vital combination of warmth and rigour to three broad areas:

1. helping the client explore the past;
2. helping the client explore the present;
3. helping the client have a more conscious connection to what I call 'the beyond'. By that, I mean whatever it is that meaningfully goes beyond the everyday and the purely rational.

Figure 0.1 attempts to represent this as an image.

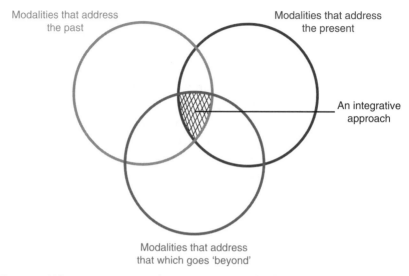

Figure 0.1 Where an integrative therapeutic approach is located

1. Modalities that help the address the past

Examples of approaches that help unpack what has crucially shaped an individual would include all those that come under the heading of a developmental approach, including:

- Attachment-based work.
- Work informed by what we know and are discovering about the physiology of how a human body develops and functions, in particular what we are learning about the nervous system and neurobiology, especially with reference to the impact of trauma.
- Psychoanalytic and psychodynamic theory/practice that offers a framework for seeing how early experiences have an enormous impact on each of us, which are lost to conscious awareness, and can only manifest via the unconscious.
- Work that looks at family systems and group dynamics, and provides insight into the relationship between an individual and the family/group/communities connected to that individual.

2. Modalities that help address the present

By 'the present' I mean the client's current day-to-day life, as well as the present of any one moment in a session.

- Gestalt therapy and other work that is influenced by the therapeutic approach of encouraging a focus on and amplification of the moment-by-moment experience of the client, in the session.
- The use of the phenomena of transference and countertransference to uncover important feelings and experiences for a client which have been buried in the unconscious, and which aid the therapist to allow the client to re-experience these more consciously and thereby integrate them. (See below for brief definitions of transference and countertransference.)
- Body-focused trauma work, that supports a client to thaw old, frozen traumas and pain, and other embodied work such as dance and movement therapies, and therapeutic approaches that incorporate the physical touch of the practitioner.
- Work that encourages a client to reflect on their current life and become more aware of the ways they think and feel which have become habitual and which may no longer serve them, in order to bring about life changes, such as the therapies that come under the heading of 'time-limited' and 'solution-focused' work, e.g. cognitive behavioural therapy (CBT).

3. Modalities that address that which goes 'beyond'
These include:

- A transpersonal paradigm that explicitly gives a place to the spiritual, soulful or mystical aspects of existence, such as work informed by the approaches of, for example, Jung and Assagioli, and by different aspects of faith traditions and from ancient indigenous wisdom, such as Shamanism or Wicca.
- Approaches that make deliberate space for the creative and imaginative, for instance by helping the client use art, music, drama, dance or storytelling, either explicitly in a session or elsewhere in their life.
- Approaches that foster a client's capacity to focus on *being* rather than *doing*, such as meditation, mindfulness, chanting, centring, grounding, etc.
- Work that supports and fosters an understanding of and ability to reflect on the larger stories against which an individual life plays out, in terms of socio-economics, ethnicity, gender, sexuality, etc. and aims to give a conscious space to this in the work.
- Approaches that foster a greater connection to the healing that comes from being in touch with, and belonging within, even larger stories, e.g. the story of being part of a line of ancestors, the story of the cycling of the seasons, and the story of being part of the diversity of life forms on this planet.

THE TERMS 'TRANSFERENCE' AND 'COUNTERTRANSFERENCE'

For anyone reading this book who is not familiar with the clinical terms of 'transference' and 'countertransference', I offer the following very brief definitions.

> **Transference** can be understood as the way that we cannot help but bring our previous experiences and the meaning we made of them from the past, into the present, as we *transfer*, more or less consciously, some of the ideas and feelings we had about a person in our past onto an individual in the present.
>
> **Countertransference** can be understood as the therapist's physical, emotional and mental reactions to some of the client's deeply unconscious feelings, thoughts, sensations and memories. The client, in effect, unconsciously puts some aspects of these (especially the ones that have been unbearably painful) out into the therapeutic space. This can convey to the therapist some vital things about the inner world of the client that the client has lost touch with and needs to rediscover, in order to be whole. The therapist aims to use the countertransference in a session, and they therefore strive to notice their feelings, their thoughts, and their bodily sensations, in order to make connections between (a) what they are picking up and (b) what the client may have experienced in their life at some point, and lacked the support at the time to integrate. If a therapist can successfully be open to, and reflect on, the meanings of such unconscious, non-verbal communications from a client, then that client feels the benefit of another person understanding, and perhaps giving words to, what has been buried away inside them, causing them such perplexing discomfort and a sense of not being complete. This enables a profound healing to take place as the client feels more of their whole self can be in their awareness.

1

CONTAINING AND WORKING WITH A MALE SURVIVOR'S RAGE

Sam

Perhaps everything terrible is, in its deepest being, something helpless that wants help from us.

Rainer Maria Rilke (1875–1926)

An account of work with a man who had endured great violence and abuse as a child and had gone on to behave in violent and antisocial ways as an adolescent and adult. How, once the nature of his past family trauma was uncovered and engaged with, as well as his struggle to manage his anger in the present, he surprised himself and others in his uncovering of richly creative, artistic impulses and an openness to poetry. How he found he could express himself through writing and make meaning of the abuse he had suffered, and thereby free himself of his terror that he would inevitably behave abusively in the future.

People who behave aggressively in antisocial ways often have three unhelpful narratives that they tend to 'tell' over and over again through their behaviours:

- I feel angry and therefore someone/something is to blame and must be punished.
- I feel angry and therefore the world is an unjust, unsafe place and I must be ready to vigorously protect myself in it.
- I feel angry and therefore I am an unsafe person to be around and had better be left alone, in case I am provoked and lash out.

Very often, these narratives came to be formed as ways of making sense of experiences of being badly hurt and abused. They helped to cope with those situations at the time, but after many years, they become part of an ongoing problem for the person who tells them. Therapy is one important way of allowing abused individuals to revisit these narratives, to look again at how they came to be formed, and explore how there might be different, more helpful stories that can be told through their lives from now on.

It seems that many communities have men in them who have complex and largely unconscious reasons to do with having been abused and hurt behind their aggressive outbursts and acts. But we have too few people in our different communities who can take the time or have the skill to get to the bottom of the rage, and help these men with containing it, before it escalates into hurting others/themselves very badly indeed. This is, in part, due to the fact that unpacking the reasons for aggressive outbursts usually has to involve allowing angry, abused men to tell the hidden stories of what has left them so full of pain, shame and rage. And there are still, sadly, not enough settings in which this feels safe or even possible for many men. Abused men who cannot access help in time and who act out their pain by being aggressive often end up either being dealt with by the police and the criminal justice system, or by trying to numb and drown out their rage with addictive behaviours that tend to lead to yet another set of problems.

Of course hurt, abused women can be full of unprocessed rage as well. But it is men who make up 95 per cent of the prison population in England and Wales, and are far more likely than women to be in prison because of transgressive behaviour that is violent and causes the most immediately apparent and aggressive harm to their environment (Allen and Dempsey 2016).

'I was bad in school' said Sam with a wary smile. We were a few sessions in to what would turn into two years of weekly meetings in my private practice.

SARAH: Were you?

SAM: Oh yeah. I was out of control some of the time. I was a nightmare for the teachers. One time, one of them was trying to get me to sit down and write something in an English lesson when I was about 12, and I … I'm not proud of it … but, when I tried to walk out of the class-room and she told me to sit down, I threatened her. Told her I was going to punch her in the head in if she ever spoke to me like that again. Then I walked out. I was not very nice.

Sam looked down at his hands and twisted them. He was a powerfully built man, who was over six foot tall. Thick set, with a shaved head, a dark, full beard and several piercings in his ears and face, he usually came to sessions straight from the building sites on which he worked, in his work clothes and steel toe-capped boots. He said that he knew he struggled with pent-up anger. That anger became unmanageable for him at times, leading him to behave in verbally aggressive ways that were damaging to him, and those around him. He wanted help with managing his anger better.

We had talked in our first meeting about how we would cope if he ever felt very angry in a session with me. I had noted how open he was to looking at and thinking about this, and how clearly he was able to acknowledge that he needed support. He had looked for a counsellor on the internet and had saved up money to pay for sessions. His manner in the first session was open and reflective. He spoke of the fact that he had the support of a girlfriend, with whom he had a close, committed relationship. She had helped to steady him, and he had been able to talk with her about how he had been abused as a child. This background information helped me in my risk assessment and subsequent decision that he could make good use of sessions.

Sam's family background had been one of outward respectability. His parents had been gregarious, friendly people whenever they were in social situations. Behind closed doors, they had behaved very differently. They each had a story of childhood trauma. Sam's father had been brought up by a cold, unloving aunt and uncle after his single mother had died at a young age of cancer. He was 'the life and soul' with his mates and co-workers, but a harsh, driven figure at home, as a father and husband. He ran a successful roofing business, worked long hours in all weathers, came home exhausted, and, once he was at home, he expected complete compliance from his wife and sons in all matters. He punished all three of them equally, for being noisy, having bad table manners, making a mess, or for giving him 'any lip'. He meted out punishments by terrifying shouting, aiming forceful smacks, slaps and kicks, or by throwing a heavy object at whomever he was annoyed with.

Sam's mother had been sexually abused when she was very small for many years by her maternal grandfather, and was by turns a joking, sweet, smiley person when out in public, and a volatile, unpredictable presence when she and her sons were alone in the house together. Sam's description of her behaviours revealed someone who had been so hurt and devalued as a child that, as an adult, she still had a very young craving to feel special, and a

narcissistic wish for her needs to be placed at the centre of everything. Sam
and his older brother were therefore invariably cast in the roles she assigned
to them: her obedient helpers in the home, her confidantes, and her little
audience for the song and dance routines she liked to perform in the living
room and be praised for. In Sam's case, she also cast him as her consort-like
companion, with whom she could live out some of her erotic life, in ways that
satisfied her needs, and were blind to Sam's feelings.

From the time he was a toddler, she had made sure Sam, the youngest
child, slept in bed with her at night, to act as a buffer between her husband
and herself, to prevent any sexual activity in the marriage bed. As Sam grew
older, she would still insist he come to bed with her when she was 'tired' in
the day time and wanted someone 'to snuggle with'. By the time he was in his
teens, while they were lying together, she would hold and stroke him when
they were on the bed together, and kiss his neck 'from behind, more like a
girlfriend than a mother'. This made him feel uneasy and confused, as well
as loved and comforted. She would also require him to give her bare back
massages from time to time, as she lay face down on the bed, during which
Sam was sure she would become sexually aroused. He felt sick and torn while
this happened. He hated the fact that the massages were so 'dodgy', but they
were also opportunities to feel close to his mother and please her, which he
desperately wanted to do.

When Adam, Sam's older brother, was 13 he found a stash of their father's
pornographic magazines in a bag under their parents' bed and showed them
to Sam who was then nearly ten. Sam remembered that he had found the
images disturbing rather than arousing or interesting, and that some of them
depicted scenes of staged violence to women which seemed very real to his
young gaze. Adam experimented with masturbating while looking at the
images and encouraged Sam to do the same, and mocked him when 'nothing
happened', meaning that Sam did not get an erection or ejaculate, as his
brother had. Sam was not yet at a stage of his development where this was
possible, but he nevertheless felt inferior and humiliated about his sexual
nature. This added to the toxic cocktail of confusion, fear, self-doubt and
anger that was the norm for so much of his young life.

A few days later, their father angrily confronted them about having 'been
at my mags'. The boys had been very frightened, but then hugely relieved
when their father had burst out laughing, made it into a joke, and actively
encouraged them to look at his magazines any time they fancied. Soon Sam's
brother was looking at them and masturbating at least once a day, and ridiculing Sam for not wanting to join in. A schism became more and more evident

from this point in the family, with Sam and his mother as one dyad, and Adam and his father as the other. From around this same time, Sam also seemed to become the chief scapegoat in the family, as his father, brother and even his mother identified him as the soft one, the weak one, and a target for teasing and blaming. He became the butt of jokes and sneering, the one who was made to do the most unpleasant household tasks, and blamed for any mishaps.

In any sessions in which Sam described his childhood, I could witness the physical strain he experienced in simply recalling and speaking about it. He would twist his hands together, the muscles in and around his face and neck would tense, he would flush, and sometimes a film of sweat would break out on his forehead, temples and upper lip. As our work progressed I was struck by how very visibly Sam's difficulty in regulating his emotions played out before me.

A basic understanding of the biology of the human nervous system is so useful for all therapy practitioners to help us make sense of the embodied reactions that we see before us in the consulting room, and which we can also sense within ourselves as we sit with clients. A key part of understanding the biology of the way humans deal with life is to know about the functioning of the autonomic nervous system (ANS).

The nerves of the ANS are intertwined with those of the central nervous system, and provide a constant, regulating flow of information around our body about the state of our organs and viscera. The key characteristic of the ANS is that it has two branches:

- *the sympathetic*, which ensures we get turned 'on' when our environment evokes the need to be stimulated, alert, active, aroused, etc.;
- and *the parasympathetic*, which ensures we get turned 'off' when our environment evokes the sense that now is the time to be calm, at rest, relaxed, soothed, etc.

Ideally, if a child has a reasonably secure start in life, and is with adults who ensure they are safe and cared for, these two branches develop normally and work in harmony together. So, for example, if a baby hears a sudden loud noise because someone has dropped a pan on the kitchen floor, its sympathetic nervous system is turned *on:* chemicals including adrenaline and cortisol are released so that the baby's muscles contract, its heart rate goes up, its breathing becomes rapid and shallow, and its pupils dilate. All of this happens so that the baby can be on high alert and do whatever it can to promote its own safety. The baby may burst out crying to ensure a carer will come to its aid. If a safe figure arrives and picks up the baby, and that figure gives the baby the comfort of knowing it is protected, for example, speaks to the baby in a soothing, calming tone of voice, and shows by the expression on their face and their general physical demeanour that all is well – that there is no terrible threat – then the baby's parasympathetic system is activated, and the baby can begin to return to a calm state. The baby may need to continue to discharge some of the adrenaline and cortisol for a while, and may continue to cry or show some distress, but if they feel safe enough, and connected enough to an attentive carer, their parasympathetic system ensures that the production of the stress hormones is turned off, their heart rate slows, their breathing returns to normal, and the baby can fairly quickly recover its equilibrium. The parasympathetic system is needed to allow someone to return to a steady state after they have been very excited or scared.

Figure 1.1 shows the cycling of the states of being 'on' and then 'off' in someone who has good enough capacity to regulate their inner states.

If someone has grown up with 'good enough' caregivers who were attuned to their emotional state, then these two states of 'on' and 'off' come to feel manageable and normal: we can just accept that we have ups and downs in life, and that's OK. We get excited, angry or frightened sometimes, and then we come out of those states. For example: one afternoon we might find we are calm or low in mood – our parasympathetic nervous system has been activated. Perhaps we are feeling a little sad because we looked at some old photos of someone who is no longer in our life; or just pleasantly mellow because we are cuddled up on the sofa with our dog, listening to soothing music. And then something lifts our mood – a friend calls and says a few others are going out for some drinks tonight, and do we want to come? Then our sympathetic nervous system gets activated: we're off the sofa, excited, pleased, anticipating a fun time. We get the idea of calling another friend to invite them along too, we hurry to change our clothes and get ready to go out. And so it goes: 'on' is followed by 'off', which is then followed by 'on', and so on, ad infinitum.

But if our start in life was with caregivers who were not attuned to how we were feeling, and who could not comfort and soothe us when we were too 'on', and seemed not to notice or care if we sank too far down into being 'off', then the 'on' and 'off' sides to our inner states don't feel as if they are part of a natural, inevitable cycle, but more as if they make up an intense, rather horrible and utterly unpredictable roller coaster. 'On' can feel scarily manic; 'off' can feel deadeningly numb. And rather than moving around the cycle in a smooth, circular dynamic, one state will tend to stay around for

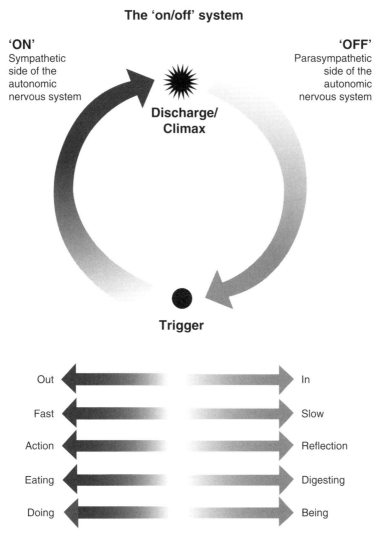

Figure 1.1 The 'on/off' system that helps humans to regulate (adapted from teaching presented by Roz Carroll)

quite some time and then suddenly jerk round the cycle into its opposite state. So we see that, for people who have not had a secure start in life, there is the experience of endless swings between intense, hyperaroused 'on' states such as anxiety and irritability, and then equally intense hypoaroused 'off' ones of depression and lethargy.

I found that, sitting with Sam, I noticed sensations of being drained from simply witnessing the sudden switches between the intense 'ons' of his heated feeling states, and the intense 'offs' of the dampened-down, dulled, dissociatively protective states that he could experience, many times, all within the space of one session. If it was exhausting to witness and track, then I could imagine how very draining it might be for Sam to be on such an extreme switchback of 'on' and then 'off'.

FROM SESSION 10

SAM: All the teachers were the same. They'd expect me to be able to sit down and do writing, or maths and stuff, but I just didn't know where my head was at. That time I flipped out at my English teacher, it was because she'd set us this task of writing something like 'The best thing I did this summer' or something. And I had spent just about the whole summer holiday in my bloody bedroom, because my dad had said I had to stay in there. He was mad because I had thrown a tennis ball up in the sitting room and broke the light in there. He got me on the floor when I done it, and he was like a terrier with a rat. He just shook me, and then, like, half threw, half dropped me. And then he said, he couldn't stand the sight of my face, and to stay out of his way, and any time he was in the house that summer I should just be up in my bedroom.

[Sam pressed both thumbs forcefully into the corner of his eyes.]

SARAH: That sounds shocking.

SAM: Mmph. Maybe. That wasn't so bad, for him, in a way. At least it wasn't a real proper beating.

SARAH: Mmm. Do you remember how it felt, being in your room over the summer?

SAM: Not really. I looked out of the window a lot. I had this one library book, that had three stories in it. I looked at that a lot. I did come down for meals. I remember saying to my mum, could I please just stay down and watch telly before Dad got back, but she said 'No' with this look on her face, that was like …

SARAH: Like?

SAM: [Looking down] Like she was pleased.

SARAH: That sounds painful. [A long pause.] How did you feel when she said no?

SAM: Fucking … betrayed, is what I felt!

SARAH: Yes. [Pause.] So, later, when you were set the task of writing about the 'best thing' about a summer when you were stuck in your room … Can you say more about that?

SAM: It did my head in! I sat there to start with, and looked at the page, and I was just … blank. I couldn't … I couldn't think of anything. Not even a bunch of lies, like the lies I used to tell when I was a little kid, about my dad being a millionaire, and my mum being related to the queen, and all sorts.

SARAH: They sound like a made-up version of your life that was a bit nicer than the one that was the reality at home.

SAM: Dunno. Maybe I was just a shitty little liar.

SARAH: That seems quite a harsh way to describe your little self. [Pause.] I wonder if you remember how you felt when you made up the stories?

SAM: Uhhh. Dunno. Better for a bit, maybe. But at the end of the day, no matter what, you still had to go home. There was no escape.

SARAH: So, when you say '*you* still had to go home', you mean '*I* still had to go home'?

SAM: Yeah.

SARAH: Would you be able to say that again, but saying 'I'?

SAM: [Long pause, while he looked up at the ceiling] *I* still had to go home. [He cleared his throat, and a sheen of tears appeared in his eyes.]

SARAH: It might have felt quite frightening and lonely for little Sam to have to go home to that reality?

SAM: Mmm. [He shifted uncomfortably in his seat] Is it hot in here, or what?

SARAH: Would you like the window open for some air?

SAM: Uhh … yeah, or … umm, I dunno. Don't ask me! I can't decide stuff like that. Huh! I can't ever give anyone a straight answer to anything. If Chelle even says, 'd'you want a tea or a coffee?' I can't ever say straight off. It's like I just freeze for a moment if anyone ever asks me anything.

SARAH: Really? Mmm. So, freezing is not uncommon for you?

SAM: Huh?

SARAH: It sounds like you can end up freezing in quite a few settings. You seemed to do something similar in the English lesson, when you were faced with two awful choices: to make stuff up about your summer, or write about what really happened. I guess both would have been painful in some way.

SAM: Sorry, I'm not following you. Can you say all that again?

I was struck at this point by the fact that I had got tangled up in trying to unpack something in a way that was far too wordy for someone who could easily feel lost when it came to words. I wondered if I had been unconsciously caught up in a dynamic where someone has to play the part of the one who is superior and unkind, and someone has to play the part of the victim who is bewildered and inferior – which is a dynamic that someone who has been abused is painfully familiar with, and which they can often, unconsciously, play a part in recreating in their interactions with others.

> SARAH: I don't think I was clear enough just then. Let me put it another way: I imagine you have a tendency to 'freeze'. And that could be linked to having been on the receiving end of abusive behaviours when you were little.
>
> SAM: Oh.
>
> SARAH: The way war veterans do, if they have PTSD and get the sense they're back in danger.
>
> SAM: Hmph. Right.
>
> SARAH: It might have felt that you were in a war, back then, in a way …
>
> SAM: Mmm. Yeah. Maybe. Maybe it was a kind of war …

FROM SESSION 20

We had been talking about Sam feeling stuck in life, not able to make simple choices as well as big life decisions, including whether or not to propose marriage to Chelle.

> SARAH: Feeling stuck usually means your *will* has been impaired in some way.
>
> SAM: My what?
>
> SARAH: Your will. The part of you that is active when you can clearly tell what you want, and then feel able to go for it.
>
> SAM: My will. Hunh. [He sighed] It drives Chelle crazy that I can never choose between two things.
>
> SARAH: Does it?
>
> SAM: [In a flat, dispirited tone] Yeah. She says she's sick of always being the one who has to make all the decisions, like where we're going to go on holiday or what we're going to have for tea, or just about anything we're going to do together.
>
> SARAH: And how are you with it?
>
> SAM: [With a sudden surge of energy, and sitting more upright] It drives me ape! Like, why can't I just … Like, last night, I was in the

7-Eleven, standing, looking at all the milks, and I'm just looking from semi-skimmed to skimmed, and back again, and for about a minute I'm like, '*Which one is best, which one should I get?*' … It's mad!

SARAH: Sounds frustrating.

SAM: Yeah! And what's it matter! Who cares! It's only a pint of milk!

SARAH: Perhaps it's more about what 'making a choice' stands for. So, it's not really about the choice between skimmed and semi-skimmed. More about being reminded of what it feels like to be faced with two choices. Somehow, that situation makes you freeze. If that's the case, I wonder what that might be about?

SAM: Do you know?

SARAH: I could make some guesses. But I'd like to hear your thoughts. What comes to your mind when you think back to times when you were young and had two choices, and neither felt OK?

SAM: [Long pause. Looking down] Like every time my mum would say, like, come upstairs with her to go and have 'a lay down'.

[There was a long silence, then he sighed.]

SAM: She always said it in the afternoons when I was back from school, before Dad was back, when I was just trying to be on my own and chill. And I would … I would look at the pattern on the carpet in the living room, and just go kind of floaty. I knew what she meant, and I didn't want to. But I knew, like, if I tried to say, *no*, or *I don't want to*, or *it feels a bit wrong*, then she would like, be … She could turn. She could just get really upset and miserable so quick. She'd get this look and then the whole evening would be hell, and she'd get me in trouble with Dad when he got back.

[Another long silence.]

SAM: Did I tell you she threw her cup of tea at me once, when I didn't say 'yes' straightaway, like she wanted?

SARAH: No you didn't.

SAM: She'd told me to look at her when she was talking to me – so I looked up at her and then she screamed, 'Take that smirk off your face when I'm talking to you', and chucked her hot tea at me.

SARAH: That sounds very frightening. So, often you just couldn't really get things right for her?

SAM: No. But I tried. I kept trying. Until I was about 20. I tried all the fucking time.

FROM SESSION 25

We had been talking about Sam's feelings towards his mother and the fact that no matter how hard he tried to please her, she often seemed furious with him.

> SARAH: I imagine it wasn't really about you – Sam, the real person – for her. Perhaps it was more to do with *who you stood for*. If, somehow, you stood for a male figure she could finally dominate or take her anger out on safely. Then, it wouldn't have mattered what you did or didn't do.
>
> SAM: Yeah. But she *did* love me. I know that she *did* love me. [A tear crept down one side of his nose and he angrily wiped it away and looked up at the ceiling.]
>
> SARAH: Yes. It was so hard for her to express that in ways that were OK for *you*, though.
>
> SAM: D'you know what? I wish it could be her sitting here now, instead of me. Or, no, that she could be here as well as me. No, really, I wish she, like … that she could have had something like this when she was my age, to help her not go on and fuck everything up when she had her own kids.
>
> SARAH: Yes. What a shame that never happened.
>
> [We sat in silence for a long while.]
>
> SAM: But it's too late for her now. She's already told me she thinks I'm pathetic for doing counselling. She messaged me on Facebook to tell me. Nice of her, wasn't it? Supportive as usual. My mum. There you go. Still trying to make it all my fucking fault and my problem. So … just … fuck her!
>
> [There was another long pause. Then Sam seemed to go off on a tangent.]
>
> SAM: Can I just ask – is the counselling actually going to help me with this thing about not being able to choose?
>
> SARAH: Ummm. I'd say … the short answer is: *yes, probably*. The longer answer is: *it will, if you can use the sessions to end up with more of a connection to the part of you that needs to sit on the fence.*
>
> SAM: But there isn't *any* part of me that likes sitting on the fence, though! I've told you! It drives me mad. I'd love to just choose whatever, and then get on!
>
> SARAH: Consciously, yes, of course. But then, you already have an OK connection with the grown-up part of you that wants to

quickly choose the milk and go home. I'm guessing there's *another* important part of you, that you don't have such a good connection with. A part that feels much younger, and gets very anxious about making any choice, however small. That part is very powerful in its own way. It might be trying to protect you from making a wrong, 'bad' choice, by ensuring you don't make any choices at all.

SAM: [Looking very uncomfortable] Well, it wasn't working very well when I was like, 21, 22. I made a lot of very bad choices a few years back, before Chelle and me got together.

SARAH: Did you?

SAM: [Looking more and more uncomfortable, shifting in his seat, twisting his hands, and flushing] Mmm.

SARAH: Are you able to say more about any of those 'bad' choices?

SAM: Yeah. I … Well, I didn't just threaten to punch that teacher I told you about: I did actually … well, not *hit* her exactly, but I did shove her. She tried to put her hand on my arm when I got up to leave, and I, like, pushed at her too hard, and she fell back onto her desk and got hurt. And … Umm. Thing is … can I just check, like, how … how confidential are these sessions, in like, reality?

SARAH: In reality?

SAM: Well, how much do you have to hear from someone about stuff they've done – bad stuff – before you, like, think … that you'll have to tell them that you're going to go to the police, or whatever?

I had given Sam a client agreement before we had started work which had stated what I meant by the word 'confidential' and we had briefly gone through the limits of that, and what might happen if I was concerned he might seriously hurt himself or someone else. But that had been some time ago, and it was in our first meeting. For many clients who have experienced abuse, the high anxiety in a first session has a considerable impact on how well they can take in or recall the details of certain agreements.

SARAH: Do you remember going through the client agreement I gave you at the first meeting?

SAM: Not really. A bit. I mean, I get that you would, like, need to say something if you thought I was going to top myself or go after someone. But what about stuff in the past?

At this point, I felt a small firework of anxiety shoot off in me, as I had a few moments to fantasise that Sam was going to tell me about something extremely violent that he had done. I searched for something neutral to say, which would open the door for Sam to say more, whilst being clear with him that this could not be an utterly confidential space.

SARAH: You sound like you're worried that if you tell me something, I might decide I would have to involve other services.

SAM: Well, like, would you have to go and report it to the police if, I had, say, beaten someone up a few years back?

I felt the flare of fear dying away, as I returned to trusting that I could guess the lie of the land ahead of us once more.

SARAH: Well, I couldn't promise 100 per cent confidentiality here, as that's never a good idea in therapy. (Anyway, you probably wouldn't believe it if I said I could). But I *can* say that I wouldn't usually see the need to break confidentiality over a client having hit another person in the past.

There was a long pause and then Sam said in an emotionless voice, while looking at me, 'Well, I did.'

We were very near the end of a session now, so I did not want to start a lot of unpacking of this new important material.

SARAH: Right. OK. I'm glad you felt able to share that with me. Sounds like it might be best to talk about it in more depth next week, rather than start now. But perhaps you need to hear from me today that this wouldn't usually be something I would break confidentiality about. [There was a pause.] Can I ask how you feel now, having told me, and hearing my response?

SAM: [With a sigh] Relieved. I feel it's a big relief. [He was starting to look visibly lighter; his gaze was steadier, his spine more erect, and the flush that had been suffusing his face and neck had subsided.]

SARAH: How about we talk more about it next time?

SAM: Yeah. That'd be good. I think. Or, well … it will be bad, of course. But in a good way. You know what I mean?

SARAH: [Firmly] I do.

FROM THE SUBSEQUENT SESSION

It turned out that Sam's assault on another person had been about three years earlier, at the end of an evening's drinking with his brother Adam and a group of Adam's mates, who were in a Sunday football team that met each weekend to play and then socialise. Sam had met Chelle for the first time a few weeks before this night out, and she was becoming his first serious girlfriend. One of the men in the group teased Sam about this, off and on throughout the evening. This man was known as a bit of a bully, and someone who would try to sow mischief in the group and be generally provoking. It was also known in the group that Sam 'had a temper', and a few of the other men were at pains to keep reminding Sam to ignore the other guy, take no notice, etc. At one point, near closing time, Sam had looked up when his name had been called out, to see the man who had been teasing him standing at the other end of the bar, grinning and gesturing at him. The man called out to Sam something about Chelle.

SAM: How he'd heard that she was up for anything, and if she ever tired me out, to let him know and he would stand in for me, and loads of other shit.

[Sam put one hand over his eyes for a few seconds and then swiped his palm over his face, rubbing away sweat.]

SAM: I knew he was bladdered, and coked up as well. He'd been going in and out of the toilets all night with my brother, doing coke. And the other guys were saying, 'Don't let him get to you, he's just being a dick.' And I was all, 'Yeah, yeah, it's all good. I know.' I was like, taking deep breaths.

SARAH: Managing to calm yourself?

SAM: A bit, yeah. But, no, not really. Really, he was getting to me, I could have … God! I was … And then, anyway, it was chucking out time, and we all went out to get taxis and whatnot. And he's standing right by me on the pavement, like, bent over to tie his shoe lace or something, and I just went up to him and stood right over him and …

[Sam did a gesture of aiming a powerful blow downwards, with one hand making a fist and punching into the palm of the other hand with a loud smack.]

SAM: I just punched him real hard on the side of his head and he went down. He was knocked out cold. Some of the other guys came straight over and got me away from him, 'cos I was going to … I would have started laying into him, if someone hadn't stopped me. Once he was just down and out, I wanted to kick the shit out of him, so bad.

One of Sam's knees was trembling up and down in a way that looked involuntary. He placed both his palms flat on his knees and the hand on the knee that was jiggling gently moved up and down, and we both looked at it as it quivered before us.

I felt disturbed at the mental images that Sam's narrative had conjured up, and felt an inner wince at the thought of being punched so hard in the head that it would knock me out.

Sam's own distress and the pain behind his actions, although largely hidden at the time, were apparent in the session. He had a stricken expression on his face. He stared as if transfixed at his trembling knee, then lifted one hand to roughly rub over the cropped hair on his head. He then put the fingers of one hand to his mouth and began to bite nervously at one of his fingernails. He cleared his throat.

> SARAH: I can see that you're in touch with some difficult sensations as you talk about that incident. It must have been quite disturbing for you, to have done this?
>
> SAM: [Uneasily] Mmm.
>
> SARAH: Are you able to tell me about some of what you're aware of now?
>
> SAM: Yuh, like in my chest?
>
> SARAH: Yes.
>
> SAM: It's gone quite tight, like I can't get my breath properly.
>
> SARAH: Uhuh. Anything else?
>
> SAM: My ... my ... I feel like something's stuck in my throat.
>
> [He put his hand up the area around his Adam's apple, and I did the same to mirror him.]
>
> SARAH: Your throat feels blocked?
>
> SAM: Like ... I just feel I could get up and ... [He punched a fist into a palm again.]
>
> SARAH: Right. You can feel a lot of energy and urge to move in your muscles. Sounds like there's a lot going on in your body. That could feel a bit overwhelming?
>
> [Sam gave me an anxious, frowning look.]
>
> SARAH: If there was one area of sensation you could focus in on, right now, what might it be?
>
> SAM: [Looking a bit lost] How do you mean?

I remembered his inhibition about choosing and realised this was rather a misattuned comment, but Sam surprised me – and maybe himself – by suddenly responding:

SAM: My throat. [He swallowed and winced.]

SARAH: Your throat, OK, good. How would it be to just allow your attention to go there? Could you just allow yourself to notice what's going on in your throat, without trying to change it, no matter how uncomfortable?

We sat facing each other, both with one hand on our throats; I consciously copied his position, in order to help him feel that he was being accompanied. To begin with, Sam had a nervous enquiring look directed at me, but soon his expression changed as he focused more and more on his own inner experience and less on trying to read my expression for approval or disapproval.

Much of the aim of therapy, whether that aim is made explicit to the client or not, is to encourage the client to be properly attentive to their own feeling sensations. When we are able to be sure of *what* it is that we are experiencing (churning guts, clenched jaw, a warmly open chest, whatever it might be) we can be more sure about how we feel *about* something (I like/don't like this situation) and take congruent action. If we are cut off from our own sensations, and fail to read the clues our body is giving out, we end up trying to have the reactions that we are guessing we are 'supposed' to have, rather than the ones we are actually having. So, we eat the plate of food that everyone else seems to think we should enjoy, even though it is not pleasant for us; or we put up with discomfort or pain in some settings, because we have learned we are 'supposed' to like certain positions or activities, and so on. We can't be authentic, because we don't feel our actions are in tune with what we feel, deep down, are the visceral truths about what we are finding pleasant or discomfiting. This invariably leads to a build up of self-blame and resentment, as we never feel we can express our true feelings or be properly understood, and are annoyed with ourselves and others because of this.

Rather than turning us into monsters of selfishness, being able to pay proper attention to how we feel and acknowledge those feelings to ourselves, enables us to take better care of ourselves, and stop expecting someone else to always attend to our emotional welfare for us. Part of the reason therapists keep banging on about feelings, (and are often portrayed in films and sitcoms as asking soppily, 'How do you *feel* about that?') is because what is good for individuals (being in touch with our feelings and feeling more able to take responsibility for caring for our own emotional wellbeing) is also very good for relationships, families and communities. Many of the most troubled, volatile people I have worked with started off by being in a state in which they had an intuition that *something* very powerful and important seemed to be boiling away inside them, but they really did not know what. A typical response from someone who is deeply unhappy and irritable, when asked about how they feel, is to reply, with complete honesty, 'I don't know.'

SAM: [Swallowing a few more times] It's like a bit of bread's got stuck on the way down.

SARAH: Mmm. Uncomfortable. Do you have a sense of the size and shape of the bit of bread?

[Sam made a gesture with the thumb and forefinger of one hand, to denote a circle a few centimetres wide. The other hand remained at his throat, and he began making gentle downwards-stroking movements around his larynx, that I saw as him instinctively trying to soothe himself.]

SARAH: What do you notice when you allow yourself to pay attention to the feeling of the bit of bread in your throat?

[There was a long pause while Sam continued to stroke his throat, the way a mother might gently stroke her baby's back to help its digestion.]

SAM: Hmm. Ahem. It's starting to feel easier, like its fading away. The lump's dissolving or something, so I can swallow the bits down.

[Pause.]

SAM: It's better now, not so sore. The lump's gone. Heh. [He coughed and swallowed a few times and rolled his head around. His focus began to shift again, from being directed inwards, back to me.]

SAM: Well, that was weird. Is that some, like, special technique you have, that works on throats, or something?

SARAH: I suppose you could call it a technique, in a way. One of the oldest in the world. It's what the Buddha taught, and the Dalai Lama recommends. It's just about giving your full attention to something, instead of ignoring it. It's quite healing in most instances, to just allow and notice all our sensations, as far as we can. After a while, they can sometimes just gently pass off, or ease, on their own, if we can allow ourselves to really notice them in the first place. That's all. Not anything fancy – more like common sense.

SAM: Huh! Well, it works on throats!

FROM SESSION 30

We had been talking again about the time Sam had punched the man who had been making unpleasant remarks about him and Chelle. He revealed that this had been a turning point, as after this he was never actually physically violent again. He described how, up to that point, he was known as someone who could be relied on to get involved if there was any fight or aggressive altercation in the neighbourhood. Throughout his late adolescence and early twenties, there would usually come a time on a night out, partially fuelled by alcohol and sometimes also drugs, when he would get embroiled in some sort of fight or dispute.

SARAH: What does it feel like, talking about all of those fights with me, here?

SAM: A bit unreal. It's like, it wasn't really me. I mean, I know it was, but I can't feel in touch with that guy when I'm sitting here.

SARAH: That's interesting. What do you make of that?

SAM: I dunno. I think … I think of that guy, the guy that got in to fights, and I just think, '*Who is he? Why is he being such a twat?*'

SARAH: Sounds like it could be hard to think that it *is* you who can act like that?

SAM: A bit. But I feel a bit relieved as well, discussing it. It is a good thing to be able to talk about it, but … [A pause.]

SARAH: But …

SAM: You would say, wouldn't you, if you thought I was, like, a danger to society or something? Wouldn't you?

SARAH: It sounds like you might be needing to check with me again about how confidential this space is?

SAM: Maybe. [Another pause.] Do you?

SARAH: Do I what?

SAM: Think I'm a danger to society?

SARAH: Well first off, society isn't my client – you are, so at this point I'm more focused on whether you're a danger to yourself. And … I think I *do* feel some concern about the situations you can find yourself in because of your short fuse. But I also know that it's been some years since you've been violent, and that you're coming here and working on how you manage your anger. And you've got the support of Chelle. So – no, I'm not thinking you're a danger at this time.

SAM: Humph.

> SARAH: How are you feeling about working with me in these sessions on what makes you angry, and trying to find better ways to manage your anger than lashing out verbally?
>
> SAM: OK. But … like, no offence, but … you're not going to try and turn me into a pacifist, are you? Because I can tell you now, if someone was to diss Chelle in front of me, or like … I can't be all … *turn the other cheek* or whatever. Because that is complete BS as far as I'm concerned!

Sam was looking quite stirred up and 'on' at this point, and I could feel the energy in him building, as he was seeming to experience me/the therapy as being potentially *against* him and his need to protect himself and stand his ground.

It felt important at this point to give Sam the chance to express himself to me forcefully, and not experience me as nervous of this. I felt he needed to know he could safely have a mild level of conflict with me, without it escalating. I wanted to model for him the capacity to be assertive, i.e. stand firmly for what you want or believe, whilst taking into account that others have equally important feelings and deeply held beliefs.

> SARAH: Of course not. I'm not suggesting you become a wimp. Everyone needs their anger to some extent – it's what makes us able to stand our ground. Gandhi and Mother Theresa must have been able to access the power of their anger at injustice. But it didn't get them into fist fights and brawls outside pubs.

I was relieved to see Sam grin at this.

> SAM: Yeah, well, just as long as you know I'm never going to be some bloke who sits around meditating all day and saying '*Hello, World*', or whatever.
>
> SARAH: [Grinning back] Noted! Let's talk more about it, next time.

For a number of sessions after this we looked at some of the times Sam had had uncontrolled verbal flare-ups more recently, and he told the story of how some of them had come about. As he talked about each one, I would slow the story down each time, helping him to reconnect to how he had been feeling and what had been going through his mind at various points throughout the incident, and also to make it more possible for him to be aware of what he was experiencing in the here-and-now, during the retelling of them. This all helped Sam to process more of the emotions that had taken him over at the times he had lashed out. It also helped him to make some new meanings out of these temper outbursts that were more useful to him than the meanings he had been tending to make out of his experiences, which were the three that I described at the start of the chapter.

The first thing that became more apparent to Sam as we looked at certain instances of him 'losing it' was that he never lost his temper with anyone he perceived as vulnerable, weaker than he was, or in need of help. His aggression was directed towards those he perceived as bullying, overbearing, cruel or superior to him in some way. So, he had been verbally abusive to a traffic warden who had smilingly continued to give him a ticket even though Sam had arrived back at his van only a few seconds after the parking time had expired. He had shouted at a GP receptionist who had told him abruptly to stop using his mobile phone in a waiting area, when he had been in the middle of turning it off in order to comply with the notice asking patients to do so. He had sworn at a man who had put a hand on Sam's arm and shouted, 'Come on, mate, move down!' on a crowded bus. He had told a woman who had been yelling at her small kids in a supermarket queue that she was being a moody bitch. Most recently, and most embarrassingly for Chelle, he had spoken rudely to the woman who managed the hairdressing salon where Chelle worked. Sam had arrived there to meet Chelle from work, just as the manager was speaking rather curtly to Chelle about a work matter. Sam's urge to protect Chelle took over and after telling the manager not to speak to Chelle in that way, and an ensuing heated exchange, Sam had insisted that Chelle leave with him immediately, even though she wanted to stay and smooth things over. As soon as they had left the salon, Sam had realised he had made an error of judgement and left Chelle in a horribly awkward position, which she was, in her turn, furious with him about.

SARAH: What happened then?

SAM: I had to eat humble pie, didn't I! I went back about ten minutes later to say I was sorry, even though she was bang out of order. Chelle kind of made me – she had a face on her like … thunder. She said she wasn't going to lose her job because of me being a wanker. So … I just had to suck it up and go back there and apologise to that cow.

Despite still needing to let off steam about these incidents, once he had let his 'on' state subside, Sam was able to be thoughtful as he spoke about what was going on for him at those times. He described a snapping sensation inside him when he either saw someone being mistreated or felt that he was being 'disrespected'. In the end he had a wonderfully clear insight into what seemed to happen each time he lost his temper:

> SAM: It's like each time, I can sort of see my dad when he was laying into my mum or me, or Adam, and I just … It's like I get a chance to *do right*, in the way no one ever did right for us at the time. I'm like, fighting my dad, saving my family, every bloody time I get into a barney!

Sam had vividly expressed what a psychodynamic perspective tells us about one person aggressively attacking another, whether that attack is physical or verbal. For a person on the attack, something has suddenly made it feel horribly possible that they will once again be made to feel small, vulnerable, traumatised, helpless and afraid (the way they were as a child or adolescent). It then becomes vital that they turn the tables and ensure that, in that moment, *they* can act out being the powerful, traumatising one in the current scenario. Unfortunately, for this coping method to 'work', they need to cast someone else in the role of the one who must play the part of the terrified, traumatised one. It can sometimes be hard for those who are unaware of the unconscious processes involved in one person objectifying another in this way to have much sympathy for the one who has lashed out. And to begin with, Sam did not expect much understanding or compassion from me for the times he had behaved badly. But the more time we spent in sessions looking at the episodes where he had suddenly been aggressive, the more Sam began to see there was a truth in the perspective I was offering: that every time he had attacked it was because he had somehow felt under attack himself, and the only way he had ever developed to deal with being under attack, rather than fall apart in terror, was to counter-attack. After a few months, Sam came to believe that he, as well as the person on the receiving end of his temper, deserved some compassion and understanding around his angry outbursts.

Running parallel to his growing ability to talk about what went on inside him when he lost his temper, Sam was also more able to speak about the effect on him of his mother's sexualised use of him, which had continued beyond his childhood into adolescence.

FROM SESSION 35

Sam had been describing how, throughout his teenage years, his mother would invent reasons to come in to his bedroom after he'd had a shower, and would then often make comments on his body hair, or his spots or the size and appearance of his genitals, in ways that shamed him deeply.

> SAM: And she'd call out if we were in the garden in the summer, on purpose, so like, other people out in their gardens would hear, 'Oooo, Sammy's got his shorts on! Careful, you don't pop out now with that big old trouser snake in there.' Or at night, she'd be like all drunk and sloppy on the sofa, and if we were alone she'd say 'Give us a kiss goodnight, then. God, some girl's going to be lucky to get you!' and be all over me like she *was* my girlfriend, before I could get away or my brother or dad would come in.
>
> SARAH: It sounds so confusing and uncomfortable.
>
> SAM: It was … [He made a throaty, exasperated sound and clenched his fists.]

Sam had become increasingly more able to tolerate difficult and painful feelings, and talk about the emotions he was feeling *while* he was feeling them, so I risked probing at this point.

> SARAH: What's happening as you make that angry sound and clench your fists?
>
> SAM: I … Ugh. I just don't want to talk about it!
>
> SARAH: Mmm.

There was a long pause.

> SAM: [Less angry and more anguished] I just can't!
>
> SARAH: You look as if you're in some discomfort right now.

Sam was looking up at the ceiling and drawing some deep breaths, which was what he typically did when he was trying to quell any expression of his deep grief and hurt at the abuse in his childhood.

> SARAH: What if there was a way that you *could* express more about this – but it wouldn't have to be by talking about it now, in this session?

SAM: Like how?

SARAH: Might you be willing to try an experiment?

SAM: Huh?

SARAH: Well, what if you could write down, in a 'pretend letter' the things you needed to get off your chest, about the way your mother was with you around sex?

SAM: What, a letter that I write to you, you mean?

SARAH: No. One that you write to your mother and you bring to the next session. It can take whatever form you like, short or long. But, and this is very important, it is *not* a letter that is actually going to be sent. You don't write it in order to actually post it to your mother. But you do write it *as if* it is a letter directly to her. [Pause.] Would you be up for giving that a go?

SAM: You know I'm shit at writing, don't you?

SARAH: That's good, because the less confident you are about writing, the more effective it is, as an exercise to help say what you really need to say.

SAM: [With an annoyed glint in his eyes] Oh you're good, aren't you! I can see how you can really turn the screws!

SARAH: You sound annoyed.

SAM: No, I'm not annoyed. I'm just … [He went silent.]

My sense was that the wasp of Sam's anger, so to speak, was now right in the room with us. I judged that he and I had enough of an alliance, and he had enough capacity to calm himself when he got into an 'on' state, to make it worth working with, in the here and now, in order to help dissolve the taboo in Sam's mind about expressing anger towards a woman he had an emotional connection with. I was aware of the charge that my suggestion had for him, given the similarities between the time the English teacher had pressured him into writing, and what was happening in the session.

SARAH: What's happening for you now?

SAM: [Crossly] What do you mean 'what's happening?'

SARAH: I'm wondering what's going on inside you, as your tone of voice and the way you're sitting and your facial expressions have all changed.

SAM: [Taking a deep breath] Honest to God, I am not annoyed at you, Sarah. But I just … I hate situations where you get painted into a corner. And it's … I've just said I can't talk about some of this stuff, and you've said, 'OK'. But now you're telling me that if I don't talk about it here, I've got to go and write about it, which for me, is probably worse! So … [He sighed out the rest of his breath, forcefully.]

SARAH: So, you feel that I'm painting you into a corner?

SAM: No! Oh, I just can't explain!

The parallels with the many times in Sam's life when he felt caught between two awful alternatives, and felt no support from his environment, were very clear to me, and very unclear to Sam in that moment.

Sometimes it is much more useful for a client to have time to come to their own awareness about something, and the best thing a therapist can do is button their lip and not break in too soon and too suddenly with a supposedly helpful insight or interpretation. At other times (and I thought this was one of those times), the client is more likely to be helped by the therapist intervening somehow when there is a significant impasse. At these times, it is likely that it is only the therapist who *can* help to move the work on. This is often to do with the therapist being the only one who can name the thing that is taboo and is therefore kept deeply down in the client's unconscious, and likely to remain there, unless the one who is more conscious about it can be proactive, to prove that the taboo can be broken without someone being punished for this. In Sam's case, the taboo was to do with feeling angry with a woman he cared for. In the past, this had been his mother. In Sam's day-to-day life, this was Chelle. In the actual moment of the session, it was me. If anyone was going to name that Sam might feel angry with me and that this might not have to automatically mean catastrophe, I thought it was going to have to be me.

SAM: [After a pause] Oh, just … all right, I'll try and do a letter or whatever. Fine!

SARAH: Well, I appreciate you being willing to try. And I do also want to give some space to the part that is uncomfortable about feeling sort of … pressured into it.

SAM: Yeah, well … it doesn't matter.

SARAH: Mmm. I'm not so sure that it doesn't matter. I wonder if you are feeling the way you may have felt at other times in your life when you felt a woman put you into an impossible position …

SAM: You mean … Chelle?

SARAH: Possibly. I was wondering if how you are feeling now is more to do with how you used to feel when your mother wanted you to be sexual with her.

[Sam's eyes suddenly filled with tears that no amount of looking up at the ceiling could prevent. He bowed his head and I could see the tears fall. He spoke in a whisper.]

SAM: I just don't want to.

SARAH: Yes. I hear that, Sam. And I want you to hear that I am not going to force you to do anything. [Pause.] I guess you already know, horribly well, how it feels to be made to do something that you really don't want to do …

SAM: I can't do it! I can't put stuff down in words about what happened!

SARAH: Yes. It's a very frightening thought – to put down in black and white what you remember …

SAM: [Lifting up a flushed, tear-streaked face] But if I don't … If I don't write it or … whatever … If I never get it all out … Then what?

SARAH: It's so painful to be caught like this. Caught the way you were with your mum, and then with that teacher, and others, where the choice seems to be to either put up with something humiliating, or lash out and cause harm. Not much of a choice, really, is it?

SAM: [Squeezing his eyes shut, putting both hands up to his face, and speaking loudly and emphatically from behind his hands] I didn't want it! I didn't want to have to rub her back and let her touch me. Why would I want that from my own mother! I was just a little kid! Why would you want to make a little kid do that?

[He sobbed, and put his hands down.]

SAM: But I didn't say 'no' to her, did I! I didn't stop it. So what does that make me?

SARAH: You think it makes you … ?

SAM: I dunno. Like, a little pervert or something. A dirty little, pervy kid, getting his rocks off. Either that or a coward … or …

[Sam suddenly stood up, and looked towards the door.]

SAM: Right, I think I'd better just go now … [He hesitated.]

I looked up at him and his pose put me in mind of an animal on high alert, like a deer that is sniffing the wind for the hunter. Not angry any more, but hypervigilant.

The session was at a turning point. There was the possibility of turning down the temperature of the work and helping take the charge out of what we were doing, in case Sam's feelings became overwhelming and he got thoroughly retraumatised. And there was the chance to keep enough heat under the work to allow us to stay with his feelings and give them a chance

to be expressed: for the whole cycle of his ANS to have a satisfying comple-
tion, and for Sam to have the experience that he could express anger in the
presence of a woman with no disastrous consequences.

SARAH: Maybe we could find a way to help you feel less trapped, while
you still stay in the room.

SAM: I think it would be better if I just went.

SARAH: I understand that, and of course, it's always your choice
whether you stay or leave. But I wonder if you *did* leave, whether
you'd be getting caught in an old pattern of feeling you have to
put a woman's needs before your own – that you have to protect
me from seeing you angry? [Pause.] I would like to be able to
support the part of you that needs to express some of their anger.
If you stay, it would be easier to support that part, than if it gets
taken away and put out of sight again.

SAM: [Still standing] I don't know if you'd want to see me angry. I'm not
very nice.

SARAH: No, probably not. I don't think I'm particularly nice when I'm
angry, either. But there's usually good reasons for me to get angry.

SAM: Hmph!

SARAH: How would you feel about staying in the room, but letting yourself *picture* leaving and doing whatever it is that you might want to
do because you're angry?

Sam gave me a bemused look and then stared down at his feet. For a few
moments his face played different expressions that suggested he was indeed
imagining something, and was concentrating on this. There was a pause.

SARAH: Would you be able to share some of what you pictured?

SAM: [Slowly sitting back down, and then continuing to stare down at
his feet] I … thought of … storming out to your hall and like, just
… trashing everything in it.

[He looked up at me, cautiously.]

SAM: I wouldn't!

SARAH: I know. But it's an energetic idea, isn't it?

SAM: [With an uneasy laugh] Yeah.

SARAH: How did it feel – imagining it?

SAM: I dunno.

SARAH: Frightening? Sickening? Satisfying?

SAM: Huh. Pretty good, actually.

SARAH: A kind of release?

SAM: Maybe. Like, knocking pictures off walls, and kicking in the door, and acting like a right nutter!

SARAH: Acting like a very frustrated person who is trying to make people aware of how upset they feel?

SAM: Mmm. Yeah. But that's not how other people would see it, though, is it?

SARAH: Maybe things would calm down more easily if more people *did* understand that when someone is behaving like that, they need some support …

SAM: Maybe.

[There was another pause. He smiled suddenly.]

SAM: You know, I'm still not doing that letter thing, don't you!

SARAH: It's your call.

FROM SESSION 40

Sam had been feeling extremely angry with his mother and father, and after talking about them both in the session he began to feel so emotional that he felt, as he said, as if he did not know what to do with himself.

I invited him to do something that could help with the huge build up of adrenaline and cortisol that had been happening in his body as he had been speaking and, in effect, reliving some of the abusive experiences he had endured. He agreed, and I invited him to copy me in simply standing up and vigorously shaking both hands at arm's length and stamping his feet, to help provide ways for his body to be active. I also invited him to make a small 'o' shape with his mouth and blow a jet of air vigorously out, as if he was trying to blow a feather hovering in the air in front of his face, away from him in a straight line. This is useful to release the tension in the mouth, throat and chest for people who feel too inhibited to cry or shout, and also for people who have a tendency for the sympathetic side of their ANS to get quickly aroused and feel too out of control if they engage with more vigorous cathartic activities like shouting or cushion bashing.

After doing this together (I did it too, so that he wouldn't feel foolish as he did these rather odd activities), we sat down again and Sam reported in a surprised tone that he felt less agitated for having done them.

SAM: So they're pretty good techniques too. Do you reckon the Dalai Lama does that one?

[I laughed.]

SARAH: I bet he does it all the time!

SAM: Yeah, right.

[We were both laughing now, which also helped with the continued dis-
     charge of the stress hormones. Suddenly Sam spoke.]

SAM: Tell you what, seeing as I'm getting so good at all this stuff, do you
     know what I'm going to try?

SARAH: No, I don't. What?

SAM: That letter-to-my-mum-thing.

THE NEXT SESSION

When Sam arrived I could see he was holding a rolled-up exercise book in
one hand. As soon as we sat down, he said, 'Right, Well, it's not really a
letter, but I've done something. D'you want to read it now?'

SARAH: I would like to. But can I ask first about how it was to write it?

SAM: Very weird. I went home feeling like, 'Why did I set myself up for
     this!' And then when I got back I remembered that when I was about
     13, 14, I was obsessed with the lyrics of, I dunno if you've heard of
     them, but – Tupac and Eminem.

[I nodded to let him know I did at least know the names of the musicians
     he was speaking about.]

SAM: I used to spend ages up in my room – I did it that whole summer
     I told you about – just copying their lyrics out into my school books.
     Maybe it was because you said it had to be a letter, like saying it
     directly to my mum, and that reminded me that there's this song
     Eminem did that was like that: a letter, a mad letter, that is totally
     angry with the person it's to. So I went and found some of my old
     exercise books and I found loads of other stuff I'd written in there
     that I'd forgotten about, as well as the sayings of Tupac and stuff. All
     weird little stories and jokes and doodles that I did all summer. And
     there was this one page at the end that was still blank, so I sat down
     and just wrote this thing to my mum. But it's not really a letter, not
     a proper letter.

I felt a poignant wave of emotion within me as Sam described having had
such a visceral reconnection with his younger self at a time when it seemed
his creative, imaginative life had been active and also part of what had helped
him cope with the dreadful traumas he was going through at home.

He held the book out to me.

SARAH: Would you be able to read it to me?
SAM: [Looking very taken aback] Oh, I'm not great at reading aloud. I thought you could just read it.
SARAH: I'd prefer to hear your voice reading your words.
SAM: Christ! All right.

He cleared his throat and proceeded to read from his exercise book in a rushed, somewhat embarrassed way, making his voice sound flat, and with occasional stumbles, which made what he was reading seem rather disjointed and without affect to begin with.

But as he read, what emerged was the immense potency, the underlying fire, of what he had been able to put down on paper in a letter to the figure of his wounded, abusive mother. It was, in effect, a long poem: 'To You, Mum.'

It began in blunt, everyday language, as a boy's raw outpouring of love, grief, longing, hatred and confusion about his mother. As it went on, the language became more adult, more poignant. Lines became shorter and more rhythmic, there were unmistakably deliberate internal rhymes, and soon a deluge of acutely evocative metaphors, including a rose growing within a coil of barbed wire, a family sitting on a sofa on the rim of an active volcano, and a child hanging himself in his bedroom on a summer afternoon, watched by a line of his toys on the bed.

With the exercise book looking tiny and insubstantial in his large hands, Sam seemed to morph before me, from a heavily built, powerful man into a physically powerful, but emotionally tender youth, and from there, even further back in time, to looking like a small boy adrift in an unsafe, attacking world.

When he'd finished, he sat back and kept his gaze fixed on the letter-poem before him on the page. There was a long pause.

SARAH: Thank you for reading that and sharing it. Such a powerful piece of writing. How do you feel?
SAM: Like … like a door got opened in my brain, or something. I read it to Chelle, and she said, 'Oh my God, it's like you're a poet!' So I … I feel …
SARAH: … maybe a bit like a poet does?
SAM: Yeah right!

SARAH: I'm being serious, Sam. Poets use words to make things that are unbearable, overwhelming or unclear become more bearable, less overwhelming and clear. And that's what you've just done!

SAM: Yeah, but I'm not going to start carrying a notebook around with me and have to keep saying, 'Scuse me a minute, while I just make a note of that!'

SARAH: Well, *that's* an interesting image! You're mocking the idea of writing things down as you go through the day, but I do know people who do that and they find it very helpful. You don't have to make a big deal of it, but you *could* find the odd time during a day to make a brief note. It could just be the odd sentence on your phone. Especially if it's about something that has upset you or annoyed you. I think finding a way to express things in written words might suit you very well. I see now that you have a real way with words!

SAM: Mmm. I'll think about it.

We sat in silence for a while. Then Sam said, 'I never thought about it in this way, before, but I reckon I got someone to write a load of poems *on* me.'

At that, he rolled up both sleeves of his top to reveal the tattoos that covered his arms. We spent some time looking at them, with Sam explaining them to me. He talked about the images he had asked the tattooist to make on him, in the light of some of what we had been exploring in therapy. He could now see and speak with a lot of insight about the symbolic significance for him of some of his image choices, such as the jewelled dagger piercing a heart that was dripping blood, and of a voluptuous woman's body topped by a grotesque, skull-like Death's Head.

Until the end of our sessions, from this time on, Sam *did* start to use writing (in a new exercise book) to give him an outlet for the waves of powerful feelings that could still come over him from time to time, especially when those were angry feelings. As time went on, he wrote about other feelings too, and gradually, over the following months, anger began to take more of a balanced place in the pantheon of other 'on' feelings he experienced, alongside his excitement, desire, anticipation, anxiety and joy.

At the end of our work Sam was no longer a man with such a dangerously short fuse. He could walk away from situations where previously he would have 'blown his top'. About a month before we finished, he told me that he had proposed to Chelle. She had accepted, and their wedding plans included reading out their own vows to each other. Sam was going to write his in the form of a poem, 'For Chelle'.

SARAH: It's official – you *are* a poet.
SAM: Do I get a badge?

2

THE THERAPEUTIC USE OF MUSIC TO HELP WITH DISSOCIATION

Jay

That Music Always Round Me

That music always round me, unceasing, unbeginning, yet long untaught I
did not hear,

But now the chorus I hear and am elated,

A tenor, strong, ascending with power and health, with glad notes of day-
break I hear,

A soprano at intervals sailing buoyantly over the tops of immense waves,

A transparent base shuddering lusciously under and through the universe,

The triumphant tutti, the funeral wailings with sweet flutes and violins, all of
these I fill myself with,

I hear not the volumes of sound merely, I am moved by the exquisite
meanings,

I listen to the different voices winding in and out, striving, contending with
fiery vehemence to excel each other in emotion;

I do not think the performers know themselves—but now I think I begin to
know them.

Walt Whitman (1819–1892)

*An exploration of how the defence of dissociating often comes into the work when there
has been sexual violation, and how this was managed in the therapy with a very defensive young man. This was done partly by looking back at how his childhood had shaped
him; partly by working with the dissociation that happened in the therapy session; and
partly through the use of music during therapy, including in the sessions.*

Jay was pretty upfront from the very beginning of our work about the fact that he felt unable to trust me.

> JAY: Sorry. Don't take it personally. I just don't trust anyone apart from my sister. Sorry.

Both 'sorries' were said in a tone of voice that did not sound at all sorry but conveyed, rather, a quiet fury.

I told him that there might be many reasons for this to be the case and perhaps it was my job, rather than his, at the start of our work, to hold the belief or the hope that therapy could be trusted.

When he arrived for his first appointment at a service that offered young people counselling, advice and a drop-in facility, I was struck by how much Jay reminded me of some of the young men towards whom I could sometimes feel quite antagonistic when I encountered them out and about in my own neighbourhood: young guys who lived near me and behaved in ways I sometimes found off-putting and intimidating when I encountered them at my local bus stops, shops and other public spaces. He had the same very low-slung trousers, the same style of wearing a top with the hood pulled up to hide most of the face, the same rather wary, sullen expression that suggested trouble could be brewing imminently.

He sat down opposite me, and as soon as he told me he didn't trust me, he went on to say he had been raped a few weeks previously by a man he had met in a club.

Jay was 21, white, working class, originally from a large town in the midlands, and had a deep mistrust of almost everyone except his sister, who was seven years older than he was. Their mother had been under the thumb of their abusive stepfather as they grew up. (The family had had no contact with the children's biological father since he left shortly after Jay was born.) Jay had always turned to his sister as the person on whom he could rely to take his part, see his side of things, and try to look after him. Their stepfather seemed to have had undiagnosed and severe mental health problems, and was an extremely aggressive, controlling man who had brutally dominated the family household for as long as Jay could remember. He seemed to hate Jay in particular: targeting and scapegoating the boy – beating him and keeping him shut in his bedroom over long periods for such things as eating the last biscuit in a packet, or not cleaning his bike properly if it got muddy.

Jay's mother appeared to have had her spirit broken by the time Jay was old enough to remember how things were at home and incapable of stopping her partner's cruel and bullying behaviour towards herself and her children, whereas Jay remembered his sister continually trying to stand up to the stepfather, for herself, and also on behalf of her mother and brother. Jay described how his sister would always risk being punished herself by sneaking into Jay's room to bring him comics and sweets, after he had been beaten and sent to his room with the order that he was to be left alone. As the siblings grew older, she continued to try and stand up for her brother even more openly: arguing with their stepfather when he wanted to punish Jay, and defying the orders to not speak to him, or exclude him from meal times. She regularly risked being beaten herself as she tried to try protect her young brother. When she turned 18 she left home and moved to London, promising Jay that as soon as he turned 16, he could come and join her. The years that Jay lived alone with his mother and stepfather were desperate ones for him, and he felt he lived for the regular calls and texts of his sister.

By the time he was 14 he had the added strain of realising he was gay, and he lived in terror of this being somehow revealed to the stepfather (whom he always referred to, in sessions, as The Prick), knowing that if his stepfather knew this about him he would use it to escalate his sadistic cruelty towards Jay. Just before his sixteenth birthday he begged his sister to let him come and live with her in London, and she and the man who was now her fiancé both agreed to this. Jay left in the middle of the night without saying goodbye to his mother, with very few possessions, knowing that if he had said anything or had made any obvious preparations, his stepfather would have tried to prevent him leaving.

To begin with, life in London with his sister and her partner, and being free to live openly and explore the gay scene, had been a huge relief and great fun. Jay had begun to feel some hope about his future, although he and his sister did both worry about their mother, now that she was left alone with 'The Prick'. But it transpired that Jay was, unsurprisingly, not very good at looking after himself, now that he suddenly had so much more freedom. After years of such brutal repression and control, he found he had an impulse to let his behaviour swing to the extreme opposite of being so constrained. He would invariably feel drawn into acting in ways that were utterly out of control whenever he went out to bars, pubs and clubs. He drank a lot on his nights out, and ended up picking fights with other men, breaking shop windows and vandalising public spaces. He would also leave himself very vulnerable to being taken advantage of. He had his mobile phone, wallet and keys stolen more times than he could count. He would often pass out on park benches or night buses and come round hours later, sometimes covered in cuts and bruises, with no idea where he was or what had happened to him.

Having been so badly objectified and brutalised by his stepfather, and emotionally abandoned by his mother, it seemed that Jay had internalised these ways of behaving towards himself, and perpetuated both, painfully and repeatedly. His sister and her partner became ever more exasperated with him, and lectured him endlessly about steadying himself. But over the next five years he continued to be reckless, party hard, and lose every job he ever got in bars and clubs because, after a few weeks, he would not turn up for his shifts, or, if he did turn up, he would still be high or drunk from the night before.

In sessions we began to look at his behaviour as not only being the result of wanting to enjoy himself after so many years of repression and denial, but also as one of the consequences of the damage done to the development of a vital adult capacity to inhibit himself when appropriate. The cruel and repressive prohibitions of his stepfather had skewed and disabled his capacity to self-regulate and he could not contain any urge for the immediate gratification of a wish, or for the immediate expression of a feeling. We also explored his behaviour in the context of understanding it as part of his unconscious drive to repeat certain elements in life that felt deeply familiar to him, even though they were also agonising, such as being punished, made to feel a fool, being objectified and being physically hurt.

A few months after moving to London, he had had his drink spiked one night in a club, and woke up in a strange flat, fairly convinced that someone had had sex with him, but not being sure, and too embarrassed to ask the other two young men who were asleep next to him, in the same double bed, about what had happened. On that occasion he had snuck out and found his way home in the early morning. A few weeks later, a similar thing happened, and before long, Jay found out that he had a reputation 'on the scene' for being an easy lay, and someone who could be depended on to be up for threesomes, kinky sex, going to saunas, cottages, chemsex sessions, orgies – anything that required a lack of inhibition. He ended up feeling that this was the way it had to be, in order to be socially accepted. It began to seem normal to him that he should drink a lot and take drugs on every night out, to dampen down any anxiety that he might feel about the fact that he was probably going to let anyone he met during a night out have sex of any sort with him. He began to build up an ever-strengthening sense that men, and gay men in particular, including himself, could not be trusted, as he continued to put himself into situations where, in the end, some individual would target him to be used as a sexual object.

The latest episode in Jay's pattern had finally prompted his sister to insist that if he was to stay under her roof, he had to go and speak to someone about what was going on and get help in putting a stop to his damaging cycles of behaviour. Jay had done his usual thing of going out to a club and getting extremely drunk and what he called 'flirty'. I could imagine he was describing, with that adjective, some behaviours that were indicating a profound longing for physical closeness and affection, and some intimacy with someone. He had ended up talking to an attractive older man once he was already a little drunk, and then had suddenly felt extremely faint and dizzy after finishing a drink this man had bought him. He later suspected the drink had been spiked. He had come round somewhat to find he was being bundled into a taxi, and had vague memories of kissing a man in the back of the taxi before passing out again.

The next thing he remembered was coming round again, this time in a strange bed, in extreme pain as he was being anally penetrated. He found he couldn't breathe properly as the other man was holding his face hard down in a pillow and the penetration was extremely rough and caused Jay dreadful pain. He could hear the other man whispering threats of violence as well as sexually excited phrases, and he lay still in a frozen, terrified state. He later managed to tell me that his terror and anguish at the time were related to his belief that he would actually be murdered once the assault was over.

In fact, once the man finished using Jay sexually, he got up and made some coffee, brought a cup to Jay and drank one himself, while sitting on the bed where Jay had been lying, chatting to him and being affectionate, as if they had just been having consensual sex. Jay was in such pain and so traumatised, scared and disorientated, that he had barely been able to speak. He accepted the coffee and numbly went along with the pretence that they had both just enjoyed sex together, for fear of provoking this man to even worse behaviour. He finished the coffee as quickly as he could and then said he would have to be going. The man who had raped him showed Jay out and blew him a kiss, which Jay returned. (He would often go back to this fact in therapy sessions, to ask me, and himself, in tears, why had he done so, and berate himself for it.) Once he was home, Jay had tried to cover up what had happened out of overwhelming fear, shame and disgust, but the rape had caused severe tissue damage and he was in such pain and had such bad bleeding that in the end he told his sister, who insisted he go to their GP, and that he also get help with his emotional and psychological distress. It was his sister who had got the details of the service Jay had come to, and she had urged him to come and see a counsellor.

Jay had grudgingly given in to his sister's pressure to see a counsellor, but drew the line at going to the police to report the rape. He was adamant that the police would do nothing. It was something he had heard from plenty of other gay men – that on occasions when they, or someone they had known, had gone to the police to report a rape or other sexual violation which had taken place during or after a night out in a gay bar, club or pub, it had not been taken seriously, with attitudes and questions from the police officers that implied the person reporting the crime had foolishly put themselves in harm's way, had gone out looking for sex, and therefore should not expect that much could be done on their behalf, or that they should get much sympathy from any official quarters.

When I discussed my first meeting with Jay in my supervision with a more senior colleague, I came up with an image for how it felt to be in the room with him: it was as if I was trying to earn the trust of a wild animal, one that had long legs, was used to being hunted and had an explosive turn of speed and could be gone in an instant, if need be – something like a gazelle or impala. It was imperative to sit very still and quiet to begin with, to allow the animal to come close at its own pace.

As the sessions continued, I felt the need to put very little pressure on Jay and not burden him with too many questions or too much input from me. This would mean there were often long periods of silence in a session, during which he stared at the ground, or his hands. He quite often needed to go to the toilet at least once or twice in a session, and left the room to do so. He would usually mention at least once in each session that there were some things he needed to get off his chest, but that he couldn't bring himself to speak about them, 'yet'.

Each week there would eventually come a time in the session when he managed to say a few things about how he was feeling or what he was thinking. He would speak haltingly but very clearly and movingly about the endless stress and frustration and fear in his early life, or about the shame he felt about many of his current behaviours. The statements were usually addressed to the floor and after making them he would sit back and look at me with an uneasy, guarded expression, which seemed to epitomise the tension between his sense that no one was to be trusted, and his urge to make himself incredibly open to others, despite his mistrust.

Something new needed to come into the work to help Jay with the awful tension he felt between longing to reveal more of himself and dreading to do so.

There are many leading clinicians who have contributed to the thinking around the need that many clients have for their therapist to be able to shift the focus of the work from the unpacking of past losses and traumas, to, instead, make quite radical efforts to make space for other things to happen in the work apart from exploring past pain, in order to build up the client's capacity to bear a revisiting of and a working through of old hurts and losses. 'There are untold men whose sense of self is so porous and fragile that we have a responsibility to construct new ways of engaging with them' (Corbett 2016).

Peter Levine (2010) and other body-focused practitioners offer a number of helpful strategies to help a traumatised client feel more resourced so that they can better tolerate dipping deeper into old wounds. This resourcing of the traumatised client, or building 'new ways of engaging', sometimes requires the therapist to extend something about their usual way of working, and make creative adaptations in order to help the traumatised client make progress.

After some weeks, I talked with my supervisor about how I felt the need to gently introduce something else into the frame to help the work with Jay move forward. My supervisor encouraged me in my sense that it could be a welcome relief for both Jay and myself if I could find a way to open up other avenues in the work, to run parallel to the work of uncovering what impact his past experiences had had on him. We wondered about different ways this could happen, and about spending more time on looking at small things that might be going well in his life, or something that he had an interest in – anything that might support him in feeling that we didn't only have to talk about things that involved him feeling vulnerable, exposed and shamed, and at the affect of what gave him such pain to remember.

One week, quite early on in the session, I asked Jay what – apart from his sister – it was that kept him going, gave him pleasure, felt worth living for. He gave a semi-nervous, semi-sneering grin:

JAY: You mean apart from getting off my tits and shagging anything that moves?

SARAH: Yes, apart from that.

JAY: [With a scowl and a defiant stare at me] That would be my music.

It emerged that a huge part of Jay's story that had been left out so far was the key fact of his being a musician. He was absolutely passionate about music, and had never once mentioned this. He played the keyboard and guitar, wrote songs, performed solo in open spots whenever he could and was also trying to get a band together. I felt both excited to hear about this rich seam that had suddenly become available to us, and struck by how much I had missed of Jay by knowing nothing of this to date.

SARAH: It sounds like music is extremely important in your life. I wonder what you were listening to on the way here.

JAY: Why do you want to know that? So you can analyse me as some massive narcissist if it turns out it was my own stuff?

SARAH: You sound annoyed that I asked. As if you found the question a bit too intrusive?

I was struck by his use of the word 'narcissist', and could feel his use of that word alerting me to another side of Jay that had not been at all obvious in the way he had presented himself to me so far. As he shared more in this session about what kept him going, apart from his sister, he began to reveal more of a side that had not been visible until this stage of the therapy. It was a side he had not let me see and I had not guessed about, which not only involved his music, but also meant that he could talk knowledgeably about politics, history, economics and philosophy, all of which he had read a great deal about and had once wanted to study. Because he had dropped out of college after his GCSEs in order to move to London, he had, he said, lost any motivation to continue studying and now wanted to concentrate on his music instead.

From this point something shifted in the work and from that session onwards I trusted that we were building up enough of an alliance for Jay to feel a little more comfortable in the room with me. He could allow me to know more of who he was, in addition to being someone who was wounded and struggling.

Much of the inner discomfort he endured was mirrored in the physical discomfort he was often in during sessions. As well as a chair in which clients faced me, there was also a sofa in the room for them to use, if they preferred. Jay had shot a look at this sofa early on in the work and said 'You're not expecting me to lie down on that, are you?' making it clear this was in no way an inviting prospect for him. However, after some months it became clear that he often found sitting in the chair uncomfortable. He would shift around a great deal in his seat, take the cushion from behind him and put it on the floor, then almost immediately retrieve it and put it back behind him, only to get rid of it again a minute later. He stood up sometimes, ostensibly to straighten his trousers, but I thought it was also a way of relieving some kind of pain he felt when he was seated for any length of time.

One day, after even more than the usual shifting around, I raised the obvious discomfort he was in.

SARAH: You look as if sitting down isn't very comfortable for you today.

JAY: Yeah. Well. Sorry about that. I'm trying to get comfortable. But …

SARAH: Some people do prefer the sofa. I wonder if you might feel easier on it?

Jay looked over at it, and for a moment I thought he was going to get up and walk over to it, so as to try a more relaxing position. But although his muscles tensed up as if he was about to stand, he remained motionless, looking at the sofa, but somehow frozen. As I watched his face, a subtle change came over it, his face became oddly impassive – apparently calm, but his eyes had a strange appearance to me, as if his usual self was not looking out of them, and there was a lifeless fixity about their gaze, directed at the couch. He remained motionless for some time.

SARAH: Jay?

[There was no response, and he continued to sit, in a position that suggested he was about to get up to go over to the couch, but he did not move.]

SARAH: Jay. I wonder if you are able to speak to me and tell me what's going on for you?

JAY: Mmm.

SARAH: It looks as if something's happened for you that makes it hard to speak, hard to do anything.

JAY: Yeah … mmm.

SARAH: I think something has reminded you of something very painful and it's triggered a 'shock' response. [Pause.] And that's very overwhelming.

Jay's eyes shifted their gaze momentarily from the couch to the carpet, which I was glad to see. He could at least move his eyes to look away from the couch that might have been part of what had triggered him.

SARAH: It can be helpful to get out of a frozen state by just allowing our-selves to look around the room and name what we see. Can you do that?

JAY: Carpet.

SARAH: Good. OK. You can see the carpet. Can you say what colour it is?

JAY: Green. Greenish-greyish.

SARAH: And are you able to notice the feeling of your own breathing. How the breath is cool going into your nostrils, and warmer as it comes out?

JAY: [After a few breaths] Mmm. Yeah.

I continued to gradually ground Jay back into a state where he felt present within his own body, and in the 'here and now' with me, which took some time.

Once he was back, I checked out how able he felt to talk about what had happened, and he decided that now he wanted to get off his chest 'the thing' that he had not yet been able to, as it was out in the open, anyway, because of what had just happened. He disclosed that he was prone to episodes of what he described as 'zoning out'. They happened at any time, but especially if he felt some pressure to get to somewhere at a particular time, or perform a particular task he had been asked to. It became apparent that these episodes of dissociating were at least part of the reason that Jay was not willing to commit to picking up his studies, or to keeping a job. He was ashamed of the fact that he had a good chance of zoning out on the way to anything where there was an expectation that he would arrive at a certain time, and that if this happened he would quite often come round on a tube or a bus or a street a long way from where he had been intending to get to, and as a consequence would either be very late, or give up trying to get to the appointment. He hated this inability to be reliable and was very ashamed of it, as well as disturbed by it. He could tell that the usual judgement people made about him was that he was useless with timekeeping and that he must not care about letting people down or keeping them waiting. Because he found this judgement and criticism so painful, he preferred to avoid anything that might lead to him being late and risk the other person thinking badly of him.

We talked about what might have triggered the episode of dissociating that had just happened in the room with me, and Jay described how some part of him had very much wanted to go and lie down on the sofa so that he could relax and feel more comfortable, but that the thought of that had also brought to mind instances when he had been invited/pressured/expected to lie down on a bed or sofa, in order to have sex with someone on a night out, when he hadn't really wanted to. Before he knew how to say anything about that, he found himself frozen, in a suspended state. As we talked about this, an even earlier memory came to Jay.

He was around eight years old, his stepfather and mother had decided to go out for the evening somewhere, and his sister had also gone out for the evening with some friends. Jay had been left alone in the house, which he had been expecting to enjoy and had looked forward to. However, once he had the house to himself, and all was quiet and still, he had begun to feel unaccountably disturbed and restless. He had felt lonely as well as alone, had cast around for something to do, and hit on the idea of washing the kitchen floor, thinking how pleased his mother and stepfather would be when they came home and found a spotless kitchen floor.

His eyes filled with tears as he recounted how happy it had made the eight-year-old boy to think of pleasing these two, and how he had begun with great energy and focus – moving all the furniture out of the room, getting a mop and bucket, rolling up his sleeves. However, it did not take long for the young Jay to feel he could not carry out the task he had set himself in the way he had imagined. Soon the floor was awash with dirty water, which trickled under appliances and soaked into the edge of the carpet in the hall. No matter how much he swilled and wiped and tried to dry the floor, the worse it looked. He began to keep a nervous eye on the clock, trying to work out how much more time he would have left to try and at least dry the floor and put back the table and chairs. He abandoned the mop after a while and tried to use handfuls and handfuls of kitchen roll to dry and wipe the floor.

As he remembered and retold the story, the tears that had hovered in his eyes finally fell, thick and fast.

He had wiped and thrown away dozens of handfuls of kitchen paper, in an increasing panic, until he had looked up at the kitchen clock, noticed it was the time that his stepfather had said they would return, and almost immediately heard his stepfather's car pull up outside the house. At that moment, Jay said he zoned out for the first time that he consciously remembered doing so. He could remember feeling a huge wave of panic, of an imperative need to try to rush and finish the job and get the furniture back in place, while another, even stronger, impulse simply overrode the urge to keep going, and had simply paralysed him. He remembered standing stock-still in the middle of the dirty, wet kitchen floor, looking at the mess he had made and feeling as if his body was filling up with some heavy substance like concrete, making him utterly unable to move, while his head seemed strangely light and buzzy and as if it was no longer attached to the rest of him. He stood, frozen to the spot, as he heard the adults open the front door, come in, take their outdoor things off and walk into the kitchen.

When his stepfather and mother came in, the look of fear and horror on his mother's face and the look of fury on his stepfather's seemed to break open his frozen state, and the eight-year-old Jay found himself suddenly shaking and sobbing. The adult Jay covered his face with his hands and sobbed in the present, as he remembered this part of the scene from the past. After his sobs lessened, we sat in silence.

SARAH: You were so upset and frightened. It had all gone so wrong.
JAY: I don't know why I even thought of cleaning the floor for them, anyway. Stupid, stupid, stupid little kid!

SARAH: You sound very angry with yourself. [Pause.] I wonder whose voice that is, that comes out when you call yourself a stupid kid? Who might have said such a thing to you?

JAY: Oh, it was what he always said, when he'd give me a beating. He'd grab hold of my collar or sleeve or something, and say it in time to when he was hitting me.

[Jay enacted it on the arm of the chair, saying, 'You stupid, stupid, stupid, stupid little kid!' and punched the chair on every 'stupid'.]

SARAH: I see. So that would be your stepfather's view: to see the action of washing the floor as stupid?

JAY: Yeah.

SARAH: So I wonder how it would feel to hear that there could be other ways of seeing that boy's behaviour on that evening?

JAY: Yeah? Like?

SARAH: I'm imagining some people might see a sensitive boy, a thoughtful boy, who got the idea to do something that would be nice for his mum, and that might get his stepdad off his back for a bit. But no one had showed him how to mop a floor before, so he found it was more complicated than he realised and he got overwhelmed. That's what *some* people might think of that scene.

[Jay looked as if he was mulling over what I had said. We sat in silence for a while.]

SARAH: Can I ask what your stepfather's reaction was?

JAY: Huh. The usual. He said something like 'What the fuck do you think you're playing at!' and gave me a beating, and made me clean the whole kitchen up while he and my mum went to watch TV in the other room.

SARAH: Right. So … What if … what if an 'adult Jay' could have somehow magically stepped into that scene, and intervened for 'little Jay'? What would he have said or done, to stand up for that boy?

JAY: You mean me? Me now? What would I do if The Prick tried to lay a finger on me now?

SARAH: Sort of, but it's also about imagining that you're there for the boy-who-was-you. So it would not only be about standing up to your stepdad, but also about looking after that little boy.

JAY: So that's more like, more like what did I wish my mum had done.

SARAH: Oh, OK. And what would that have been?

JAY: It would have … I wished she could have … just … [More tears fell and his voice cracked as he went on] I wanted her to just say, 'No. Don't. Stop it. You can't treat us like this. We're leaving.'

SARAH: Yes, I see. And what can you imagine she would do then, to take care of little Jay?

JAY: She'd just … come and put her arm round me and say, 'Get your things, we're going, and we don't ever have to come back.' And if he tried anything she'd …

[He broke down sobbing again.]

JAY: But she never did! She never did stand up to him, not once!

SARAH: No. That was so awful for that little boy. His sister tried to. But his mother never did.

JAY: And we could have just gone, and left him the fucking house! It was horrible anyway, like living in hell. She wasn't happy. Why? I'll never understand why she didn't just get our stuff together and go!

[He looked furiously at me.]

SARAH: Yes. It seems incredible, in one way. [Pause.] But maybe it's a bit like your sister can't understand why you keep getting into fights and losing your jobs?

This was a bit of a gamble of an intervention, but I decided to risk it, as I thought our alliance was strong enough by now for a bit of a challenge. Jay pulled a pained face and grunted as if I'd scored a point, and he was conceding it reluctantly.

SARAH: If our self-esteem reaches rock bottom, it's very hard to exert ourselves, even a little bit. Which I think you know about.

JAY: [Gloomily] You mean I'm like Mum? I take after her?

SARAH: Well, we all take after our parents to some extent. I think I meant more that … that maybe you understand more than you think you do about what got in the way of your mum standing up to your stepdad and stopping the abuse.

[We sat in silence again, and after a few minutes Jay sighed deeply.]

JAY: She always puts everyone else before her. She never even felt confident to sign her name on forms, or speak for herself if someone phoned the house. And … it's like … me … when I say to myself, 'I'm going to get to the gym this week. I am going to cut out the booze, and maybe just stay in and just get an early night, one time in the week', but then it comes to it, I'm like ... 'Why bother? What's it matter if I get smashed again, really. Who cares?'

SARAH: Mmm. Yes. I hear the way your commitment to your own self-care can easily get undermined. It's not easy to keep believing that we are of worth when we are also carrying lots of unresolved, unprocessed trauma from our past.

I chose this moment to offer some context for how we could understand Jay's response to overwhelming stress.

As well as needing compassion for how distressing and disorientating episodes of dissociation can be, most clients who experience them also find it very helpful to have them normalised and explained, in terms of what goes on in our bodies when we are traumatised or extremely stressed. I gave him a brief explanation of how our bodies attempt to keep us in a state of reasonable balance, and how having been traumatised can badly knock out the usual systems that regulate our bodies. This gave Jay a way of understanding what was happening to him when he zoned out, which reduced the acute shame and dread he felt about those episodes, which had become a part of what he had to manage living with every day.

JAY: So I'm not a basket case then?

SARAH: No, that's right, you're not. In fact, your body is responding completely normally and as we would expect in a situation of feeling acutely at risk. It's just that you've now developed an extremely sensitive 'on' switch to any potential danger. A bit like a house with a smoke alarm that goes off at the slightest thing, even if it's just someone making some toast.

Of course, to intellectually grasp that dissociating can happen because something has triggered a hypersensitive response to a perceived threat is not the same as being able to stop oneself from getting triggered. If someone has been brought up from their earliest years, as Jay was, in ways that mean they could not feel a basic safety with their caregivers, they can certainly find it helpful to understand what lies behind their extreme responses to even mild stress. But then they also need long-term input of many different kinds – physical, emotional, cognitive, creative – to help them bring about some changes. When these different sorts of input can happen over time, and in the context of feeling cared about and consistently supported by others, they find that their body can eventually be fundamentally reprogrammed in its responses to stress. Such clients can eventually learn how to feel at home in their own body, and manage their tendency to defend against painful emotions and sensations in better ways than by numbing out, but it often takes time.

My supervisor and I once more discussed some ways that Jay and I could do more in sessions than simply sit and talk *about* stressful things, and to do this in ways which would not be at risk of triggering his dissociating defence. Because he loved music so much, I wondered about gently introducing the subject of music into the sessions again. The first time I had asked him directly about the music he liked he had been prickly – both angry and defensive. But now that we had been working together for some months and had more of an alliance, might returning to the area of music feel more bearable? If so, my supervisor and I agreed that talking *about* music was not quite enough.

I asked Jay in the next session how he would feel about us listening to some music together. He looked interested, if a little wary.

JAY: How would that work?
SARAH: One way could be if you have some music on your phone, then you could choose a track for us to listen to. And I have my iPod here, so then I could choose a track for us too.

Different expressions played across Jay's face as he took in my suggestion. He looked amused, pleased, excited, then a little suspicious. We sat in silence for a while. After some minutes a sadness seem to creep over him and into the room. The atmosphere in the room somehow seemed to become darker and heavier. He put his hand up to cover his mouth and spoke through the bars of his spread fingers.

JAY: Yeah. I can do that. I could do it now. [He fished around in his hoody pocket.] I'll play the thing I used to listen to a lot after that guy …

He didn't finish the sentence and let the silence stand. He never said the word 'rape'. There was a pause while he untangled his earphones, and I noticed how surprised I was that he was willing to go straight for the jugular, so to speak, and play something that he associated with that traumatising incident.

I readied myself for some music that was pretty alien to me. Jay was considerably younger than me and I knew from experience with my adolescent sons that their taste in music had lost me some time ago.

JAY: Shall I just play it from the phone speaker, or … ? [He looked enquiringly as his earphones dangled between us.] Or … you could just listen with my earphones, and I'll … Oh, I dunno.

[He began to look disheartened. It didn't take very much for him to feel sure that something wouldn't work, or that someone wouldn't keep being interested and engaged.]

SARAH: I think it would be good if we could both listen to it together at the same time. What if I had one earpiece and you had the other?

JAY: [Brightening again] Yeah. Yeah. Ok. That could work if you … [He gestured that I would need to move my chair a little nearer to his.]

Once I had repositioned my chair, with his guidance, we were obviously and suddenly sitting much closer to each other than we usually did. He plugged one of his earpieces into his left ear, and proffered me the other one. I felt the intimacy of sitting closer and of sharing his earphones as I fitted the plastic nubbin of the earpiece that had recently been in Jay's ear, into mine. I found myself thinking of how he had often been violated by having something pushed into him that he had not wanted, both literally by his rapist and by other men, and psychically and emotionally by his abusive stepfather as a boy. Now here was a tiny role reversal, in as much as he was now arranging for something to be put, both physically and psychically, *into* me. In this way, he could be the more powerful one, but in ways that were tolerable for and allowable by me. My thoughts swirled on to the role reversal that had happened at times when my kids had been very small infants, in their high chairs: after I had been helping them to eat by spooning mashed-up food into their mouths and they were full up, they would often then want to feed me. How clearly their concentration and delight showed on their faces as they became the feeder and I the one fed!

Italian scientists Rizzollatti and Ciaghero have explored the specialised cells in the frontal cortex of the human brain that seem to play a part in enabling us to intuit an embodied sense of what it might feel like to be another being, simply by looking at that other being. These specialised cells have been called 'mirror neurons' and play a central part in a capacity to empathise (Van Der Kolk 2014). Simply watching another person turns out to be an activity during which a very great deal is going on for us, and this can be detected in our brain's activity. When, for example, babies and their carers gaze so intently at each other, there are layers upon layers of important learning going on, at both a conscious and unconscious level. As it feeds, the baby is, in effect, sensing into the reality of, *I wonder what could it feel like –*

being that one, the one doing the feeding? As the adult spoons the mush in, they are, in effect, sensing into the reality of, *I wonder what could it feel like – being the baby, the one who is fed?*

A capacity to intuit or imagine how it is to *be* another person is at the heart of being empathic – of being able to realise that, although not everyone and everything in the world feels exactly the same as 'me', we can nevertheless feel into what it *might be like* to be 'the other' and find points of sensate similarity. The attunement of a caregiver, and the give-and-take of imaginative play, was what Jay had lacked and been left so hungry for, while growing up. It was what being able to share some music with me was giving him a tiny taste of.

He pored over the screen of his phone, searching for a particular track, and I watched him as he did so, frowning with concentration. I had been preparing for a piece of music that would need me to bracket my judgement about taste, and which might be opaque to me, but in fact I suddenly found myself listening to a track that I already knew well, by a 1970s New York punk band. My surprise that Jay knew this piece of music was intermingled with my own memories of listening to the song when I had been a young adult, and also with the poignancy of hearing the lyrics in a new way – as a communication of Jay's inner response to his rape and abuse.

As the track played I felt very sensitive to the fact that, to begin with, Jay was scanning my face, perhaps in order to read something about my response to his choice of music. After a while, however, he began, instead, to look down at the ground. After a while I too looked down, at first deliberately and then unconsciously, mirroring him, as we both became increasingly absorbed by the music. It seemed to me that we were deeply involved together in allowing this powerful song to enter us and have an effect. There is a long guitar solo in the piece that is janglingly, piercingly plaintive, and which continues for a long time, building in a crescendo that wails spikily on and on, and evokes in the listener both a longing for it to peak and stop, and yet an awe and scratchy enjoyment of its relentless power and expressiveness.

When the song ended, Jay looked up at me, once again with a wariness, a cautious expectation – the wild creature was ready to stay if the reaction to his offering was fitting, ready to flee if it wasn't.

SARAH: It sounds like the guys in the group really know something about the complicated feelings that someone who has been sexually hurt could be left with.

[Jay gave a small assenting nod. We sat in silence for a little, letting the
intensity of our joint experience subside.]

JAY: [Suddenly] I can't think what you would pick for me.

SARAH: Mmm. I wonder what you'll make of it. It's by ... [I named a
band I liked].

JAY: Oh, yeah, I know them. They were good a few years ago, when
I saw them on the Glastonbury highlights.

SARAH: Ah. So you might already know this track.

I fished out my iPod from my bag. It had no earphones with it and I felt
moved when Jay simply unplugged his earphones and held them out to me
so I could put them into my iPod, which I saw as a small but significant act
of trust in what we were doing together. I found the track and played it. It
was a sweet, simple tune with the female vocalist singing powerfully from
the heart in a sound that was raw, but ultimately hopeful. The lyrics included
a reference to being so low sometimes that the singer had felt she might not
continue to live, and yet some life force had pulled her onwards.

Now it was my turn to watch Jay's face as he listened. Different expressions
passed across it, and although a slight frown was a constant, it seemed to be a
frown that was to do with deep absorption, rather than displeasure. As soon
as it had finished, he looked up at me and I was surprised, as well as pleased,
to see a lopsided grin appear.

[He gave a short cough.]

JAY: You picked it to be encouraging!

SARAH: I think I *did* have that in mind. It is encouraging. But it's made
by people who've been through some stuff. Some very dark times.
Yet they still hope.

JAY: Mmm.

SARAH: Perhaps there have been times when you thought you wouldn't
make it?

JAY: [With an uneasy laugh] Really? You think that I must have thought
I wouldn't make it? Do *you* sometimes think I might not make it?

I pondered his comment. As I did, I felt the acuity of Jay being able to hone
in on the darkest part of what may have been unconscious in my choice
of a track for him. I did indeed sometimes fear for his safety and had on
occasion wondered if he would 'make it' through another day. In his book
on working psychotherapeutically with men who have experienced sexual

violation, Alan Corbett highlights the risk of suicide that is often in the frame with this client group. He highlights the severe depression that runs 'like a thread through the fabric of a male survivor's psyche', and refers to the research indicating that if there has been abuse in childhood, whether violent, sexual or both, there is a greatly increased risk of suicidal behaviour for such men.

> Girls who have been sexually abused have a threefold increase risk of suicidal thoughts and plans, compared to non-abused girls. Boys who have been sexually abused have a ten-fold increase for suicidal plans and threats, and a fifteen-fold increased risk for suicide attempts, compared to non abused boys. (Corbett 2016)

Tempering the need to be aware of the reality and depth of Jay's depression was my awareness that an unhelpful pattern in Jay's life was that others would always think the worst either *of* him (as I had, when I first met him, and his stepfather always had), or think the worst *for* him (as I sometimes did now and his sister obviously also often did). And at least some of my thinking around this choice of music track for Jay had actually been linked to how hopeful it was: how much it spoke to the redemptive side of having something to live for, some creative potential to fulfil. So I chose now to focus on this aspect of the song and why I had chosen it in my reply to his question.

SARAH: I *do* think it's important that the singer names that she sometimes thought that she wouldn't make it. But she is singing about the fact that, ultimately, she *did* make it. She's singing about how sometimes we have to hold on to a trust that our life's path *might* change for the better. [Pause.] Maybe I chose it because it's a song about someone who has a lot to offer, even though – maybe even *because* – they have been through the mill. [Long pause.] And I think that's true for you. That *you* have a lot to offer.

JAY: Oh! Well! Thanks. [He picked at the seams of his jeans, and stood up to straighten them and sat down again.] You're probably the first person who's said that for … a long time.

SARAH: You haven't been told encouraging things about your potential for a while?

JAY: Nah. Well, not by anyone who knows what they're talking about. My sister thinks I'm wasting my time with the music stuff. The other guys in the band are pretty dumb, really. They're all convinced we're going to make the big time, no bother. They've no idea!

SARAH: Mmm. So how would it be if you could believe that I do see something of your creative potential?

JAY: [A long pause] If I could trust it, that would be … good. I suppose.

SARAH: How would you know it was good? What sensations in your body would tell you it felt good?

JAY: Umm. My shoulders would drop. Umm. My guts would feel easier. My chest wouldn't be so tight. I could just be … just feel … My jaw would … I dunno.

As he named sensations in the different parts of his body, I could see subtle changes in those parts. As he described that his shoulders would drop, they dropped slightly; his posture softened, his face softened and brightened slightly.

The approach of getting a client to wonder what it would be like *if* something more positive could be true, and then really helping them to focus on what the imagined physical sensations would be *if* they felt happier, more confident, appreciated, and so forth, is a very simple but effective one. It can be a very good intervention for clients who have been badly let down many times and therefore have every reason not to hope for good outcomes, and who don't yet dare to take on board affirming and appreciative feedback, in case they are horribly let down again. It gives these clients the safety of knowing they are 'only' being asked to imagine what it would feel like *if* they were cared about, are happier, etc., and that they are not being asked to trust that this is definitely going to happen.

JAY: It would just feel … good.

SARAH: Mmm. So it would be a *good* thing to hear that your creative potential is seen and valued, if you could trust it. Yes. I get that it would feel good.

We sat in silence together, for a few minutes, until the end of the session. At the end, as he packed away his iPod, Jay said, 'I might have to write a song about this.'

SARAH: About the session today?

JAY: Nah. About what happened. About the rape.

I was taken aback by the sudden clarity and ease with which he could name the act.

In my notes after the session, I first wrote about how the music seemed to have opened up profound areas for the work. How it had helped both reveal and then contain deep levels of thinking and feeling that might not have otherwise emerged, culminating in Jay suddenly being able to name what had actually happened to him for the first time, and for him to envision a way to contain his felt experience of it, by making a song about it. But when I read back over the notes, I saw I had missed something. On reflection, I saw it was not simply the music itself that had been so significant. It was the *sharing* of the music that had been so affecting and effective: it was listening to a piece of music *with another person* – thinking about it and talking about it *with another* who was respectfully engaged in the process alongside him – that had been an important part of the healing experience.

Listening to the songs with another had woven an intricate web so that Jay could feel he was held by a number of supportive, connecting threads that stretched way beyond the consulting room. These threads connected him to his past self, to his present self, and to me, for sure. But, beyond that, it had connected both of us to the individuals who had created and performed the songs we had just listened to, and, even more widely, to every person who had ever listened to and been touched by those songs. Jay had had, it seems, a profound and helpful experience of feeling he was not alone in those minutes of listening. And this helped his whole body have a vital experience – one that meant that the world could be trusted on occasion, that others in the world, apart from his sister, might be people who would not hurt or exploit him, and with whom it might be safe to play.

Of course, therapy is often not so much in the business of compensating clients for their terrible losses, as it is about helping them properly feel and metabolise the reality of the impact of their loss; 'It's less about trying', as one of my senior colleagues once said to me, 'to make everything all right for the client, and more about making it all right that, on occasion, it has been absolutely *not* all right for them'. But sometimes, especially with clients whose ego strength is extremely underdeveloped and who have very limited support outside sessions, it is so helpful for the sessions to be places where they also have an opportunity to contact and experience something that feels genuinely good. For Jay, having the visceral experience in the session of listening to music with another, and thereby taking part in a form of play and openness during which nothing went horribly wrong, during which he was not shamed or blamed or hurt, was very potent. It was a tiny but important step in re-educating his body so that he could begin to know the felt sense of it being possible to trust someone else in addition to his sister.

He did indeed go on to write a song that was about the evening he was raped. A few weeks later he brought his iPod to the session to play me a rough version of it. It was very moving to sit with him once again, sharing earphones, but this time listening to his own creation, into which he had poured some of the excruciating thoughts and feelings he had been carrying since the rape and trying to hide. Thoughts that he was to blame, that he was disgusting and deserved to be treated like dirt, that he was too sick, too perverted, too broken to be loveable. The song contained his agonies, and gave them a shape and form that made them both bearable for Jay, and wholly palpable to another.

As his sense grew that he could put into songs more dark experiences which he could not communicate about in any other way, his hope for the future and his sense of himself as someone who had something to offer both grew. Once Jay had an embodied experience of himself as someone who could be creative and successfully produce a song that was valued by someone whom he now (cautiously) trusted and respected, he began to find it easier to bear the truth that, as well as being creative and inspired, he also had some problems that needed serious attention. He was more receptive to his sister's and my suggestions about returning to the GP to ask for more help for his pelvic pain and recurring haemorrhoids. He felt able to acknowledge that his dissociation was a problem that wouldn't just disappear on its own. He was more open to experimenting in sessions with me around techniques to help him to ground and soothe himself if he got triggered. They included: slow, deep breathing; picturing a calm, safe place and having 'an anchor' such as a thumb squeeze to prompt the memory of that calm place; and physically grounding himself with gentle pats and taps on different parts of his body to reaffirm his sense of the actual space and solidity of his body. After a month or so of practising these strategies, both in and outside our sessions, he became much quicker at getting himself out of a dissociated state, and eventually even some-times managing to nip an incipient episode in the bud.

Jay carried on seeing me for nearly a year once he was feeling more hopeful and on an even keel, to build on the support and containment of the therapy. He continued to benefit from the support of his beloved sister, her husband, and his music. A few months before we ended, he found himself a job behind the bar in a gay club run by two older men who became good figures and mentors in Jay's life. They encouraged Jay to do 'open mike' spots in the club whenever possible. Jay also began putting his music out into the world online, and grew a small but loyal fan base.

He named two wishes that were unfulfilled at the time we drew our work to a close: that his mother would extricate herself from the toxic bond she had with Jay's stepfather, and that he could feel able to risk another intimate sexual encounter at some point. Although neither of those wishes seemed to Jay as if they were going to happen any time soon, he felt able to accept that this was the case. In our last session, he said that he thought his future was 'looking better', and I agreed.

3

THE NEED TO BOTH RESPECT
AND DISMANTLE DEFENCES
George

This is the curse of life: that not
A nobler calmer train
Of wiser thoughts and feelings blot
Our passions from our brain;

But each day brings its petty dust
Our soon-chok'd souls to fill,
And we forget because we must,
And not because we will.
            Matthew Arnold (1822–1888)

*This chapter helps to explore the typically engrained habit for many men of cutting off
from any vulnerability; this can prevent men who have been abused from getting support.
It explores how working with ways to let go of being 'the hero' helped one man develop
a different sort of resilience and strength, more useful than the brittle strength of needing
to appear invincible to harm. It illustrates how there was a need in the work to address
(1) past woundings; (2) current family difficulties; and (3) the suppressed need for emotional self-expression.*

Many men and boys have been trained to be very contained and suppressed
around their emotions. Some would argue that males also have an in-built
predisposition to be so. Whatever the origin or flavour of the nature/nurture
balance, in terms of masculine identity, the result tends to be the same –
many boys and men feel a deep inhibition about connecting to and showing
certain feelings in their everyday life, especially those feelings to do with
fear, vulnerability and sorrow.

   Any therapist working with a man who has been sexually abused is
facing a person who has an impressive set of reasons for being ambivalent

about therapy, and may be both dreading and yet longing for a process in which he will be invited and encouraged to revisit certain extremely painful feelings.

Some men may be trying to protect their core self from uncomfortable feelings with alcohol and drug addictions, compulsive behaviours, eating disorders, or other obviously problematic ways. But ego defences can also be more subtle. Trying to ensure we are always seen in a good light, for example, is a powerful and common ego defence. Striving for excellence, attempting to always be helpful, tidy, on time, agreeable, etc. – all these can be ego defences that have been unconsciously put in place to ensure we will never feel a whiff of shame, rejection or criticism. Those sorts of coping strategies, which are employed to help to protect someone from the agony of being rejected or ridiculed, can be acting as ego defences, just as vigorously as, say, the excessive use of alcohol and drugs can.

George had some powerful defences against feeling the shame and pain of the sexual abuse and trauma he had experienced, that took the form of being very focused on the needs of others.

When I opened the door to him for our first meeting in my private practice, I had an immediate impression of his ease and assurance. A tall, broad-shouldered white man in his mid-fifties, he was dressed in a smart but sober suit. He shook my hand with an air of confidence and an awareness of his status. We had spoken briefly on the phone, so I already knew that he had a quietly authoritative way of talking.

GEORGE: Sarah? Good to meet you.

When he came to sit facing me, he crossed one leg elegantly over the other, smoothed one hand down his dark blue silk tie, and shook his other arm slightly, so that a heavy and expensive watch changed position slightly on his wrist.

He gave me a small, inviting smile after a moment.

GEORGE: So?

I noticed a feeling of the tables being somehow turned, and that it could almost be the case that George was now in charge of the space.

I smiled back. 'So.'

George cocked one eyebrow at me with an almost amused expression.

GEORGE: You'd like me to begin? Where should I start … ? Well, as you already know, I found your details online. And … I think I chose to come and see you partly because of where you are. Geographically speaking, I mean. My wife and I have just helped our eldest get her first property in this neck of the woods. Not far from here. It's good for her to get her foot on the ladder, even if it's a modest first rung. And it would be very convenient, very quick, to come here after work, and then go straight on to Lexi's and give her a hand with doing her place up.

As George finished his sentence a soft, thrumming cheep sounded from his jacket's inside pocket. He drew out a very large smart phone and glanced at the screen briefly, before jovially addressing the phone – 'No way, my friend! You can wait.' He turned the phone off, placed it face down on the low table by his chair, and then drew out a second, even larger smart phone from one of his jacket's outside pockets, and turned that one off as well.

GEORGE: Sorry about that. Work following me round! Where were we?
SARAH: You mentioned it might be convenient to come here.
GEORGE: Yes, right. It would be a way of combining, um … *this* [he gestured to the room we sat in] this umm … *therapy business* with seeing Lexi. Lexi is my stepdaughter – Alexa's her given name. I married her mum, Steph, when Lexi was ten, so I've been a dad to her for the last 12, 13 years.

George had mentioned on the phone that part of why he wanted to explore having some sessions was to do with problems in his family at the moment, although there were also some other things he wanted to be able to talk through.

SARAH: Is there something about yours and Alexa's relationship that has prompted you to …
GEORGE: [Interrupting] No, no!
[He looked almost shocked at the thought.]
GEORGE: Lexi and I get on very well, very well indeed. She's a super young woman – really together, and doing ever so well; working in a law firm and … No, no, she's not the problem.
[His open, affable expression changed subtly, and became ever so slightly troubled as he went on.]

GEORGE: Part of the problem is to do with, well … my son, Franco. He's 13 and he *is* mine – biologically speaking, I mean. He came along almost immediately after Steph and I got together. She said she didn't want to be one of those old mothers, and she was looking at 40 when we got involved, so there was no point hanging around, and so there we were, ten months after we got married: with Franco. And … he's … He's a bright boy, a lovely chap in many ways. But … a handful for his mother. A complex character. Yes.

In settings where there is some explicit sense of the most obvious issue for a client, such as in a bereavement or an addiction service, then the difficulty the client wants help with tends to be at least partly implicit in the fact of them having come to a specific service. In private practice, or more generic services, it often requires a little more 'digging' in the first sessions, to get some clarity about what the client is most troubled about, and what it is that they need some support with. I was aware as George spoke that if he had found my details 'online', this might have meant he had seen my website, on which I mention the areas in which I specialise, including working with male survivors of sexual violation. I knew, from past clients who were male survivors, that this had been the deciding factor in them making an appointment. This was in my mind as George continued to speak.

GEORGE: Anyway, just recently, he's been a bit … Things have been pretty … shall we say … umm … they've come to a bit of a boiling point with Franco. His school have made it clear he's drinking in the Last Chance Saloon.
SARAH: I see.
GEORGE: And … [George smoothed his tie again.] I have said to my wife, who is of course at her wits' end, that now might be the time to call the professionals in. But we're not really very keen on the whole psychology thing. I mean, the school did offer various sorts of support and so on … but … I think, that the thing is … Well, anyway. Now, I would say, it's all got beyond what we can reasonably be expected to manage on our own … And it seemed to me that there could be nothing lost by making a discreet professional appointment to talk a number of things through. And perhaps there could be something to be gained.
SARAH: Right. So some things are difficult in your family at the moment. Can you say more about the impact this has on you?

[George looked slightly puzzled. He gave a slight frown and smiled at the same time.]

GEORGE: Well … I … We haven't …

[He cleared his throat.]

GEORGE: One always want to do one's best for one's family, of course. But it can be quite … draining to get back from a full day's work and find one's wife and son at loggerheads, yet again. But … I should make it clear that I am not the one most impacted by all this. So I'm not quite sure what else to say.

SARAH: No?

GEORGE: No. I should say that it is my son and wife who bear the brunt of the … the troubles. I am … more in the way of a helpless bystander.

There was a long pause while I waited to see if something else would emerge to help me get a clearer grasp of what George might be coming for. After a short silence he gave me a small, rueful smile.

GEORGE: I have the feeling you're waiting for more.

SARAH: And is there more?

GEORGE: Well, absolutely! You name it! His school work's gone down the pipes. General attitude – very poor. He was at a very good school that finally called 'time' on him last year, after all sorts of silly she-nanigans. Using marijuana and nitrous oxide and what not. We found a good school for him in London where he's a day pupil now, but the problems have gone on. Lots of the time he's just up in his room, on his Xbox. I think the current school's about to pull the plug if he doesn't buck his ideas up.

SARAH: Mmm. It sounds a very stressful situation. So, would it be correct to say you're thinking that coming for some sessions with me would be in order to somehow, indirectly, benefit your whole family?

GEORGE: Well … No. Not quite. I … perhaps there is a little of that. But, no, there is something that I, myself, would like to talk over and … in a way … lay to rest. I think if it was purely a question of how to support Franco, we would … you know, there are other avenues we would, in fact we *have*, pursued. Various things – trying to find him hobbies, and so on.

SARAH: So there might be something you would like to gain from having sessions that is *not* directly related to anything you have already mentioned?

GEORGE: Absolutely, absolutely. [George's tone was almost soothing, as if
   he was attempting to reassure me.]

I could feel myself really struggling to catch hold of what it was George
might be coming to therapy sessions *for*. This is not so unusual in a first
session, but there was a way in which I felt I was being subtly managed by
George – a mixture of being built up and yet a bit put down and sidelined
by him – which left me feeling unusually rudderless. It was as if every
time I attempted to steer a particular course, George would gently make it
apparent that we in fact needed to go in a very different direction.

SARAH: I wonder if you could help me out a bit here, George. I don't
   seem to feel quite clear about what it is that you might like to get out
   of coming to sessions with me. Would you be able to try and put that
   in a nutshell – sort of … sum it up?
[There was a pause. George uncrossed his legs and then crossed them
   again.]
GEORGE: [Taking a deep breath and letting it out with a large sigh.]
   I have thought, well … *wondered* for some time, if certain events in
   my childhood have … left their mark in some way. And I think that
   it is these that I would benefit from being able to speak about with
   to a professional person, rather than a family member.
[He cleared his throat and smiled in a way that invited me to be amused
   by him, and spread his hands apart.]
GEORGE: You can tell I'm a bit of a novice at all this *unburdening myself*
   business!

I did not smile back as it seemed that to do so would be buying in to
George's view, which had emerged as we talked, that while other people's
problems were important and deserved to be taken seriously, his were
amusing and could be taken lightly. I did not want to collude with that particular narrative.

GEORGE: But I have to confess, I'm not really clear what the benefit
   would be of disclosing certain events to you. I suppose I have a hope
   they could be laid to rest and … Not that they aren't already in the
   past, and well-nigh forgotten, most of the time, but … Anyway …
   I … I've lost the thread a bit now. I don't quite know what else you
   want me to say.

SARAH: Perhaps … you have some mixed feelings about whether or not it would be helpful to come here and talk. A part of you might be willing to believe that, and a part may not be so sure?

GEORGE: Yes. That's quite a good way of putting it. A good way of cutting to the chase! Perhaps I should do the same. So … to put it bluntly – I was, as the term goes, *abused* as a boy. I have to say I really have given this very little thought over the years. It didn't seem to be such a dreadful thing that it needed to be dragged up and gone over. The chap who, I suppose you would say 'molested' me was not a monster or anything of the sort. In many ways (perhaps this will sound odd, but I think it's true), he was a decent man. He was a teacher at my prep school and … you know, I think he was a rather gifted teacher, and very devoted to the school. He gave many of us boys a very good start in a lot of things – music and tennis and photography. And the way he was … I mean, what he did … Well, let's say, it wasn't the very worst way these things can play out. A while ago I bought the autobiography of that music chap – do you know him? Pianist. Umm … Scruffy-looking. I can't think of the name. Anyhow, his abuse sounded absolutely dreadful, I mean at the age of four or five, being, you know, actually sodomised. Dreadful. Absolutely dreadful. I mean physical damage being done to him and so forth. And I'm not talking about anything like that. No indeed. [See Rhodes 2015.]

George cleared his throat and took a sip of water. It would have been easy to doubt that he was in touch with any difficult feelings as he talked in his even, calm manner, with a hint of a twinkly, smiling friendliness underlying whatever he said. But the way he had coughed and needed a sip of water alerted me to the possibility of tension in his throat that he was attempting to dampen down.

GEORGE: You mustn't misunderstand this … I mean, misunderstand my reason for coming. I'm probably not like the majority of people who come and see you. I'm not all knotted up with some dreadful sense of hidden pain or what not. There are plenty of things that can happen to a person in life that are much worse than what has happened to me in my life. And all us boys knew, you see. We made jokes. It was the older ones he went for. You had to be about ten, and it was almost like a badge of honour, in an odd sort of a way – to be singled out by him.

George gave me another rather rueful but gently wry smile, inviting me once more to be amused along with him about the abuse.

GEORGE: We all joked about it, in a pretty brutal way. Sort of, 'Oh there goes Price – off to have his trousers taken down by FF.' That was our nickname for him. He was called Mr Fisher, and we called him Funny Fisher or FF for short.

There was a short silence. In it, I found myself picturing a ten-year-old boy. I could still remember my own sons and their school mates when they had been ten, even though that was some years ago. I had also just recently spent time with a friend and her ten-year-old son. I connected to a vivid impression, as George spoke, of the combination of strength, resilience and resourcefulness that ten-year-old boys have, alongside a certain sweetness and vulnerability. I connected via these memories to my sense of how capable and strong ten-year-old boys can be, and yet how much they still need the support of adults to steer them through tricky situations. I felt for the ten-year-old George as the adult George spoke about the abuse in a way that made it sound so trivial.

To make light of some experience – to minimise it, rationalise it and make the recalling of and describing it a purely intellectual or cognitive activity – can be part of a vital defence against the painful feelings surrounding it. In some ways it is a very effective strategy for the survivor of a traumatic experience, as it enables them to continue with at least some level of ego function, which is preferable, in many obvious ways, to allowing the ego to simply be shattered by a depth and breadth of pain. However, always making light of painful experiences is a strategy that begins to reveal its drawbacks once a dangerous and traumatising event is long past. Then the tactic of a stiff upper lip, and making past pain into nothing more than an amusing anecdote, can begin to become a problem in itself.

It is analogous to a soldier in a battle having a serious injury: while in the battle, he will clearly fare much better if he is able to simply slap on a dressing and fight on, in order to get through the fight and live another day, than if he allows himself to stop, focus on and possibly be overwhelmed by his suffering. However, once he is safe, and able to attend to his wound, if he cannot admit to himself or anyone else that it is serious and painful and he chooses instead to continue to make light of it, he is in danger of not attending to the wound properly and of it becoming ever more serious, and causing him severe problems in the long term. George, along with many other male survivors of abuse, had been able to find a way to soldier on heroically at the time of the abuse. This deserved some appreciation and a kind of honouring; but it also needed to be carefully challenged, as it was not likely to be the best possible tactic for George now that he was out of that dangerous situation.

The dismantling of a defence is a sensitive business. Another military metaphor is apt: if a faithful and loyal guard has been standing at the city walls, ensuring no enemies can pass the gate into the central courtyard of that city, he is not going to take kindly to someone suddenly coming along and telling him he is no longer needed, and that he must hand over his weapon and stand down immediately. He has served faithfully for many years, even decades, and may only be willing to relinquish his weapon if he can be convinced that the city really no longer needs his protection. It will help him greatly to stand down willingly and with dignity, if he can be shown he is no longer needed in a way that offers him an acknowledgement of, and appreciation for, his long years of service.

> SARAH: Mmm. And can I ask you to say a bit about what is making you wonder if your experience at the school where Mr Fisher sexually abused you and other boys in his care, is still having an impact on you?
>
> GEORGE: I … It's hard to say exactly. I have dreams … There are certain things I can't really … I have a hard time with … anything … like a situation where I … well, let's say there are certain consistencies of things, like porridge or custard or … anything gooey, if I have to look at them or come into contact with them, then I … find that … difficult.

Here George winced slightly and gave a subtle sort of gulp that was very slightly suggestive of a retching motion, which prompted my wondering if this could be to do with the teacher having put his penis in George's mouth, and perhaps ejaculating in or near this part of George. George cleared his throat again and took a sip of water. He then put one index finger to the corner of one eye and then the other, as if he was getting a speck of dirt out of each of them, skillfully disguising the fact that tears had come into his eyes.

> GEORGE: And … I somehow feel I'm failing my son, rather, at the moment.

[He tightened his lips, to disguise the fact they had slightly trembled.]

GEORGE: I, myself, behaved in a very similar way to the way Franco's been
behaving when I was about the same age, I … But … I mean, there
were other problems for me back then. My mother was, shall we say,
unwell, and her's and my father's marriage was sadly coming apart by
the time I was about 14, so it would be unfair to lay all my difficulties
at the one door of, you know, abuse. But I too went somewhat off the
rails, at about the same age as Franco has. And I would like … I think
I need to be able to speak to my son and ask him, straight out, 'What's
been going on? What has … Has something upset you?' And I can't.
I simply can't bring myself to … to have that sort of conversation
with him. Now, do you think you can help me work out why this
should be so, and do something about that?

Part of what George was struggling with was related to a recurring phenomenon that many practitioners have observed when working with abuse
survivors. When adults who have been sexually violated as a child have
intimate contact, later in their life, with a child or young person (particularly
if the child is the same gender as them) it is extremely affecting for them.
The visceral, bodily experience of witnessing, listening to, touching, sharing
a space with someone who evokes their own child-self, stirs up emotions,
memories, thoughts and anxieties that tend to be in a sort of potent but
undifferentiated swirl. The adult survivor finds it understandably hard to
tease out what might 'belong', emotionally speaking, with them and their
past, and what might belong to the child and the present. They can easily
start to worry that the child whom they are close to may be at risk of some
harm or abuse, when it is possible that they are getting in touch with their
own memories of how it was for them at around the same age. I wondered
if George's defence against feeling the pain of his own abuse had stopped
being so effective around the time his own son hit the age that he, George,
had been when he had first been violated by his teacher.

SARAH: Can I ask you a question before I respond to yours?

GEORGE: Go ahead.

SARAH: Do you have a worry that Franco has been sexually abused by
someone?

[George frowned, and then spoke.]

GEORGE: No. I have wondered … but, no. I don't think so. I think, that's
more my … stuff – that I can't get it out of my head sometimes that

he … sort, of must have. But, no, I'm sure he would have said something to his mother or sister. They're very close. Talk about all sorts. No. It's just that whenever I think of trying to talk to him about what's bothering him … it makes me think of *my* life … my, you know, school days. And then … I just feel I can't be of any use to him. I can't talk to him. Help him with whatever he's going through. Can you help? Would coming here help with that?

SARAH: I expect that you can guess therapists often don't give straight yes or no answers to direct questions, in case it closes down certain avenues of exploration too quickly. But there are some questions it's important to try and give clear answers to, and 'Can you help?' is one of them. So, I would say: I *would* expect you to find benefit from some sessions, in all sorts of ways. But it is not always an easy or quick process. Things can often feel a bit worse for a time before they feel better. And therapy doesn't help for every single person. So my 'yes' isn't in the nature of a cast-iron guarantee.

[There was a pause.]

SARAH: How does the answer strike you?

GEORGE: Fair enough. And would you concur with my hunch – that there is a link between me not being able to ask Franco about … about what's bothering him, and my own … my … abuse?

SARAH: I can imagine that's likely. It wouldn't be unusual for a parent who has experienced abuse to find it hard to speak with their child about things that may be troubling the child.

GEORGE: Right. [He sighed.] So. What do we do next?

We agreed that George would come for an initial ten sessions and we would then review the arrangement.

There followed nine sessions during which more details emerged of both his past story, and the pressures he was currently facing. Throughout, there was always a sense that our meetings were at a superficial level. I felt as if George treated his sessions almost as if we were having a friendly chat or a good-humoured interview. He deftly sidestepped all my attempts to stay close to any points when he came close to being in touch with his deeper feelings. George was at pains, from time to time, to affirm to me how appreciative he was for 'all this' and how helpful he was finding it to simply come and talk and be listened to for an hour each week, and I did not doubt this. But I felt as if we were skating over the surface of a vast and dark lake, and that the real substance of what George and I needed to look at together was a long way down, and would require something to break through the ice if were ever to get to what lay beneath.

This idea of a break *through* (horribly close, of course, to a break *down*) was a delicate area. Not only did George have an enormous amount invested in keeping his current circumstances on an even keel, he had also been vigorously trained from an early age to put away messy, inconvenient, spontaneous emotions and their expression, in favour of being a polite, obedient, correct little boy. With very little connection to any current feeling about what he described, George would mention various facts about his early childhood that, in effect, gave me snapshots of what may have been going on internally, for his younger self, as he had first learned and then unconsciously internalised the lesson that any of his more intense or troubling feelings were of no importance, value or interest for the adults around him.

He had been the only child of wealthy parents, and his mother had been artistic, sensitive and a great beauty. She had sunk into a quiet, melancholy alcoholism shortly after George's birth, finding herself alone with a tiny baby while George's father, an athlete and workaholic, was continually away from home. He worked long hours in the City during the week, and went off at weekends with male friends in order to play cricket and rugby, or go mountain climbing and sailing. When George was six his mother made what might have been an attempt at suicide: she took 'too many of her sleeping pills' one night when drunk. At that point George's father insisted his son should be sent away to the same prep school that he had attended himself 30 years previously.

With the rueful smile he often had when recalling times from his childhood, George spoke of his prep school. Some of his memories (invariably recounted with his trademark, semi-amused expression) included:

> Yes, well, the homesickness was pretty awful to begin with. If you were a 'new bug' you could pretty much count on wetting the bed for the whole first term, at least. Pretty grim!
>
> The headmaster's wife was rather sweet to the new boys. She could tell it was all pretty confusing for us to begin with. If she saw one of us looking a bit lost, she would pop a mint humbug into our mouth, and say, you know, something like, 'Come on, chin up! What would Mummy and Daddy say if they saw you all down in the dumps like this!' And, d'you know, it worked like a charm: it's pretty hard to cry with a whopping great mint in your mouth!

> Sometimes at night in the dorm, you could hear one of the other new boys crying in bed. They'd be trying to disguise it, you know – putting a pillow over their heads, or burrowing down under the blankets, or what have you. But if you heard it, you just … well it was awful, because it would set you off as well. But it made you sort of despise them as well, because if only they hadn't been so wet and weak, you wouldn't have heard it and been set off too, so it sort of made you hate them. Terrible, really.

And then there would be the inevitable smile at me, inviting me to also be slightly amused by a story that had been sad, but was over, and long past now.

On one level, George absolutely needed to forget what it had felt like to be that little boy at his boarding school. He needed to be able to continue to function in the present without any cracks in the façade: he had a role in his bank that meant he was responsible for huge amounts of currency being transferred successfully from one country to another, every day. His elderly, fragile, widowed mother continued to be depressed and alcoholic and she looked to her son for most of her emotional and practical support. He was also the rock that his wife, stepdaughter and work associates all seemed to lean on and turn to, when they had problems. Only his son seemed to be resisting George's offer to be the helpful protector. In so doing, he was, unconsciously, doing George a very big favour, by forcing George, thereby, to realise how caught up he was in a pattern that Alice Miller outlines in her writing on narcissistic wounding. Her description of a man who has been brought up by those who cannot really relate to him as his own real person, but only as a sort of object that they can invest with something of their own, denied inner life, seemed a fairly accurate description of George.

> He cannot rely on his own emotions, has not come to experience them through trial and error, has no sense of his own real needs, and is alienated from himself in the highest degree. Under these circumstances, he cannot separate from his parents, and even as an adult he is still dependent on affirmation from his partner, from groups, and especially from his own children. (Miller 1987)

George's outwardly robust, but inwardly shaky, sense of self relied very heavily on being the Good Husband, Good Son, Good Colleague and, very importantly, the Good Father. He needed to feel the reassurance of his own goodness by lavishing the good fathering he had hardly ever received onto his children.

But luckily for the therapy, George had a tiny but persistent hunch that it *might* be important to look back at the fact that he had been abused, and to wonder how the impact of this could have some part to play in his current difficulties. Franco's ability to stay true to his own needs and emotional life (rather than obliging his father by dutifully being a nice, appreciative son) helpfully boosted George's own small urge to be alive to the fact that he, George, might also need to pay attention to his own deep needs and feelings.

However, George's powerful ambivalence about opening up to what he had felt as a boy, as well as to what meaning his painful experiences might have had, was the reason that our sessions remained so frustratingly at the surface. He came to each appointment on time, and was unfailingly thoughtful and amiable, and often assured me how helpful he was finding it all. But it didn't matter how sensitively I attempted to begin to deepen the work, something vital about his inner life would somehow always slip away out of our focus. After each session I would sigh: the coping, avuncular persona that George had developed and honed to perfection would have headed me off at the pass again.

At our ninth meeting, I attempted to broach this pattern with him.

SARAH: It was in my mind before you arrived that today is our penultimate of the ten we arranged.

GEORGE: Gosh, yes, that's right. The time's flown by!

SARAH: Maybe now would be a good time to think together about how the process has been going and what the next steps might be.

GEORGE: Mmm. Yes. Well. I'm in your hands, really. What would be your thoughts?

SARAH: I can certainly let you know my thoughts. But I'd like to hear from you first. How have you been finding the sessions?

GEORGE: Well … It's been very helpful, on the whole. It's always good to come and talk and get things off one's chest, and speak to someone who's objective and professional.

[He blew out his lips in a puff that conveyed an 'I don't know what else I can say' attitude.]

SARAH: How is it for me to ask you how you have been finding the sessions?

GEORGE: Fine. Of course. As I say, it's been very good. I ... I don't think I quite get what you want me to say, in addition to what I've said. I'm very glad to have had a calm, professional space to reflect on certain things.

SARAH: Yes. And in terms of getting what you originally came for – do you think that has happened?

[George looked ever so slightly pained.]

GEORGE: Umm. Not quite. Don't get me wrong – I do get that this isn't a sort of magic bullet, of course. But perhaps I thought I would have felt more equipped by now to make some changes in the way I'm feeling about trying to talk to my son about, you know – what's going on for him. And ... [George cleared his throat] ... and I can certainly say it's been good to talk over a few things in confidence. But on reflection, now you have brought the question up, I do think this is probably a good point to draw these sessions to a close. Perhaps we could make tonight the last meeting?

I noticed my reaction to George's rather abrupt decision and how he voiced it. He seemed to have no feeling about what he had just said, which was in stark contrast to my feeling response which was that I felt almost as if he had suddenly thrown his glass of water in my face. I felt a kind of shock and tried to gather my thoughts. It seemed it could be time to take a small risk.

SARAH: I wonder ... I wonder what little ten-year-old George wants to do about the sessions?

GEORGE: Little George?

SARAH: The ten-year-old part of you that still, in effect, lives inside you and struggles to make his feelings apparent.

GEORGE: Umm ... Not sure.

There was a long pause. It seemed that if I did not do something that stirred things up a bit more radically, then George might leave without getting what a very wounded part of him had come for.

SARAH: Mmm. If the 'little you' had found someone at school to whom he could have talked openly, back at the time that Mr Fisher was taking you off for all those special tennis sessions, I wonder what he would have wanted to say?

George seemed to instantly respond to this tack of me explicitly trying to make space for the little boy he had once been and speak more directly to that young part. He did not hesitate in his reply.

GEORGE: He would have wanted to … He would have said, 'I want to go home.' And he would have said that he never wanted to have to see FF ever again.

SARAH: Can you picture your ten-year-old self, as you talk about what you wanted?

GEORGE: Mmm. I can actually. In the jakes behind the tennis courts.

SARAH: The … ?

GEORGE: Some lavatories near the tennis courts, on the way back into the main school buildings.

SARAH: Ah. And what are you picturing?

GEORGE: I'm … standing in one of the cubicles. On my own.

SARAH: How do you seem?

GEORGE: Not happy. I'm…I'm crying.

SARAH: Are you? So, you see a very unhappy little boy?

GEORGE: Mmm.

SARAH: And if there was a way for some adult who could be supportive, to step in to the scene, what might they say to that little boy?

GEORGE: Some adult? A real person? But there wasn't anyone!

SARAH: There wasn't anyone to help him at the time. But, now, in your imagination, if you could have anyone there to help your younger self, who could you picture?

GEORGE: [Doubtfully] My father?

SARAH: What would he say?

GEORGE: Oh, you know. Something like, 'Come on, now, old chap. It's all right. Chin up!'

SARAH: I'd like to interrupt him, because it wasn't all right for Little George, was it? It wasn't 'all right' at all.

[There was a pause.]

SARAH: Perhaps you could picture someone else. Someone who would be able to properly acknowledge how upset Little George felt, and who would let the little boy speak about his feelings.

GEORGE: Mmm. Don't know. I don't know who that could be.

SARAH: Could it be your adult self, as you are now?

GEORGE: Me?

SARAH: Yes. Could you picture the 'grown up you' being with your little self, to offer him some support and understanding?

GEORGE: Mmm.

SARAH: If Little George could trust that *this* adult will listen to him, what would he say?

[George's voice changed as he spoke with a new urgency.]

GEORGE: 'I don't like it here! I don't know why Mr Fisher wants to ... I don't want to keep going off with him to the tennis courts. I want to go home. I don't want to go on holiday with Mr Fisher. Don't let me go on holiday with Mr Fisher. He'll put me in his bed and do the thing with me and I hate it.'

[George put a hand up to his face. There was a long silence. I saw his shoulders give a few heaves as he made a great effort to keep his crying silently smothered.]

SARAH: That little boy sounds very frightened and alone.

George continued to cry silently. He would let out an occasional, anguished, 'Sorry', and wipe away the tears on his cheeks as if each wipe would be the final one, before a fresh wave of tears seemed to take him by surprise.

GEORGE: Sorry. Don't know what's come over me.

SARAH: Tears are a very important way for the body to regulate itself. They are a very good release. Thank goodness you were able to find somewhere to cry when you were little. [Pause.] Perhaps crying now is also a very healthy, important release.

Maybe it was because I had explicitly stated that crying was not frowned on in sessions, but indeed was actually accepted and even welcomed, that George broke down after I said this and cried freely and noisily for some time. After a while his sobbing lessened, and then there was a long silence. After some moments, I offered a statement designed to help him return to a more day-to-day type of exchange, as a way back from the powerfully regressed state he had just visited.

SARAH: Perhaps it's been some time since you last cried?

GEORGE: [With a deep sigh] I can't remember the last time. It was ... No, I can't call a time to mind. It might even have been when I was at that school. I don't know.

SARAH: Many years, by the sound of it.

GEORGE: Yes. Probably. Even back then, you didn't cry if you could possibly help it. You had to keep your tears to yourself. Well, I've told you about that.

SARAH: Mmm. Can I ask how you are feeling after you have cried here?

GEORGE: It's a bit embarrassing, obviously, but also, I have to say, I do feel ... a bit, sort of ... lighter.

[We looked at one another.]

GEORGE: But there's still a doubt, you know, about all this. I do get that too much of the old bottling everything up and putting a brave face on thing isn't good for one. But, the thing is ... I can't see myself ever ... Because I have to keep things together a bit here, you realise? I can't start falling apart all over the place. I have a lot of people depending on me.

SARAH: Of course. We're not working at you falling completely apart. That's no use. Perhaps it would be more helpful to think of sessions as being like the valve you can open at the top of a pressure cooker: we're not aiming to just take the lid right off in the middle of cooking and let everything that's boiling hot spill out. Just gradually relieve some of the pressure with the special valve. Bit by bit.

GEORGE: Hmm.

SARAH: You look doubtful.

GEORGE: No, not doubtful. I just had a funny thought. It's probably not relevant but ... I actually have high blood pressure. I don't know if I mentioned that. And ... It makes me wonder, you know. I mean, plenty of people do in my line of work – and they have stuff like tension headaches and irritable tummy stuff. I get those sorts of things too. I wonder about it all being connected, you know?

SARAH: What an interesting connection to make. There's plenty of evidence that there certainly is an important impact on our bodies when the chemicals related to stress just hang about in our systems and don't get properly metabolised so that they can dissipate.

GEORGE: Hmph! I grind my teeth at night too.

SARAH: Do you?

[There was a pause, then George gave one of his rueful smiles.]

GEORGE: I'm a mess! [He said this in a tone of voice that had a brightness in it. He looked as if he was not altogether averse to describing himself this way.]

SARAH: Sort of ... outwardly tidy, inwardly a mess?

GEORGE: That's it! [He looked almost delighted.]

SARAH: And what's that like?

GEORGE: How do you mean?

SARAH: Can you say something about how it feels to be you, living like this – so different on the inside from what you show on the outside?

[George frowned, not as if he was unhappy, but as if he had been given an interesting puzzle to solve. After a while he spoke.]

GEORGE: It feels … as if there's always a … gap. A gap between things.

The word 'gap' that George seemed to have dredged up from somewhere deep inside him was a wonderfully evocative word that suggested he was intuiting the operation of one of the most primal and unconscious defences within himself: splitting (Freud 1938).

Internal splitting enables some of the most fundamental pairings of human experience (love and hate, good and bad, success and failure, clean and dirty, beautiful and ugly, etc.) to be kept separate, so that they do not have to come anywhere near each other in our inner world, let alone have any link or common ground. This enables the person who is terrified of the more knotty, shadowy side of these pairings to have the relief of believing that the shadow side will never intrude, overwhelm and spoil the lighter side of life. Good can be preserved and badness can be exiled. In George's case, he had been able to split off a sad, hurt, frightened and dependent little boy, so that he could manage in the world purely as a cheerful, assured, independent little person who was well able to smoothly attend to all his own needs, as well as other people's.

But splitting, like all defences, is most useful at the time of the pain or trauma, and afterwards, actually often becomes part of a problem. George had recently been discovering the limitations of splitting. He had been forced to realise that he was simply unable to keep at bay the reality that his life included anger, sadness, failure and ugliness, when it became undeniable that his son was unquestionably troubled and causing others trouble.

I thought there was something very hopeful that such a split inside him was coming more into George's conscious awareness, as he spoke of a 'gap'. I wanted to foster that awareness.

SARAH: That sounds important. [There was a pause.] Would you be able to draw something that gives a flavour of that gap?

GEORGE: Draw it?

I gestured to some large sheets of blank A3 paper and pots of crayons, pencils, pastel and felt tips that I kept on a low table, near the chairs we were sitting in.

George stared at them as if he'd not only never noticed them in the room before, but also that he'd never seen such things in all his life.

GEORGE: Oh. Gosh. I don't know.
[There was a silence filled with a tension.]
GEORGE: [Suddenly] OK. I'll give it a go!
[I put the art materials on the floor between us and then sat on the floor near them.]
SARAH: You OK to sit on the floor?

George took off his jacket and loosened his tie, before he sat opposite me. Sitting on the ground, and in his shirt sleeves, he suddenly had a much younger appearance and a slightly softer presence. He picked up a crayon and looked at it with an almost boyish interest.

GEORGE: I haven't had a crayon in my hand since I don't know when!
SARAH: Oh?

There followed a long silence as George rooted through all the drawing materials, taking a few out and examining them, rolling them in his fingers, tearing little shreds of paper off the outside of some of the crayons, and even taking the tops off the felt tips and smelling their inky nibs. He looked as if he was beginning to enjoy himself. He then looked at the paper for a while and smoothed one hand down his tie in a characteristic gesture which I was starting to recognise as one of his key self-soothing activities that he did when he felt some inner agitation.

I gave his inner boy a gentle encouragement.

SARAH: It doesn't have to be a great drawing, so I recommend not over-thinking it. Just seeing what can happen when you put some marks on the paper is all that's needed.
[George immediately picked up a maroon pastel, bent over the sheet and made two large emphatic downward slashes of colour down the page, perpendicular to each other. Then he lent back and looked at me.]
GEORGE: Best I can do, I'm afraid.
SARAH: Great. Can you say something about what you've drawn?
GEORGE: Umm. It's the gap.

[There was a slight pause, then he searched in the felt tip pot, found a black marker and scribbled roughly with it so that the space between the dark red lines was filled with zig zags.]

GEORGE: There's the space in between, that is just all dark and ... where there's a big drop. So that things fall down into there, and are ... lost.

[Then he searched in the pencil pot and selected an ordinary graphite pencil and drew a small stick figure at the top of the left-hand line, with one foot on the line and the other foot hovering over the top of the black scribbles.]

GEORGE: That's me. Sorry, I'm terrible at drawing. Hmm. I'm right on the edge of the gap, aren't I?

SARAH: Yes. And you're quite a little figure, there.

GEORGE: Mmm. A bit precarious. 'Mind the gap!' Huh! That's something I hear almost every day. Every day I head in to work, at Bank tube station, you know. The warning about the gap between the tube platform and the train.

SARAH: Oh, yes! Another interesting connection!

[There was a pause.]

SARAH: How do you feel about what you've drawn?

GEORGE: How do I feel about it?

[He blew his cheeks out in a puff that was part of one of his 'I don't know' expressions.]

GEORGE: I feel ... well, as if it's not very good, really. And also that I'd like to sit back up now – my knees aren't what they were.

We both sat back on our chairs. I wanted to support the parts of George that had been largely relegated to the depths of unconsciousness for so long, and that his tidy, controlling, capable ego didn't give much room to. So I continued to look down at the drawing that his consciousness didn't see much worth in. Eventually George seemed able to take the cue from me and he too gazed down at it. After some moments he said, 'It's quite big, that gap. I think it suggests to me that there is more to do. More down there than I thought! Perhaps this week need not be the final session. If that will be possible?'

SARAH: Sure. We can look at extending the time you would come, if you wish. I'd support that.

GEORGE: OK. Good. There's probably more to this business than meets the eye.

[I nodded.]

SARAH: I think that's a good way of putting it – 'this business'. Maybe it's taken you some time to work out quite what the nature of this way of working is like.

GEORGE: Yes! True. I certainly wouldn't advise buying shares in a company that I knew nothing about. Not a wise investment.

SARAH: But now that you know something about 'this business …'

GEORGE: Mmm. I think I did have an idea that maybe it would all be about getting me to beat cushions and yell 'I hate you' at an effigy of my mother, or some such.

SARAH: Hmm. That wouldn't really be … your thing, would it?

GEORGE: No. A bit … lacking in a bit of credibility, that sort of stuff, I think. For me, at least. Maybe it suits other people who come and see you. But then, I do see that just having a bit of a chat doesn't really … reveal very much. One needs something that shakes one up, just the right amount. Imagining me at school, and the drawing … they both … umm …

SARAH: … bridge the gap between being too serious and not being serious enough?

GEORGE: I think so.

SARAH: They help Little George feel he's being listened to and taken seriously, but not so much that Grown-up George can't have his say too?

GEORGE: Grown-up George and Little George! [He gave a short laugh.] That does sound a bit … um … I don't know … a bit *unusual*.

SARAH: Unusual for them to both be in on a project together?

GEORGE: Mmm. [He glanced at his watch.] I see time's up. So … I'll see you next week?

SARAH: Yes.

I was encouraged about the use that George had been able to make of me and the session on that day. Not surprisingly, it was not simply a case of plain sailing from then on. Defences are not built in one day, and they do not come down in one either. But the process had begun.

Over the next year, although George would return, from time to time, to the place where he wanted to make light of both the sexual abuse he had experienced in the year when he had been ten, and of the emotional abandonment he had experienced throughout his childhood and adolescence, he was increasingly able to move on from that place and allow himself much more contact with his feelings. The more he was able to do this, the less terrified he was at the thought that Franco might also be having some very painful and powerful feelings about something. The prospect of opening up a conversation with his son in which the dark feelings might spill out became less overwhelming and more like something he imagined he might be capable of managing.

George began to wonder aloud in sessions whether he had been unconsciously keeping himself at a distance from Franco, ever since his son had become the same age George had been when his sexual abuse began. He also reflected on the impact on him, on his son, on their relationship, and on the whole family, of the fact that he worked such very long hours. He was not quite as much of an absent father as his own father had been, but George came to the conclusion he was 'not far off'. In sessions, he was able to get in touch with the truth that he felt lost at the prospect of spending time with Franco – that he really did not feel confident about how to be with his son these days.

Once he had been able to acknowledge this, we spent time in sessions imagining what it was that George would like to be doing with Franco, how they could spend time together in ways that could feel OK. After imaginatively playing through certain scenarios in his mind's eye and exploring them with me, and also imagining that his son was in the room and that George could speak freely to him, he decided that a way forward would be to plan to do something active with Franco. Just sitting with him, trying to have a heart-to-heart did not feel the right thing. So George took a risk and bought a bike for himself and suggested to Franco, one weekend, that he and Franco could train to go on some long bike rides together. He was extremely pleased and moved that Franco was immediately open to the idea. They both found that cycling along together, around a park or on cycle tracks, seemed to be the perfect way to exchange a few comments now and then. Rather than one, big, emotional showdown, George found that he and Franco could chat, exchange trivia, tell jokes and that, after a while, every now and then Franco would open up a bit about what had been making him so unhappy at school.

As far as George could gather it had been a combination of finding it hard to fit into a new school where everyone was in established friendship groups; finding the academic work hard and being too proud to admit this and get help; and feeling sure that something was up between his mother and father and worrying that his school failure was the source of the tension and that he, Franco, was responsible for the fact his father was so absent and his mother was so stressed and unhappy. Although it pained George to hear how unable Franco had felt to try and talk to him or his wife about any of this, he was also vastly relieved that it was nothing worse. He told me later, 'I really tried to take a leaf out of your book, you know and do a bit of what you do with me in sessions. I mostly just listened and said stuff like, "I see" and "That sounds tough". And by golly, you know, that stuff can really do the trick, can't it! I mean, Franco has been opening up in a way he never normally does. It was a great relief, I think. For him and me!'

As George continued to make efforts to spend time with Franco and do Dad-and-son sorts of things together, the closer they became and the more rewarding George found being a dad to Franco. Having benefited, himself, from being given space, time and understanding in therapy, he felt that he had more resources and confidence to offer the same to Franco, and that he could stop putting his son under an unconscious pressure to be the perfect son, and himself under pressure to be the perfect father. He similarly began to experiment with not being the perfect colleague, manager, son and husband. He did not become someone who could exactly relish the prospect of conflict, but it did not seem so taboo or wrong to admit that sometimes he could, for example, get irritated or bored with someone else's behaviour.

He also did not find that he was someone who would ever actively choose to eat things that had a sloppy, gooey consistency. But he no longer found that being faced with something of that sort was quite so revolting and disturbing. He could do the calm breathing we had practised if he came across a gooey food or substance in his day-to-day life, and did not find himself feeling nauseous or panicky when that happened.

He also found that the more he connected with and gave space to the messier, darker parts of his emotional life, the less he feared those parts of the lives of others around him.

Over the year that George came for therapy, his son Franco made a gradual but unmistakable improvement in mood, behaviour and willingness to stick at his school work. He began to include himself in more family activities, such as meals out, trips to the cinema and even helping with the DIY jobs at his half-sister's new house. His school work improved, and he began to spend more time out of school in a small friendship group he began to be included in. George and his wife began to trust that Franco could be out of the woods, as far as getting expelled or needing to see a child psychologist were concerned. Things got a lot easier and happier at home.

Towards the end of our work together George wondered aloud about this.

GEORGE: It's a curious sort of thing, isn't it? Almost like magic – if you help someone in a family, you sort of seem to help the rest of the family as well as them, without anything ever being directly said or done to anyone else outside the sessions.

SARAH: Yes, that does seem to be the way it often goes. Help a parent and you help that parent's family.

[There was a long silence.]

GEORGE: Do you think I'll ever really get over … all the stuff in the past?

SARAH: Hmm. What do you think that would look like?

GEORGE: What, me completely being over the abuse?

SARAH: Yes.

GEORGE: Oh, you know the usual clichéd stuff – me wandering about in some meadow filled with flowers.

SARAH: Could you draw it?

GEORGE: Righty-oh. I'm good at this now!

[George sat on the floor and quickly drew a green swirly field with dots of many colours and a large stick figure in the middle with a smiley face, and each hand holding a bunch of flowers. He looked at it and then commented.]

GEORGE: Hmph. Not very realistic.

[He studied the drawing, and then chose a black pastel. He drew a small round shape about the size of a ten-pence coin in the left-hand corner of the 'meadow' with it and then coloured it in with a continuous circling motion, so that a dark blot sat in the green, among the brightly coloured dots.]

GEORGE: That's more like it. There's going to be the dark stuff, no matter what.

SARAH: I notice the dark spot doesn't take up the whole picture.

GEORGE: No. It doesn't, does it! There. That'll do. [George put down the pastel and dusted his hands together.] What do you think?

SARAH: I think 'That'll do' sounds like a position that's realistic. Something that can be trusted.

GEORGE: Yes. It's not far from 'I'll do.' Even if I'm not getting it spot on all the time.

[At that he looked down and laughed. We both saw at the same moment that he literally now had got a spot on him: a wee smear of black pastel on his smart tie.]

GEORGE: Bugger! This was a present from Steph. Italian silk. She'll have my guts for garters! [Then he put his head back and laughed heartily.] There you go! That's exactly it, isn't! No way to completely get away from all the messy stuff!

And, to my delight at seeing how far he had come in being able to push against his tightly restricting defences, he lifted the black pastel up to his tie and deliberately made another small mark on the beautiful silk.

GEORGE: I'll never not have it as part of me. But … it'll do.

This time, as George grinned at me, I felt it was absolutely right to smile back.

4
USING THE IMAGINATION TO HELP RECONNECTION WITH A TRANSITIONAL OBJECT FROM CHILDHOOD
Dami

The land of counterpane

When I was sick and lay-a-bed,
I had two pillows at my head,
And all my toys beside me lay
To keep me happy all the day.

And sometimes for an hour or so
I watched my leaden soldiers go,
With different uniforms and drills,
Among the bedclothes, through the hills.

And sometimes sent my ships in fleets
All up and down among the sheets;
Or brought my trees and houses out,
And planted cities all about.

I was the giant great and still
That sits upon the pillow-hill,
And sees before him, dale and plain,
The pleasant land of counter pane.

Robert Louis Stevenson (1850–1894)

This chapter centres on how working imaginatively with trauma allowed an addicted and chaotic client to reconnect to the psychological and emotional containment that a childhood toy once gave him, which in turn allowed him to gain more psychological and emotional safety as an adult, and begin to turn his life around.

Dami had had such a rocky start in life that, when he first referred himself for therapy, his ego strength was wafer thin. He was a 30-year-old, straight, mixed-race man, with a mother who was white, and a father who was part Nigerian, part white. Both his parents had been troubled young individuals when they had met and got briefly entangled with each other. Dami's father was already dependent on alcohol and drugs at the time he moved in to Dami's mother's bedsit with her. Soon she was pregnant with Dami, and Dami's father was unsupportive and eventually downright aggressive, leaving her highly stressed at the time she was expecting her baby. He was violent to her, and also to Dami once he was born. He eventually began to dip in and out of their lives, as he went in and out of prison. In the end, he left them, never to be seen or heard of again, when Dami was about seven years old, which was a form of relief for the boy and his mother; but by then a huge amount of damage had already been done. Dami's mother was now chronically, profoundly depressed and anxious, and with a crushed self-esteem; and Dami had had almost no opportunity to ever feel safe and contented in his whole short life.

If the vital early work of providing a secure-enough environment for a baby so that it can develop a solid sense of self is not completed, then the adult that such a baby becomes will not have developed a wholly functioning ego or personality and is not yet capable of feeling they confidently know who they are, nor how they can look after themselves in the world. They are still at a 'pre-ego' stage of development and therefore need lots of support that is related to what an attentive parent/carer would offer a baby: lots of warmth, lots of input around basic care (e.g. support with eating, sleeping, staying safe), lots of affirmation, mirroring, and a kind of reliable, predictable holding. In talking therapies this holding is not usually the physical sort that is given by the embrace of encircling arms, but it is nevertheless a form of holding that can be of great benefit to a client who is not yet, emotionally speaking, an adult.

For such a client to be able to discover that each week they can come to the same place, at the same time, and see the same person, and that they can be given a space by that familiar person to say and do whatever they wish (within certain limits), will be a radically new experience. It can help to start build up their ego strength, bit by bit. If they have the repeated experience that the person who keeps this space for them will reliably try, every single week, to understand them, support them, not attack, shame or reject them, nor use them to get some sort of gratification or fill an emotional need, then the client can begin to trust this experience, and internalise what is being demonstrated to them by their therapist's attitude to them: that they *are* worth caring for, being interested in; they should *not* be harmed or exploited. They can, in the end, learn to behave towards themselves in a similar caring way; at first, perhaps, only in the therapy room, but eventually also outside, in the rest of the world. It can be slow work, and often feels pretty unrewarding on both sides to begin with. It is not a gratifyingly immediate process. For the therapist, it can evoke feelings to do with caring for a very young infant. Repeatedly feeding, changing, dressing and making sure a baby is safe and comfy in its cot is, of course, extremely worthwhile and can be a source of pleasure to the carer. But it can also sometimes feel a bit of a chore and a slog, if the carer is honest.

Dami's unsettled start in life meant that, to begin with, our work together certainly felt to me as if it was an uphill struggle in many ways – a replay, perhaps, of how, first, his parents had struggled to care for him, and then of how hard others had found it to manage the troubled person he was becoming.

By the time he started primary school, he had witnessed his mother attempt suicide a number of times, and regularly self-harm by cutting herself on her arms and hitting her own head repeatedly on the kitchen wall. Dami recounted in therapy sessions how reluctant he had always felt to leave her in the mornings to go to school. He was aware, even at that very young age, of how vulnerable his mother was, how terribly lonely and unhappy and anxious she was. He would worry about her, off and on, throughout the school day while he was away from her. When he was in Year 2 of primary school he was given a diagnosis of Attention Deficit Hyperactivity Disorder (ADHD) and put on the drug Ritalin. Even after this he was still constantly in trouble in the classroom for being unfocused and uninvolved with school activities in the ways his teachers wanted him to be. He told me angrily that he had not had any idea how to convey to them that he was in fact often absorbed in a silent ritual he had developed, which required him to chant to himself, in his head, 'Please let my mum be OK, please let my mum be OK', for a set number of times, before giving himself a break and then starting again, which obviously made it almost impossible for him to give much of his attention to anything else going on around him as he did so.

Dami was a tall guy with an athletic build. He worked out, and it showed. Whenever I came to collect him from the client waiting area in the community-based counselling service where I saw him, he was invariably the coolest-looking person there, dressed as he always was in the latest designs in leisurewear and trainers, and with his hair shaved into striking designs at his temples. He would always have his smart phone in his hand as he walked with me to the counselling room, checking messages and sending texts up to the moment we sat down and faced each other. Then he would slide his phone into his pocket and become suddenly very still and stiff. He never took off his 'snap back' baseball cap, nor whichever freshly laundered hoody he was wearing, whatever the weather. He also tended to keep his designer backpack resting on his feet, close to his body, so that he could hold the top handle of it throughout the session. It made him look as if he was always on the verge of getting up and leaving.

At the start of each meeting, he would examine my face with a searching, piercing look. He seemed to be scanning me in an attempt to read something about me (maybe some sign that would show him whether or not I could *still* be relied on, this week, not to be too sad and fragile, nor too short-tempered and agitated, to endure listening to him). He would sigh as soon as he had given me this once-over look and then say something like, 'I dunno what to tell you. It's been another bad week.' I would make some sympathetic acknowledgement of this with a facial expression or a sound. There would then often be a long silence. After that, the litany of the week's disasters would begin.

Dami worked as a minicab driver during the day, and as a DJ in a couple of clubs most nights, and his life was a swirl of chaotic, money-hustling busyness and edginess. He seemed to be constantly on the edge of law and safety, as he associated with untrustworthy, chaotic men and needy young women. Dami would start off by falling for and trying to take care of these women, then begin to feel emotionally dependent on them, and end up by mistreating them when they failed to take utter care of him. He would frequently exhaust himself, working for 18 or 20 hours non-stop, keeping himself going with coffee, energy drinks and, when he could afford it, cocaine or speed. I often found myself absolutely hating to listen to the frantic mess of his life. It was so painful and anxiety-provoking and frustrating for me to hear about his restless, unhappy, unsafe existence; to feel the dissatisfaction inherent in it; to hear about the callous way that he could behave to others, and was, himself, often treated. It was depressing enough to hear of Dami's day-to-day existence; all the more so whenever I reflected on how likely it is that many people in our communities are feeling and behaving as badly as Dami invariably was, due (in part, at least) to the amount of unresolved and deeply rooted trauma they are carrying around.

When he wasn't recounting the muddle and upset of his past week, Dami would often reveal how profoundly numb and exhausted he was. I found that my attempts, however gentle, to help him make any links between how things were for him now, and what had been going on in his early life, would often fall on stony ground. He would tend to yawn hugely and apologise for being too tired to think, if I attempted to help him make links between his past and present experiences. Sometimes he would try for a few minutes to reflect on aspects of his early life, and then bits and pieces would, thankfully, emerge that meant we could usefully put together a bit of collage as to why he might now be so unable to care for himself, or regulate and manage his own emotions, or find trustworthy people to be around, or feel hopeful about his future. But often he would report feeling very confused as to what the context of a particular snatch of memory was. He felt on shaky ground about many of his thoughts about his childhood – he didn't know if they might be from a dream, or something his mother had told him about, rather than something about which he had formed a memory for himself. Like many people in our society, Dami only knew *something* was amiss, but often he didn't know much of *what* was amiss or *why*.

Luckily he had the capacity to know enough facts about his early life for us to be clear about a few things, at least. It was apparent that many of the early experiences he could remember and describe meant that he had not been able to have the secure attachment to his carers which would have enabled his nervous system to develop in a way that meant he could regulate his emotions in a steady manner, now that he was physically adult. He could certainly remember the violence of his father, the ugly fights and shouting matches between his parents, and the frightening physical, mental and emotional collapse of his mother after his father had been violent again, meaning she would retire to her bed, sometimes for days, leaving Dami to fend for himself, aged four or five, while their bedsit sank into squalid chaos.

After a few months of sessions, it became clear that Dami was, in effect, unconsciously recreating a similar sort of environment for himself in the present that he had been deeply and agonisingly familiar with as a child. He was always falling foul of some violent drug dealer and being threatened or beaten up – just as he had been by his dad as a boy. He was always being unfairly blamed for some wrongdoing in his workplaces, even though it was usually not his fault or was due to a minor mistake or some inattention to detail, not some gross dishonesty on his part – just as he had always help-lessly found himself in the wrong at school. His hook-ups with woman were always replays of the relationship he had had with his child-like mother as a small boy, where he was pulled endlessly between the urge to take care of the pretty, waif-like 'maidens' he was always coming across, and the urge to vent his hurt and frustration on them when he found himself let down by them – just as he had loved his mum when he was little and yet also felt an awful rage and sorrow when he was around her because she could not or would not properly look after him.

I would often find that, as we came to the end of a session, the only noticeable thing that I had done in the hour was offer a few comments, every now and then, that were reflecting back to Dami how painful he must have found a particular incident that week, how hard things were for him, how tough it was that he had tried so hard to build something up for him-self, only to have it crash down all round him again (as it always did when some deal fell through, or when some girlfriend slept with his best mate, or when his mother texted him yet again with a complaining message about the doctor not giving her enough pills and could Dami please get some for her from one of his 'contacts'). It never felt enough to offer him one hour during which I mostly offered comments that were intended to help him feel that I was really trying to be *with him* – really listen to what he was saying, really imagine what it felt like to be him, and make links to his past experiences when he was a boy. This seemed like such a minuscule drop in the ocean of his days of turmoil and anxiety and fury, that I often doubted its worth to him. Dami needed so much more.

I found myself longing for a cross between a social worker and a superhero to magically swoop into his life to take control and sort things out: from his housing to his bank accounts, from his mother's treatment for her depression to all his missed schooling. He needed so very much more than one lone ther-apist sitting opposite him in a consulting room for an hour each week, saying things like, 'Mmm. That sounds very frightening/disturbing/irritating for you. What happened then?'

I described this to my senior colleague supervising the work with Dami. We explored the possibility that I was at the affect of Dami's mother's longing, as the young single mother that she had been, for someone to swoop in and magically take charge. My supervisor suggested I could check out with Dami how useful he was finding the sessions, when there was a good opportunity to do so. It was a surprise to me to hear from Dami, when I did so, how unequivocally he valued the hour a week we had together. When I asked him how he was finding the sessions, and whether he thought they were helpful to him, he mumbled, in a rather shamefaced tone, 'Yeah, good. I just get to say everything that's been, like, weighing me down. I know you can't, like, just sort it. I know that's gotta be me, at the end of the day. But, I can just say it all here, and you'll just listen. That's good. Clears my mind, like.'

There were some things that Dami remembered, with razor-sharp clarity, and wished he didn't. He remembered being sexually abused over a number of years by a teacher at a residential school.

The school was an institution he was sent to by his local authority. A number of educational specialists were brought in to assess Dami after his school came to the end of what they could cope with in terms of his disruptive behaviour, including him throwing a chair at a teacher. According to Dami, his mother was told that he was out of control and needed to have specialist residential care at a school for other troubled boys. He was eight or nine when he was sent away. He couldn't remember exactly when, but was sure he had celebrated his tenth birthday away from home. He could describe to me, in great detail, the expression on his mother's face as she waved goodbye to him, standing on the pavement by his primary school, while he sat on the back seat of a local authority minibus, looking down at her through the back window, numbly waving goodbye. He watched her as she started out by trying to smile encouragingly, and gradually broke down, so that by the time the bus drew away she was in hysterical tears. He could hardly bear to recall and describe the agony he saw on her face that day, 'Because that's my mum, you get me? My mum. She was my world.'

The school turned out to be a fairly brutal environment, with older boys often bullying younger ones while staff turned a blind eye. The boys were given the clear message by most of the teachers, who were exclusively male, that they were seen as troublemakers who needed to be licked into shape. But one teacher had seemed a little more friendly and approachable. He had taken special notice of Dami, who was one of the youngest boys there, and who had felt, from the moment he arrived, wholly lost: overwhelmed, homesick, confused and scared. This teacher had found Dami crying in one of the corridors near the dormitory he was supposed to sleep in, one evening, soon after he had arrived at the school. Dami had lost his way back to his bed from one of the bathrooms, and the teacher had been kind and consoling. He had invited Dami back to his own bedsit room to 'have some hot chocolate and be cheered up'. Once Dami was there and feeling a bit better and somewhat comforted, the teacher had suddenly taken Dami's pyjama trousers down, masturbated him for a while 'to take your mind off things and get you ready for sleep'. He had told Dami, 'This is what bigger boys do to cheer each other up. Now, you do it to me and then I'll make us some more hot chocolate.'

Dami told me bitterly, with a level of disgust and rage at himself which was painful to witness, that from then on, for three years, this teacher would come and find Dami at regular intervals of an evening, to 'invite' him back to his rooms, where the same process of Dami being given sympathy and interest, along with hot chocolate, or sweets, or cake, followed by mutual masturbation would ensue. This special attention suddenly ceased after a summer holiday during which Dami hit adolescence and suddenly became quite tall, as well as much more muscly and spotty. He could not bear to talk very much about these abusive experiences with the teacher, but he was able to talk about the fact that, as horrible as he had found it, he had also found the sudden ending of their connection deeply painful. For, even though he had always hated it, those episodes in the teacher's rooms had been the only form of special attention he ever received at the school, and from an adult man, and then even that horrible but special attention was gone.

What we know from the varied work of those who have specialised in how to help those who have been traumatised (e.g. Levine 2010; Rothschild 2000; Van Der Kolk 2014) is that there is a fine line between, on the one hand, opening up and revisiting frozen, unprocessed material, in order for it to be thawed and metabolised; and, on the other, simply triggering a flashback-type experience of being back in the traumatising scenario, and getting overwhelmed all over again in the present, or, in other words, retraumatised. Effective therapeutic work with someone who has been traumatised (and sexual violation is always traumatising to some extent) aims to avoid this 'all or nothing at all' split. The 'nothing at all' is where old trauma simply remains split off, encapsulated, unprocessed and unavailable to the therapy; in this case the therapy gets stuck and grinds to an 'impasse', and the client often leaves therapy at this point, either somewhat frustrated, or a bit grateful for what they have received and erroneously convinced that this is as well as they are ever going to be. The 'all' is when traumatic material is thawed out too quickly, and it unhelpfully overwhelms the client and therapist; and the therapy usually also breaks down if this happens, as the client leaves in order to maintain the tiny bit of the capacity to cope that they still have.

To avoid either of these dead-ends a therapist has to work out, slowly and gradually and with the client's guidance, what pace of work helps to thaw the traumatic experiences in a manageable way so that they can finally be truly felt and finally metabolised without being overwhelming.

The process of gradually thawing out the frozen, traumatised experiences is one that Peter Levine refers to as 'graduated renegotiation' or 'pendulation' (Levine and Frederick 1997).

It can feel counterintuitive, on occasion, that in order to address abuse, violation, neglect, etc., there must be an initial stage of revisiting and strengthening the client's connection to some good feelings and memories, before attempting to dig around deeply in the traumatic material. But good memories and thoughts are a powerful and necessary resource in any work for a traumatised client. They are nothing less than small but vital anchors to the shoreline of survival, enabling them to feel they can venture into a sea of difficult memories of feelings and sensations, and still come back again. Without some connection to *something* good in their life that they can remember, no matter how small, the client may feel that when they are invited to revisit painful times in their life, they are being asked to simply sail off, untethered, and that there is a chance they will get blown away in a storm of their sensations of pain or terror, and simply be lost at sea forever.

For Dami, some of the positive memories that I was on the lookout for, to help us gently thaw out some of his trauma, turned out to involve his teddy bear. It was the only cuddly toy he had ever had, and was given to him by a cousin of his mother who had let them stay in her house for about a year. Teddy had been his constant companion throughout childhood and adolescence. Dami recounted how he had sometimes been extremely rough with his faithful bear – he had thrown Teddy violently around the room (a replay of what his father had done regularly to Dami and his mother), cut bits off its ears, shaved parts of it, and pulled one of its button eyes out. Each time he would feel remorse afterwards, and attempt a repair: clumsily sewing back on the missing bits; or, in the case of the missing fur, making a tunic for Teddy by cutting up the sleeve of one of his own tops. The bear sat on the pillow of Dami's bed, no matter where they ended up: the bedsit where he and his mother and father had lived at first; the women's refuge they had stayed in for a while after that; Dami's mother's cousin's house, where they had lived until they were finally housed by the council; and the council flat where Dami's mother now still lived. The only place he had ever not had his teddy on his bed was at the residential school. This seemed to have helped Dami with the defence of splitting off the abuse and putting it away from his consciousness when he was at home during the school holidays.

Whenever Dami talked about Teddy, he became more animated, which I saw as an indication that at these times the regulation of his nervous system was functioning better than it usually did, to ensure he could have some equilibrium in terms of his bodily responses to different stimuli. We established that the bear had been an invaluable transitional object (Winnicott 1956) – almost the only constant and reliably safe thing to which Dami had had access while growing up. It reminded me of the little wooden man that Jung had made for himself when he was a boy and had been experiencing an awful anxiety and confusion. Jung had made a tiny suit of clothes for his figure, and kept it safely in the attic of his family home. Knowing the little figure was there had given him a profound sense of ease and comfort (Jung 1963b). Indeed, Jung later maintained that it was the making of this little man that had saved his sanity at the time. I noticed how comforted I felt, myself, whenever Dami spoke about his bear. It felt like proof that there had been *some* good things in his life, and that there might be again. Most of what he could describe about his experiences seemed so abusive, violent, chaotic and hopeless that I would sometimes feel quite desperate after our sessions. The Dami that felt bad because he had been rough to his bear and tried to make amends was a Dami I could feel tender towards, and a little hopeful about.

In some ways, the fact that it opened up the possibility for me to feel more warmly towards him, and eventually grow fond of Dami, the grown man, opened up a different set of problems for me to manage and make meaning of. I noticed that a few months into the work with Dami I would often feel quite desperately preoccupied about his wellbeing after a session. I knew that after a session he would often return to situations where he would be with people to whom he referred as his 'messy friends': people who tended to cheat him, lie to him, and with whom Dami would put himself in risky situations. One week, for example, I asked him how he had been after the previous week's session, in which we had discussed the fact he had found out, via some social media group, that his old residential school was being closed down and that police were now investigating allegations of historic physical and sexual abuse by the staff. Dami had been wondering if legal aid might be able to help him pursue a case against the teacher who had sexually abused him, so he could receive some compensation, and we had talked about what this might be like, and what it might entail.

> DAMI: Oh, man. That session messed with my head. I went to a friend's house for, like, moral support, after that.
> SARAH: Uh huh. And were they able to be supportive?
> DAMI: [Looking suddenly sheepish] Well, he tried. He like skinned up for me and … [The rest was mumbled.]

SARAH: He tried to be supportive by sharing a joint with you. I guess that's the way *he* soothes himself when he's distressed?

DAMI: Yeah, and then … Cos it was like *really* bad, and I said I *really* needed de-stressing, he like, well … we smoked a pipe.

SARAH: A pipe of … ?

DAMI: [Looking down, like a teenager in trouble with an adult authority figure] Just one rock. But it was just that once. I'm not going to, like, make a habit. It gave me a headache, man! He was trying to be nice, but … no. No more. I'm sticking to the puff. Just puff.

At this point I actually put my head briefly in my hands at hearing Dami's friend had tried to help by giving him the chance to smoke crack cocaine. When I looked back up at him, having tried to regain a reasonably contained demeanour, Dami was grinning, as if he was really quite pleased that I had initially registered such an undeniably strong reaction to his news. He held up both large hands, palms towards me as if I was holding him at gun point.

DAMI: [Grinning] I know, I know. No more. I promise. No more crack. Ever.

SARAH: [Unable to prevent a mirroring smile] That sounds like a pretty good idea.

I would talk with my supervisor about how I felt such a ghastly worry about Dami in between our sessions. Sometimes I even dreamed about him in potentially violent situations where I would be trying to warn him or protect him, but find myself unable to speak or move. The dreams seemed to mirror how excruciating I often found the experience of sitting and listening to Dami in sessions, with such little sense that I could intervene meaningfully and help prevent his continuing self-harm. My supervisor and I discussed my worried preoccupation with him using three different paradigms:

- a frame that foregrounded an understanding of the effect of unprocessed trauma on the human nervous system and the ability to regulate oneself;
- a frame that used a psychodynamically based, attachment perspective, that gives insight into how one person relates meaningfully to others; and
- a transpersonal frame, that allows for the idea that some things in life have elements that cannot be described or given meaning in purely concrete and cognitive ways.

We therefore looked in supervision together at:

1. How much I was at the affect, vicariously, of so much trauma in the frame of our work. We talked about the sense of feeling overwhelmed and paralysed in the face of unstoppable and catastrophic awfulness, which I felt when I listened to, thought about or even dreamed about Dami, and how this was such an accurate mirroring of his own experiences in early life, and how Dami might be evoking these feelings in me as part of an unconscious drive to make himself understood. In this way, my horrible feelings could be appreciated as ways that opened up my understanding of aspects of Dami's inner world.

2. In psychodynamic and attachment terms, we explored how my worried inability to stop myself dwelling gloomily on how awful Dami's life was in between sessions could be seen as a form of what Winnicott (1956) called 'primary maternal preoccupation'. Any attentive, caring mother has a vital preoccupation with her tiny, new infant that is wholly normal and desirable in a mother with a helpless newborn baby. Such preoccupation only becomes a neurotic phenomenon once a child is not in need of such moment-by-moment vigilance by its carer in order to survive. The fact that I was at the affect of such an urge – that I would get caught up in the type of preoccupation with Dami's wellbeing that would really only be appropriate to have for a tiny baby – could be seen as a pointer to the time when a depth of care and attention had been desperately needed but not provided in his early life, leaving him with this profound unmet need. He was therefore, unconsciously, needing to evoke in the women he encountered, including me, the urge to worry about him and take care of him. His own mother had been too stressed, frightened and scattered to be able to simply focus on her baby son, and be confident that she could do whatever was needed to make everything all right for him. Dami was consequently still hungry for a woman to do this. My supervisor encouraged me to think that it was a measure of the successful connection I had established with him that that was enabling Dami to evoke this longing in me to take care of him, or wish to organise for him to be taken care of.

3. Third, we used the Jungian notion of the necessity of the client being able to not only *affect* the therapist, but also to *infect* them, as we talked over the work with Dami. Jung used the story of a shaman who was a rainmaker and could affect the weather by quietly focusing on where his own, internal 'weather' was disturbed and thereby restore his own

inner equilibrium, which would then bring about a mysterious mirroring response in the outer weather (Jung 1963a, Vol. 14, 604n). Jung used this as a metaphor to illustrate the strange yet natural process, by which the therapist allows their client to put a form of their sickness *into* the therapist, and of which the therapist must then somehow heal themselves, thus simply embodying for the client that such a sickness *can* be cured in a person. The salient point in using this as a paradigm is that the therapist must do their own processing and their own meaning-making, related to what has been stirred up by the work, *within themselves*, in order to model for the client that it is possible, for instance, to be at the affect of great distress, or agony, or rage, despair, hatred, desire, etc., and yet also tolerate and make a space for all these feelings to be felt. This allows each feeling state in the therapist to simply blow through and make space for the next emotional weather system, and this in turns manifests the possibility for the client that such a process can happen – is possible.

All three approaches helped me to do the hardest thing when working with Dami, which was to bear the anguish I came to feel about his safety when I was with him or thought about him, and not either lose heart that there was any point in what we were doing or decide that I must change tack and start finding ways to be proactively getting him more help.

Rather than get pulled either of these ways, I would decide to simply sit still after Dami had left at the end of a session. Before reaching for my notes to write up my thoughts, or rearrange the room for the next client, or whatever I usually had been doing, I would simply sit in my chair, breathe slowly and deeply and allow the feelings that were awash in me to have full rein. Sometimes I would find myself shedding tears of pure frustration and anxiety. I would find myself saying things to myself along the lines of, *It's ok to feel so upset and worried and outraged on Dami's behalf. Those are natural feelings for a person to have about someone they care about, who is having such a hard time. These are the sorts of feelings the people looking after Dami could have,* should have *been having about their little boy; the sorts of feelings he needed them to have, so that they could be motivated to look after him and protect him. Why wouldn't I feel heartbroken about a life that has been largely spoiled and wasted, so far?* After a minute or so of this type of self-soothing I would find that I could begin to feel calmer and more hopeful about the work, and about Dami's capacity to take something useful from the sessions and, perhaps, eventually bring about his own changes in his life. The gloomy, crushed, panicky feelings would recede and I would be able to connect to some hope again, and the memory would return of Dami as an affectionate, tender-hearted little boy, who could feel remorse for having shaved his teddy bear and take pains to make amends for it by giving up his own clothing to provide a top for the bear.

One week, the teddy bear was a particularly valuable resource during a session. Dami arrived late, which was not that unusual, but his habitual lateness was in the order of a few minutes, whereas on this day it was more like 20. When he finally arrived and a colleague let him in and alerted me to the fact that he was here, I came down to the counselling rooms and saw at once that he did not have his usual air of fashionable cool, as he sat in the waiting area. He looked rattled, scattered, his hair had not been looked after, and his skin had a sickly, ashen tone. He seemed disorientated and actually stumbled as we walked to the counselling room. When he took his seat, he did not do his usual scanning look at me, but immediately sat forward, put his elbows on his knees and his face in his hands, as if he was oblivious to anything except some inner turmoil. I took my seat opposite, feeling a concern that had a dread at its edges. Dami's life was usually horribly chaotic, but he managed in it because that was his normality. I was imagining things would have to be really dire for him to find things so unmanageable as to be reduced to the state he was clearly in. He made a sudden burping, retching noise in his throat, and breathed in sharply.

SARAH: I'm guessing you don't feel at all well, Dami. Do you feel as if you might be sick?
DAMI: Mmm.
SARAH: I'll go and get you a bucket in case, OK?
DAMI: Yeah. Thanks.

I had learned my lesson some years ago that it was wise to know where to quickly get a receptacle so that a client can have something to hand, if they suddenly feel very nauseous. It tends to feel reassuring for someone if they realise their therapist is properly prepared for the eventuality of them throwing up in a session; and it is reassuring for the therapist to know where to get a container for someone to be sick in, so they won't have to risk needing to clean up a big mess.

When I came back into the room with a plastic bucket from the cleaning cupboard, Dami was crying – something I had never seen him do. He had put his hands onto the top of his head, his baseball cap was on the floor, and he was looking down and weeping quietly and desperately into his lap, like a child who has no hope of any comfort or assistance. I put the bucket gently down near him and sat down. I found myself leaning forward in my seat and breathing slowly and deeply in a rather exaggerated way, in the same way I used to when my children had been young and felt sick, so as to help remind them that they too could breathe slowly and steadily, and did not need to start panicking because they might throw up.

> SARAH: [As softly as would still make me audible] I guess you must be feeling so bad and hopeless today.
> [Dami screwed his face up and shook his head with one brief jerk, as if in response to some sudden increase in pain, as he might have if I had suddenly poked or kicked him.]
> SARAH: I'm wondering what I can do to be a support to you right now …
> [Dami shook his head sharply again and said nothing.]
> SARAH: Sometimes when people feel really overwhelmed here, it can help to just have a very little bit of physical contact. Would it feel helpful to, maybe, just hold the tip of one of my fingers?
> [Dami put both hands up and covered his face. He made no response to this for about ten seconds, and then gave a very small, almost imperceptible nod.
> I held out one index finger, and while one hand was still covering his face, he groped the air between us until he located the tip of my finger and held it tight.
> Once he had hold of it firmly, he took a deep, quivering breath. There was a short silence, then he began to speak into the palm of the hand that was still covering his face.]
> DAMI: I don't know what I'm going to do. I lost my job at the cab place. I told my girlfriend and she just screamed at me and chucked all my stuff in the street, and my mum … she's texted to say she's in the hospital again, and this time it's cancer for sure, and …
> [Dami suddenly made a sound somewhere between a groan and a retch. He continued to hold my finger, put his other hand down from his face and lifted his agonised, tear-streaked face to me.]
> DAMI: The boss said I'd been stealing! He'd left a load of cash on one of the desks in the office while he went out, and there was only me and his cousin there for an hour. Then I went on a call. I didn't touch his fucking money! I did not touch one penny of it, Sarah! It was that other fucker. His stupid, fat, lazy fucker of a cousin. The lying shit!

I didn't do a thing, and now I've got no money, no job, no home, and I … oh, what's the fucking point … I …

[He sat forward suddenly, still holding my finger, pulled the bucket to him with his free hand and retched violently into it.]

He let go of my finger when he'd finished being sick and leant back in his seat. He looked spent. He closed his eyes and I could see that behind his lids, his eyeballs were making odd, trembling movements, as if he was trying, behind his lids, to focus on and track an object that was oscillating rapidly in front of him. His breathing was becoming more rapid and shallow.

SARAH: Are you able to tell me what's going on in your body right now, Dami?

DAMI: [In an uncharacteristically high-pitched, childish tone of voice] I … I … I don't know. I don't know where I am.

SARAH: Do you know what day it is today?

DAMI: [Shaking his head] I can't … I can't really see. I can't see anything. I don't know. I can't say.

I was now working with an assumption that the crisis in Dami's present life had presented him with so much stress that it had overloaded his coping mechanisms and had triggered a sudden and very disorientating 'thaw' of frozen, traumatic experiences, to do with being unfairly blamed, unsafe, unsupported and at the risk of losing his mother. He was now, in effect, reliving the experience of being a small, vulnerable child in the middle of a frightening, abusive and utterly overwhelming situation, in which the body's instinctive survival mode had kicked in. This meant that the amygdala in Dami's brain would have taken over his functioning to ensure his basic survival and all his nervous system's activities were focused on shutting down all non-essential functions, and attempting to allow Dami to simply hover in a sort of suspended animation, until the life-threatening figure or situation had passed.

I sat running different options through my mind while watching Dami, frozen in his seat, breathe in little shallow gasps, as his eyes quivered in such an odd, disturbing way in their sockets. The two main things I wanted to support Dami with were to, first, help him reconnect to a sense that he was actually alive and in his body; and, second, that he could find a way to connect to the fact he had some agency and control about what was happening around him, to help keep himself safe from harm.

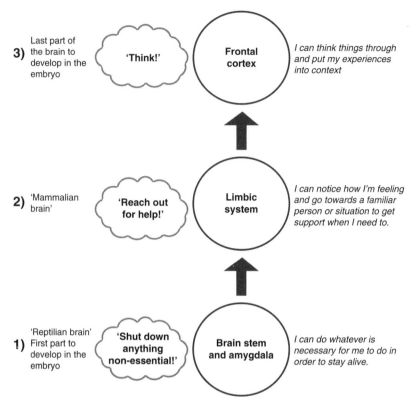

Figure 4.1 Three levels of what the brain enables humans to do (adapted from the proposition of a Triune Brain, by neuroscientist Paul MacLean)
Copyright S. Van Gogh and G. Richards

In the past, I had used the fact that people who have become triggered into some old trauma can feel soothed by being able to hold a soft cushion or be wrapped in a fleecy blanket. But Dami seemed to me to be so particularly deeply dissociated and was re-living such an abusive situation, that any attempt I might make to provide some physical comfort would run the risk of being experienced as threatening and invasive, and might trigger a further intensity of the retraumatisation. His eye movements were really concerning me. I wondered if he had once received a blow to the head as an infant, perhaps from his father, that had had a horrible, jarring impact on his skull, eyes, optic nerve and brain, which he was now helplessly re-experiencing. I racked my brain for something that Dami might find soothing – sound, words, smells? Comfort. Comfort. How could he feel comforted?

And then, with a gush of relief, I thought of his old teddy. Perhaps the warm sweetness of imaginatively catching hold of the one thing I felt would be helpful in this situation was not dissimilar to how Dami, himself, might have felt about his bear in times of distress.

SARAH: I think you're feeling so awful – upset and scared. I wonder if there could be something nice to think about instead of all the bad stuff? Something that helps you feel a little stronger, calmer?

DAMI: [With eyes still closed but a slight lessening of the terrified tone in his voice] No. Yes. I mean, I don't know what you mean.

SARAH: Well, I was remembering how you talked about your teddy bear when you were here a few weeks back.

DAMI: Oh. [Pause.] Yes.

SARAH: Mmm. Your teddy who went everywhere you went. Can you remember him?

DAMI: [A whisper] Yes.

SARAH: Can you? That's good. He's a *good* thing to think about, isn't he? Your teddy. How he always sat on your bed, no matter where you were sleeping. And how you made him a top to cover up his bald bit.

DAMI: Heh. Mmm. Yeah.

SARAH: Your dear old teddy.

Was it my wishful thinking or could I detect a very slight softening in the stiffness of Dami's facial muscles?

SARAH: If you were going to picture your teddy, right now, where would you see him?

DAMI: On my pillow.

SARAH: [Hugely relieved that Dami had answered so promptly, and was able to picture his bear] Mmm. That sounds good to think about. Teddy's lying on your pillow?

DAMI: No; sitting up. He's sitting on it.

SARAH: I see. Sitting up.

DAMI: His paws are facing the door. The bedroom door.

SARAH: Right. Sounds like you can really see him in your mind's eye.

DAMI: Yeah.

SARAH: How would it be if I asked you to imagine you were there with him?

DAMI: Hmph. OK. Yeah. Heh.

SARAH: That you can be in the room with just him, and it's safe.

DAMI: [With a tiny nod] Mmm.

SARAH: Can you imagine that you're with Teddy?

DAMI: Mmm.

SARAH: Mmm. And can you imagine you go over and pick him up?

[A pause and then another small nod.]

SARAH: You can pick him up and hold him. Your teddy. What does he feel like?

DAMI: Soft. I can feel the hard bit that was, like, his nose.

SARAH: Mmm. Soft fur and his hard nose. Yes. And can you imagine cuddling him?

DAMI: [With a new, and slightly more animated tone of voice] No! I don't cuddle him. I never cuddle him!

SARAH: I see. You don't cuddle Teddy. Right. What do you like to do with Teddy?

DAMI: I sit on the bed with him. He sits, like, near me, and I talk to him.

[Dami's breathing had slowed somewhat during this exchange, and his quivering eye movements seemed to have stopped.]

SARAH: It sounds nice, just sitting and being with him.

DAMI: I get to say whatever I want.

I remembered, when Dami said this, that being able to say whatever he wanted was one of the things he had already identified as being helpful to him about our sessions. I must have often been a stand-in for Teddy in our sessions.

SARAH: Teddy just listens.

DAMI: Yeah. Mmm. I get to say … whatever.

SARAH: Absolutely whatever you want to say – Teddy will listen.

DAMI: Yeah. I tell him what they're doing in the other room, and I tell him what we'll do later when they've finished with their stupid shit; when they've shut up and gone away.

SARAH: Mmm. Sounds like you feel a lot better knowing you've got Teddy there.

DAMI: Hmm.

Dami's voice and posture had been subtly changing as we'd been speaking, and by now he had more energy in his voice and was less physically collapsed. He had a slight edge of testiness in his voice that I felt pleased to note – anger tends to have some energy and self-preservation in it, which may be troublesome for anyone who is the focus of the anger, but it is at least a sign that the person feeling the anger can be in touch with some sense that they are of worth.

SARAH: OK. Here's a funny suggestion for you, Dami: just suppose Teddy could talk; what do you think he would say to you, right now?

Dami suddenly opened his eyes and stared at me in what looked like utter amazement. He rubbed his face slowly and wonderingly with one hand, as if he was waking up. When he spoke, his voice sounded more like his everyday self, but was both a little softer and a little more animated, more expressive of emotion, than usual.

DAMI: Fuck. That was so weird. That is so weird – what you just said. Because that is what I used to really wish would, like, happen. God. I wanted exactly what you said.

[He shook his head slightly and rubbed the top of his head. He looked down on the ground and saw his hat, and stared at it and then at the bucket for a few moments.]

SARAH: If you're feeling a bit less sick now, I'll just put this to one side.

DAMI: Yeah, I'm good now.

I put the bucket in the corner, and Dami leaned down to pick up his cap and put it back on, carefully adjusting it so that it was at the right angle. A little of his old pride and cool was returning, which I was pleased to see.

I wanted to take advantage of this new, softer state that Dami was in and there was a window of opportunity for a connection with the Dami who existed somewhere between the extremely shaky Dami who was super-vulnerable, and the old Dami with his tough, outer coating back on, armoured against the world again.

SARAH: So, you really wished your old teddy bear could talk to you. That sounds very important.

DAMI: Yeah? A bit fucking stupid too. But I was just a little kid. I wished he could, like come to life and we could do stuff together! Ha! Have you ever seen that film? That, *Ted*?

SARAH: Where the boy wishes his teddy would come to life, and he really does, and turns out to be quite crude and gross?

DAMI: That's the one! Oh man. That fucking freaked me out, like, when the trailer come out. I couldn't go and see it, because that's exactly what I imagined. That's what I fucking (sorry, 'scuse my language again) *prayed* for when I was a kid.

SARAH: Wow. It must have been very strange – seeing what you'd longed for being played out on the big screen in the trailer.

DAMI: Totally! It was totally weird!

There was already a different, much less desperate feel to the session now. It seemed that Dami's connection to his security-promoting object, even though it was 'only' in his imagination, had helped him enormously. So I felt it was OK to risk returning once again, tangentially, to his current crisis, and make a link.

SARAH: So, if you could have had your wish granted, like the boy in the film, and have your teddy come to life, I wonder what he would be saying about how things are for you right now?

DAMI: [Rubbing his hands together] Oh man! He'd be, like, 'Just gotta keep focusing on *you*, bro! Just on what *you* want. Never mind about all that other shit!'

SARAH: He sounds like a very 'no nonsense' type of bear.

DAMI: Yeah. He'd be all 'Come on, man. Ditch that bitch if she be like that. Plenty more fish', and like … 'Chin up, my man.'

I nodded. Although I felt a pang for Dami's long-suffering ex who had obviously come to the end of her tether with him, I was pleased to see him reconnecting with some more sense of hope and resilience that he would be able to get through this current crisis.

SARAH: And just suppose he had something very kind and very wise to say to you today. That would help you get through this bad time. What would it be?

There was a long pause. Tears appeared in Dami's eyes again, but they seemed to be gentler tears – tears that arose because he was connecting to his feelings in a meaningful way, rather than because he felt catastrophically overwhelmed by them. He cleared his throat and spoke softly.

DAMI: He'd say, 'You're all right, man. Deep down, you're a good guy. At heart. You've got a good heart.'

[Dami blinked away his tears and rubbed his face hard with one hand, and then looked up at me, with a dubious expression.]

DAMI: Am I just making stupid shit up?

SARAH: You sound a bit like me when I was training to work with images and dreams. I remember saying to my trainer, 'But if I imagine a peacock, it's not a real peacock, is it! It's just an imaginary one!'

DAMI: Tch! Exactly! What did your teacher say?

SARAH: She said, 'Well, Sarah, what if we could say: it's a real imaginary peacock?'

[Dami sucked his teeth in an expression of disparaging exasperation.]

DAMI: Meaning what?

[A pause.]

SARAH: I think she meant that what we can imagine is not a replacement or magical 'stand in' for the reality 'out there', but it can still have its own meaning and worth for us. So, even if, in one way, you are 'just making stuff up' it doesn't have to mean that stuff is stupid or has no value. What if the things that you made up for your teddy to say had some kind of truth in them, some meaning, something useful for you?

[A long pause, while I could see Dami seemed to be allowing in what I had just said.]

SARAH: What if you do, in fact, have 'a good heart'?

Dami smiled at me, a rare and rather beautiful smile that was not wry or ironic or knowing, but which simply lit up his face and made me want to smile back. Perhaps we were in touch in that moment with how things had sometimes been between his mother and himself, a long way back, in moments when she was safe enough to be delighted with her little boy when he smiled. Perhaps she had sometimes been able to instinctively smile back, and their delight with each other would have beamed back and forth in a gratifying loop of mirroring smiles.

DAMI: Is that what *you* think?

SARAH: Is that what I think about what?

DAMI: That I have a good heart?

SARAH: I think … I think you can tell, deep down, what I believe about that.

DAMI: [Slapping his thigh with an open hand with a loud smacking noise, and in a tone of both delight and exasperation] I knew it! I knew you wouldn't give me a straight answer to that. You therapists! You crack me up!

He laughed and shook his head, and we sat smiling at each other for a little while longer.

By the end of that session, Dami had made a sort of a plan as to what he was going to do next to get through the next 24 hours, which he assured me, wryly, would not involve smoking any crack cocaine, and he was true to his word on that.

He continued to have sessions with me for a further ten months after this session, during which he was able to recount more of what he remembered about the abuse at the school, and express more of his rage and sorrow about what his child-self had had to endure both at the school and beforehand. He grieved for the lost little Dami, without feeling so entirely shattered by his own grief. Shedding tears in a session came to feel less like a disastrous failure of his manhood, and more of a natural response to connecting to his losses and a healthy release of many of the held-in feelings he had been carrying for years. He talked over the possibility of trying to get some compensation for the abuse he had endured at the school, and of contacting the police to see if there was an ongoing investigation he could give evidence to. After revisiting these possibilities many times in sessions, he made his peace with the decision he made, which was to do neither of these things.

He also began to show subtle but significant changes in the way he dealt with stressful events, including being able to be more assertive, rather than aggressive, with various acquaintances when they were dishonest with him. He started going, of his own accord, to a drop-in support service for drug users he had found out about, which was in a service based not far from his mother's flat. This led him onto having some honest conversations with his mother about not wanting to prop up her addiction to painkillers and antidepressants anymore. In turn, this was the impetus for his mother being able to admit she had an addiction problem, and go to her GP to get her own support in addressing this.

I noticed a waning, as more months went by, of my dreadful, almost crippling anxiety about Dami's welfare, which I understood as the reflection of a parallel process within Dami himself, that indicated he was feeling less lost and incapable of taking care of himself.

In our last session he showed me a small present his mother had recently bought him: a tiny teddy bear that fitted onto his keyring. He was by no means out of the woods but he did at least have a map and a compass.

5

DISSOLVING THE ILLUSION THAT ABUSE WAS LOVE
VJ

[The grass is beneath my head]

The grass is beneath my head;
and I gaze
at the thronging stars
in the night.
They fall … they fall …
I am overwhelmed,
and afraid.
Each leaf of the aspen
is caressed by the wind,
and each is crying.
And the perfume
of invisible roses
deepens the anguish.
Let a strong mesh of roots
feed the crimson of roses
upon my heart;
and then fold over the hollow
where all the pain was.

F. S. Flint (1885–1960)

An account of some work with a young adult who felt that their true identity was female, but that they were trapped in a male body. How the sexual violation that they had experienced was interwoven with a hatred of their masculine body, and how the therapy had to sensitively address both the issues of sexual abuse and the wish to change gender. How the therapy helped the client to unpick the knot that prevented them from being able to think deeply about some of their experiences, and to go forward with their wish to remain fluid around their gender identity, without being haunted by the dread that they only wished to do so because of past abuse.

VJ was late for our first appointment. When I eventually opened the door of my house for our first meeting in my private practice, it was already over halfway into the session time. I saw a very tall, slender young man, with thick, shiny, shoulder-length black hair, dressed in loose, dark clothes as if he could be off to a yoga session or martial arts class. He was late because he had got lost on the way to his appointment. As soon as I opened the door he began apologising, in a gentle tone of voice with crisply articulated words.

VJ: You must be Sarah? I'm VJ. Nice to finally meet you. I'm really sorry that I'm so late! I went completely wrong at the station, and then my phone battery died, so I couldn't call you for directions. I kept asking different people and none of them seemed to know your street. One of them sent me completely the wrong way! In the end, I was just wandering around, for about quarter of an hour, a few streets from here. I thought I was completely lost, but I was literally around the corner. I'm really, really sorry. I'm never normally late for anything.

[VJ took a seat, brought a plastic bottle of water out of a small shoulder bag, and had a long drink. He continued to hold this bottle in both hands throughout the session, constantly tapping the lid with a fingernail, or picking at the label on the bottle and then rolling the bits of label into tiny sausages of paper and letting these drop so that they landed on the carpet round his feet.]

SARAH: Well. Good that you made it in the end. Perhaps you can get your breath while I say a few practical things. This appointment is for an hour, which now leaves us about 25 minutes. It'll be helpful if you can tell me just a bit about yourself and what's making you wonder about having some therapy sessions at the moment. And then we'll make space at the end of the time we've got left today, to talk about how it's been for you and what the next steps might be. How does that sound?

VJ: Fine.

He didn't look fine. He suddenly looked upset, with tears filling his eyes. He glanced sideways at the tissue box on a low table.

VJ: Sorry. Can I … ?

SARAH: Yes, of course. They're there for you to use.

[He took a tissue, swallowed and wiped away some tears. 'Sorry', he said again.]

SARAH: I don't think you need to apologise for crying. It's quite usual here for people to shed some tears, or let out their feelings in other ways.

[There was a long pause, during which VJ continued to look anxious and upset.]

VJ: One of my sisters found your details. She thought I should come. I didn't really think there's much point in talking about … in talking. I don't know. I know I'm very unhappy. But maybe there's no point in going over everything that happened. I just have to try and get on, and live with it. [He paused.] But I can't. I've tried and tried and tried. And I just can't get rid of the feelings that I need to get rid of. I can't.

SARAH: So you feel hopeless?

VJ: Yes, I do.

[He blew his nose. Outside on the street a motorbike went by noisily and VJ started and then glanced anxiously at the door to the room we were in.]

SARAH: You also look as if you're feeling some anxiety. That sounds a very uncomfortable mix – to feel hopeless and anxious.

VJ looked at me, as if he might be working out whether I intended what I had said to be supportive, or whether I might be saying it as a way of being critical or sarcastic. He nodded after a few seconds, and replied, 'Yes. It's pretty horrible. But I'm used to it. This is my normal, now.'

[He blotted his eyes with a tissue and gave a deep sigh. I nodded.]

SARAH: I do hear that you're not sure that therapy is for you. But perhaps you could, nevertheless, fill me in on a bit of your story – your family background, and current circumstances – and that could help us work out if further sessions could possibly be helpful?

As VJ told me some more information about himself, the pile of tiny bits of rolled up paper at his feet grew and grew.

He was 25 and was working as a manager of a shop in the West End that sold musical instruments, sheet music and various musical accessories. Whenever he finished work, he went back to North London, where he rented a room in a house with other professionals in their twenties and thirties and which was on a very busy road where heavy traffic was constant all day and most of the night. None of the house-mates knew each other socially, or were friendly with the others in the house. VJ would spend evenings alone in his room, eating a microwaved meal for one, watching episodes of a drama series on television, sometimes into the early hours of the morning, and chain-smoking. ('I'm addicted to *Desperate Housewives*'). His day-to-day routine sounded like that of someone struggling with depression and anxiety.

He was the youngest child in a family, and had four older siblings, all sisters. His mother's family were from India and his mother had come to London, as a young woman, to live with an uncle's family and study law. She had met VJ's father, who was studying medicine, and had become pregnant shortly after they started seeing each other, which neither of them had planned. VJ's father's family were also originally from India, and his parents, who lived in North London at this time, were very focused on their only son making a success of his career, and being a respectable, respected figure. They had been very displeased that VJ's mother was pregnant so soon and outside marriage. They pressured VJ's parents to get married while they were both still students, which they dutifully did. In the end, VJ's mother felt so unwell during her pregnancy, with a dreadful nausea lasting months, that she dropped out of her studies. The baby, the couple's first son, was born in the month just before VJ's father took his final exams. Sadly, by the time VJ's father had heard he had passed with flying colours, the baby had suddenly and unexpectedly died, of what was officially recorded as a tragic case of Sudden Infant Death Syndrome.

Over the years that followed, VJ's father worked incredibly hard to build up his medical career and establish his own practice as a GP. Meanwhile VJ's mother kept the home and gave birth to four children in succession, all girls. There was then a long gap and finally, as VJ described it, 'they tried one more time for a boy, and I came along'. In the brief time available to him in the session, VJ gave the impression of a childhood in which he was surrounded by warm, clever, funny, sparky female figures, who made much of him as a favourite and the baby of the family. His father sounded like a more complicated presence for VJ – a figure whom VJ looked up to, and of whom he was a little in awe, but whom he also found aloof, distant and often disapproving.

When I asked him to tell me about something from very early in his life that had stayed with him, he offered me the following scene. He was perhaps around four, and had been enjoying being the centre of attention with two of his sisters who were then around nine and ten. They had all been spending time together, dancing and singing along to music tracks in the family living room, dressed in different outfits. The sisters had included VJ in what they were doing, and had dressed him in a sequinned top and skirt, put a big bow in his hair, made up his face and painted his toenails and fingernails with glittery varnish. He remembered being very happy, feeling surrounded by love and prettiness and playfulness. Then he remembered his father coming in to the room, and the atmosphere suddenly becoming cold and somehow rather frightening. He recalled the music being turned off and his father taking him wordlessly to the bathroom where VJ had to take off his sparkly outfit and the bow. Then, still in silence, his father had grimly removed the make up and the nail varnish, rubbing roughly at VJ's skin in a way that felt slightly punitive, all in a thunderous silence.

VJ added that throughout his early childhood there were regular simmering rows, conflicts and disagreements between his mother and father. These were often about how VJ was treated by his mother and sisters, with his father accusing them of spoiling VJ and treating him 'like a girl', and his mother and sisters arguing back that VJ should be allowed to join in dressing up and dancing at home for fun, and that the father was being unfair to VJ by forbidding this.

> VJ: There was a lot of expectation on me, from my dad. Like there was on him, from *his* parents. I felt like I had to make up for the son that died, and be, you know, the epitome of manhood, or something, and make my dad proud. [Pause.] Umm, I ... How much time do we have left?
>
> SARAH: About ten minutes.
>
> VJ: Because ... There's something that I think I maybe ought to mention. I mean, I don't really want to, but I don't think there's any point in coming here unless I tell you about it ... But the thing is, I'm not sure I can tell you, anyway. And not now. But then, if I don't tell you, you won't really be able to work out if you can help me. So ...
>
> SARAH: Mmm. That's hard, isn't it?
>
> VJ: Yeah. It would be a kind of relief to leave here without having mentioned it, because I really don't want to talk about it. [Pause.] But then it would be a different kind of relief if I could manage to tell you, because then you would know. And you really can't help me if you don't know about this thing.

He gave a small sigh, and stared at the carpet. There was a long silence. Eventually, with the time in mind, I decided to trust a hunch I had formed and say something that might help.

SARAH: It can often be better for people to reveal things here at their own pace, but perhaps because time is of the essence now, and you seem to need some help working out if therapy could be for you, it might be helpful for you to know that I am imagining that part of what you might be ambivalent about disclosing could be to do with some sort of unhappy sexual experience. Would that be in the right area?

[VJ sat in silence, looking at the bottle in his hands. Some tears fell down on to the bottle and he wiped them carefully away with one index finger.]

VJ: [Hesitantly] Yes. That's sort of part of it … But there's … It's not just that. I mean something did definitely happen when I was 15 that, maybe you could say was abuse. Well. No, it probably was. Well, it was. Clearly. In one way. But then … I mean, do you say something is abuse when, at the time, you think, 'yes, I want to do this'? Like … if you think you love someone, and you think they love you … then, it's not so easy to work out what's abuse and what isn't, is it? And anyway … Oh, what's the time?

SARAH: We still have a few minutes.

VJ: I … I *do* want to tell you the … the *thing*. And, actually, that thing is worse in a way than the … abuse. If it *was* abuse. It's all tangled up with … what happened to me. I'm only the way I am now because of the abuse. And I wish I wasn't. But now I can't change this … this *thing* now. The abuse ended a long time ago. But it's left me with this other *thing*, that will never go. Does that make any sense?

I hadn't, in fact, been able to make clear sense of what VJ had been trying to communicate, at this point. I felt as if I was trying to follow him around a maze of corridors to reach some important final destination with him, but that he was always just ahead of me, disappearing around a corner, leaving me having to hurry in order to keep up with him and keep him just in sight.

SARAH: Mmm. I don't think I can say I have *exactly* followed everything you've just been saying. There's clearly such a lot in what you need to unpack and look at. I do hear that you have experienced something that *might* be seen as sexually abusive; also that something you feel is connected to that possible abuse is also making you feel unhappy and ill at ease at the moment.

VJ looked down at the ground at this point again, and seemed to suddenly notice the pile of paper crumbs he had created. He bent forward and began picking them up meticulously, one by one.

SARAH: You don't have to clear that up. It's fine to just leave it.

[VJ gave an uneasy laugh, and continued to pick up the result of his nervous label-peeling. He stuffed them in his jeans pocket.]

VJ: Sorry. It's a bad habit: fiddling with things. It used to drive my dad crazy. He used to shout, 'Stop bloody picking at stuff! What are you? A bloody monkey?' [Pause.] That's it now, isn't it – that's our hour?

SARAH: Yes, it is. Do you have a sense of what you might like to do about further sessions?

VJ: Can I let you know?

He suddenly looked as if he could barely wait to get out of the room and be away. He paid me and left in a hurry and I thought, as I shut the door after him, that he probably wouldn't be back. I was sorry to think that it seemed likely that some awful shame had VJ so thoroughly in its grip that I would not be hearing again from him.

However, I was wrong. Several months later VJ emailed me. He wrote that he had decided he *would* like to come back. One of his sisters was offering to give him some money to help pay for therapy, and he had made his mind up that he was going to have to face 'the thing' and talk about it.

When he arrived for our next meeting he was wearing a top with shorter sleeves than last time. As he sat down, I noticed several long, parallel scabs on his left forearm that made me wonder if he might have been cutting himself.

To begin with in our sessions, despite VJ's intention to name 'the thing' that he believed was so central to his difficulties, he could still only allude to it, obliquely. Naturally enough, I found myself wondering from time to time (both to myself, and out loud in the peer supervision group at which I discussed my work with VJ), what this 'thing' might be. My wonderings included whether it could be in the areas that some other clients had struggled to talk about, such as: being caught up in the heavy use of pornography, visiting sex workers, or working in the sex industry.

I wondered about darker things than these, too. Might VJ be drawn to or actually have perpetrated some kind of abuse, himself? Might he have committed some act of gross violence, or been involved in some illegal activity, which would be outside the bounds of the confidentiality I could offer? I didn't get a sense of VJ as being at all capable of cruelty or violence; I liked him and found him warm, sensitive, bright and often very funny. But the possibility of something shadowy hovered in the background of my wondering what it was that he couldn't tell me.

I talked with my supervision colleagues about the constant tension I felt in VJ's presence between needing to offer him a space in which he could feel it would be OK to tell me about the 'thing', whilst also making it a space in which he could feel accepted without ever disclosing any details about 'the thing'. I described it as feeling as if I was part of a rather awful game with VJ: a game in which I had to be both keen to know his secret, and yet also willing to not pry, and accept that I may never know it and still trust that our work would be valid. In the group, we all found ourselves imagining that there had been something in VJ's life that had felt like some kind of strange game he was caught up in, which was getting played out again between him and me, that might explain the pull I felt to simultaneously know and not-know what his perhaps-terrible secret was.

These two themes of needing to keep a secret which is both exciting and yet burdensome, and of having to know and yet not-know, are both threads that often run through sexual violation. And sexual violation did indeed turn out to be part of VJ's story.

By the time he was 15 VJ was quite a talented guitar player. In addition to his music lessons at school, his parents paid for him to start extra private music lessons with a teacher who was recommended by the parents of another pupil at VJ's school. The teacher lived only a few streets away. VJ referred to him in sessions as 'Mr X'.

Mr X was a charismatic, handsome, talented white man in his early forties. He seemed to take a great shine to VJ almost immediately. VJ quickly felt at ease in Mr X's home, and enjoyed not only the lessons, but the times before and after, when they would both sit at Mr X's kitchen table with a coffee and talk about music and books and films. Soon VJ found himself opening up to Mr X about his more intimate thoughts and feelings, including the difficulties he felt in his relationship with his father; his hopes and ambitions about travelling and perhaps living in India in order to reconnect with his Indian heritage; and about a long piece for acoustic guitar and string quartet that he was composing, based on T.S. Eliot's poem 'The Wasteland', which he was studying in English lessons. He was immensely flattered that Mr X listened sympathetically and, in turn, told VJ lots about his personal life, his own ups and downs as a youth with his family, and generally began to treat VJ more and more like a friend than a pupil.

vj: I suppose, now, you would say it was grooming. But back then, it felt wonderful – to be with someone so, you know, cool, and worldly wise, who was making you feel so special, and that they really wanted to hear what you had to say about stuff.

SARAH: So when you say 'you would say it was grooming', do you mean that you, VJ, would say that now? Or do you mean that you think that *I* would call it that?

vj: I don't know. Both, maybe. I mean, it was! He *was* grooming me! Wasn't he?

SARAH: Maybe a part of you still can't feel sure about that.

vj: No. I am! I mean … [He pointed an index finger to his head.] Up here, I'm sure. [He placed a hand on his chest over his heart.] But, here, I still can't help remembering how … what it felt like at the time. Because, I did really … See, this is the part, that, makes me think, 'Am I sick, deep down?' Because I did really love him. And if I just say, 'Oh, yeah, he was an old paedo and he groomed me', it just …

SARAH: It sounds as if that very blunt way of naming what happened doesn't give much place to your tender adolescent feelings of falling in love with this man.

vj: I guess. But was it really falling in love?

[VJ suddenly rubbed his face with both hands and made a sound of frustration and exasperation, almost like a growl.]

vj: He told me after a few months that he had fallen in love with me. That he had tried not to, but he couldn't help himself. He seemed really upset, and worried. He said he would understand if that meant I didn't want to come anymore. He knew I was too young for him, really, and that there was this huge age gap, we were from different cultures, but that he'd never met anyone like me before, blah blah blah. And I … I completely believed him. I was so …

[His sentence trailed off.]

SARAH: You were so … ?

vj: [Wearily] Happy. I was so happy when he said all this.

Mr X and VJ began having sex several times a week at Mr X's house, after school. Mr X described it as having to keep their relationship secret for the present, until VJ was old enough for society to accept them as a couple. In our sessions I could see that VJ's continued confusion and ambivalence about what had happened caused him a dreadful anguish. In some ways, the memories of what had happened were very precious to him – he talked about how he had felt that someone had suddenly 'turned on the colour in a black and white world'. I thought this as a very poignant metaphor, given that VJ's family were Indian, and Mr X was white.

It was a situation full of intensity and confusion for VJ. He was having his first ever satisfying sexual experiences with another person. He felt loved and wanted by a man he admired and adored. He was the happiest he had been since he had been a very small boy, whenever he and Mr X were together. And yet, with the benefit of hindsight, he was compelled to see that he had been taken advantage of and used by this man.

In psychodynamic terms, I thought that VJ's susceptibility to Mr X's grooming could be understood as the result of a hole that had been left in VJ's psyche because of the lack of a satisfying emotional connection with his father. This meant that VJ had a particular hunger to be close with and really matter to a male figure whom he could look up to. I imagined that Mr X had consciously and/or unconsciously intuited this hunger, and had thus been able to exploit it. This is a dynamic that seems to often play out in some stories of abuse: a boy has lacked warmth and attention, and the feeling of being prized by a father, or older male figure in his life, and is therefore extremely vulnerable to being persuaded into believing an older man likes them and finds them special, when in fact that older man is targeting them as an object that they can use simply for their own erotic gratification.

There was also the fact that VJ had been starting to feel that he was gay around the age he began having private guitar lessons. He had, naturally, picked up on the homophobia surrounding him in society, from his father and in his secondary school. He therefore felt he had to keep hidden from others his sense of himself as having a desire nature that meant he found other males attractive. For Mr X to be so open and frank about one male desiring another was another factor in VJ finding his declaration of love so utterly compelling, exciting and liberating.

I imagined that the power imbalance inherent in the fact that Mr X was white and VJ was not, would also have played some part in Mr X being able to manipulate VJ into beginning a sexual relationship.

For about six months, VJ lived a double life. For the most part, he played the part of a fairly quiet, studious school boy, with not many friends, who was still the baby of his family, and often sent to his room by his father for being 'cheeky' or 'disrespectful'. But for two or three heady afternoons a week, he could be the special secret lover of an older man who was opening the door for VJ to a whole new brilliant world and future. The difference between these two modes of existence was vast, and the effort it took VJ to keep them both going, whilst ensuring they stayed utterly separate, showed in the fact that his school work began to go downhill. He also withdrew more and more from his mother and sisters in order to spend time alone in his room, daydreaming, playing his guitar, and working on his 'Wasteland' composition. He lost his appetite and became very thin. He took up smoking, and bought the same brand of cigarettes as Mr X.

VJ did not know it at the time, but Mr X had a habit of telling certain of his teenage students, male and female, that he had fallen in love with them and that he had never felt anything like what he felt for them in his life before. In fact, he would continue to abuse other students, long after he ended the sexual relationship with VJ. But the extent of Mr X's abuse of his pupils only came to VJ's attention many years later, long past the time he and Mr X had been involved. VJ happened to see a piece in a newspaper about the trial and conviction of a Mr X for the serial sexual abuse of music students in a school in another part of the country, where he had been on the staff for about six years. The newspaper coverage had included what a number of witnesses had said as part of their evidence, and their accounts of how this man had seduced them were all very similar to each other, and sounded almost identical to what Mr X had done with VJ. By the time VJ came across this, he had already resigned himself to the fact that Mr X had not, after all, loved him. But to read the stark facts about him being a serial abuser had been deeply upsetting.

In one session, while angrily plucking repeatedly at the hem of his T-shirt, VJ told me, 'I really loved the sex I had with him. I can't pretend it was awful, because it wasn't. It was the best! But what am I supposed to do with that? Because it's shit, isn't it! It's … wrong to have to say, "Oh yes, the best sex I ever had was with a convicted child sex abuser!"'

SARAH: It sounds so very hurtful and confusing. I guess that's part of how an experience of being sexually exploited can often still keep hurting, even long after the event. Perhaps it wouldn't surprise you to hear that it's quite common for someone who has been sexually used by another person to keep feeling an awful lot of pain and self-doubt about their experience of the abuse, sometimes for many years after the abuse ended.

VJ: Huh. [Pause.] But then, I think sometimes that maybe ... just maybe ... he *did* mean some of what he said to me. I mean, at the time. I know he said it to a lot of other people too. But maybe he really *did* love me, at the time.

VJ looked up at me with a questioning air. I felt the heaviness of a responsibility to say what I thought was a hard truth, and yet make it bearable for VJ to let in.

SARAH: Mr X sounds to me as if he's a man who hasn't actually done his own, important emotional growing up – for whatever reasons. Maybe in the moment of saying he felt love for a student he wanted to have sex with, he *did* feel some intensely loving feelings, and that included towards you. But, you know, VJ, it was his role, as the adult and the teacher in those situations, to contain those feelings and not let them spill out, carelessly and selfishly, all over the young people in his care. And that also included you. When we really love another person, in an adult way, we include in all our dealings with them a recognition of how the things that we do and say to them will have an impact on them. And we keep bearing in mind what will be best for them. Even if it that would definitely *not* be what would suit us best.

[VJ looked up from his T-shirt-plucking. There was a long silence. Then he sighed.]

VJ: I guess. But there's always a tiny bit of me that wants to hang on to the thought that he did really love me. That what we had was real.

SARAH: Yes. Of course.

VJ: But ... You're saying he should have kept his dick in his pants?

I was struck by the simple strength of how VJ said this. I hoped this could be a reflection of him beginning to feel less tortured by a kind of doubt about whether what had happened to him was actually abuse.

SARAH: You could put it that way, yes.

In a later session, I heard the story of how Mr X had suddenly and cruelly ended his connection with VJ.

One afternoon near the end of the school summer term, when they were lying in bed together, Mr X told VJ he would shortly be going away and would be teaching at a summer school in Switzerland for international young musicians over the whole summer holiday period. He would miss VJ terribly and think of him every day.

VJ: He promised he would bring me back some of the best Swiss chocolate ever.

That afternoon was the last time VJ ever spoke to him.

VJ: When September came, I waited for a call or a note or something, to say when the next lesson would be and when to come round. But there was nothing. I made myself think maybe the school holidays in Switzerland went on into the middle of September or something, but by October there was still no word. I felt like I was going crazy. I thought maybe he'd died abroad and I'd never know. I couldn't imagine what had happened. I went to his house and knocked at the door, I tried to peek in through his blinds. I started to walk by his house maybe three or four times a day, just desperate to see him.

[VJ began to cry as he spoke.]

VJ: I wrote to him, to say 'What's wrong? Did I do something? What happened? I still love you. I'm waiting for you. What about all our plans?' Nothing. He'd started seeing someone new – I know that now. I had to just guess what was going on in the end. Some rumour started going round in school about this girl in my school, who was in the year below me, and how they were in some relationship with a music teacher, and that this teacher lived near me. So I knew. He was with someone a bit younger than me now. Fresh meat. A girl. And that was it. We were finished.

SARAH: What a terrible shock for you. What were you feeling?

VJ: Like I was dying. So … so … I just couldn't get my head round it. And I couldn't say a thing to anyone. I just explained to my mum and dad that I wasn't going to have lessons anymore, so I could concentrate on my GCSEs. That's what he had counted on. He must have known that I would just be so … so fucked up about it all, that I wouldn't tell anyone the truth. I don't know what was worse: losing him, or me starting to wonder if he had meant any of what he'd said. I felt like I might be going mad. All I could think to do was try and act like the whole thing hadn't happened. But my mum and sisters kept saying, 'What's wrong? What's the matter? Are you ill?' I started just spending all my time up in my room, I cried loads at night. I had days when I couldn't get up and go to school. I messed up all my GCSEs later that year. That meant I couldn't get into the 6th form to do music A level and stuff. I had to go to this crappy FE place to resit all my exams. But I couldn't be bothered. I couldn't see the point. I dropped out after a bit, with nothing. [There was a long pause.] And that's when it started … I began having all these weird habits, like having to touch things in a certain order before I could leave a room. And picking at my nails and stuff. My dad prescribed me all these anti-anxiety tablets. I used to take them from him and then flush them down the toilet. And it's when the … *the thing* really started up in my mind. And it got so that I couldn't stop thinking about it all the time. It felt like that was the only way out of what was happening to me.

[VJ suddenly glanced sideways as a draught made the door make a very faint vibrating sound in the door frame.]

vj: No one's going to come in, are they?

sarah: No.

vj: I'm just very … I'm a bit paranoid about anyone hearing any of this stuff.

[I nodded.]

vj: Mmm. [His gaze wandered up to the ceiling. It seemed he suddenly could not bring himself to look at me. His voice became very low and monotone, with little feeling in it, as if he was giving a hurried report about something, the way a spy or a soldier might pass on some vital information about a threatening situation.]

vj: OK. I think I'm ready to tell you now. You'll probably think this is very weird, but … [there was a slight pause and then he said, very quickly and quietly] I started to think that the only way I could be happy was to actually be someone else.

[VJ took a deep breath in, after he said this. He closed his eyes, pressed his lips tightly together and seemed to be holding his breath.]

sarah: Right.

[Quite a pause followed as I waited to see what else he might say. When it looked as if nothing much more would be coming, I spoke as carefully and gently as I could.]

sarah: If it's OK, I'd like to get a bit clearer about what you mean by 'someone else'? Someone like … ?

vj: [With his eyes still closed, and on an outward gasp] Not *like*. Actually *as*.

He suddenly opened his eyes and looked directly at me, and I felt an immense pressure to convey enough understanding to enable him to say more of what he needed to, and yet also be congruent about the fact that I wasn't yet sure I *did* fully understand what he had told me. As I waited to come up with a phrase that could communicate this, VJ spoke again, with a growing note of urgency.

> VJ: I started to think 'I'm unhappy because of *this* and all it stands for.' [He placed both his palms flat on his lap.] I thought, 'I can only be happy if I can have a different life, a different … body.' But I was already over six foot and pretty much looking like how I look now. It was never … it was never going to happen. Do you see? My dad wouldn't have been able to accept that his son wanted to have sex with another guy, so he would never in a million years have accepted that his son would actually be happier as another daughter.

The penny dropped. I realised that VJ was talking about feelings of being in the wrong body as far as gender was concerned, and of a wish to live as a woman, rather than a man. I felt an enormous rush of clarity once he had managed to make me understand this – my constant background wonderings about what the nature of VJ's supposedly awful secret might be came abruptly to an end. His actual secret felt so much less troubling to me than some of my darker imaginings had been that I was aware of a definite sense of relief.

> VJ: I'm sure you're shocked. I mean … I know it's just the fall-out from everything with Mr X. That I'm probably only this way because I've been the victim of abuse. Wouldn't you say? I don't mind if you're honest.

I had never experienced VJ as so direct: he was suddenly sitting up straighter, frowning slightly and his voice had a bite and edge in it that I had not heard before. My mind seemed to be turning unhelpfully blank as he waited for my reply.

> SARAH: I … don't think that 'shocked' or believing you are 'crazy' are quite the reactions I am having. I think I am more in touch with being very glad you have been able to tell me about something so important about yourself.
> [VJ's demeanour softened ever so slightly.]

SARAH: And I don't think I can offer you an opinion as to the origin of your wish to be a different gender that would be very meaningful. In my experience, profound questions about *why* we feel the way we do about ourselves can't usually be answered as simply, as 'Yes, it's because of *this*', or 'No, *that* has nothing to do with how I am.'

VJ: But that's what a lot of people (experts and, like, proper doctors) *do* think, isn't it? That if someone wants to change their gender, that's because something like abuse must have screwed them up?

SARAH: There *are* people who think like that, yes. And, as I understand it, there are also people who think that if a person feels they are the 'wrong' gender it is because that's simply the way that individual is, from the word go. And then there is a third view: that we are each a unique mixture of some predispositions we are born with, plus the totality of our all our experiences, and so it would really be impossible to simply say that one thing or another definitively causes a feeling of being the 'wrong' gender.

VJ: And whatever it is with me – do you think I'm too screwy to come to therapy? Are you going to try and talk me out of it?

SARAH: Well, no, on both counts. I think therapy should be a place for anyone, (anyone who is up for reflecting on their life, I mean) to wonder about everything and anything that has shaped them. About how they feel and think about any aspect of themselves – their loves and hates, their desires, how they fit in their families, how they feel about their bodies, their jobs, their dreams. And that could include how they feel about their gender, too. But none of that freedom to really reflect and explore can happen if we feel there is some specific aim in therapy to change a certain aspect about ourselves.

VJ: Yeah, Well. OK. But … It's not normal, really, is it? [He sighed deeply.]

SARAH: Mmm. I remember an older colleague saying to me, 'Most of our problems aren't caused by our feelings, but the feelings we have *about* those feelings.' I think she was right. It's not usually our sadness, or our fear, or our longing to see someone, or a wish that we were thinner, or, in your case, a wish to be a different gender that causes most of the pain; it's the feelings of shame or anger or doubt we get *about* those feelings that tend to mess us up. And those secondary feelings that cause the problems tend to come along mostly because of other people's reactions to what we were feeling in the first place.

[There was a long silence. VJ took a couple of long, deep breaths.]

VJ: Well, maybe. But I still think I'm weird. And, if I'm honest, I think you probably think I'm weird too, deep down.

I had learned the hard way that trying to explicitly reassure clients of the truth that I did not find them odd/disgusting/silly/weird, or whatever it was that they believed I thought, tended not to work. And clients who have been sexually used in the way VJ had tend to be particularly impervious to wordy reassurances about being liked and accepted, even when they are the truth. After all, they have already been seduced, manipulated and betrayed by someone saying appreciative, affirming things to them, and they never want to be taken in and betrayed again. The most meaningful reassurance a therapist can offer is by providing them with a consistent, regular, reliable and respectful presence over time.

SARAH: Perhaps we're all a little bit weird, in our own way. Wouldn't you say?

[VJ gave a tiny smile and shrug. He glanced at the clock.]

VJ: Time's up.

And in a matter of moments, he had picked up his bag and bottle of water and was out of the door.

In later sessions VJ described in more detail how it was that, in the weeks following Mr X's abandonment of him, his longing to change gender began to take a firmer hold within him. He stayed in his room, going over and over in his mind as to why Mr X may have suddenly withdrawn from him. One thought that presented itself and carried a great weight, was that if he, VJ, had been a girl, then perhaps their relationship would not have been so taboo in society; that Mr X might not have given up on them because he knew that people would never accept them as a couple, in the way they might have accepted a couple that was an older man and young woman.

VJ began to dwell on the idea of being female instead and how that could have smoothed a path for him and Mr X to have a future together. He said this seemed to open the floodgates of feeling sure that if he had only been born a girl, then so many things would be easier: his father would not be so angry and demanding with him, he might still be with Mr X, and his life could include more colour, fun, adornment and grace than seemed possible as a man.

He continued to stay in his room, and spent a huge amount of time listening to music about lost loves, betrayals and yearnings for another. He found that all the images he associated with that theme were of a lovely woman, who is heartbroken and pining beautifully for the man who has loved and left her. He would wedge his bedroom door shut to make sure no one would come in and see him, and then stand in front of his mirror, enacting the part of the stricken woman singer, mouthing along to the words with Dusty Springfield or Amy Winehouse or Maria Callas, as tears poured down his cheeks.

> VJ: It was the women in all the songs and operas and stories I loved who were in the position I was in. Only *they* were saying what I felt. Never the men.

After about six months of weekly sessions, there were signs that VJ was feeling the benefit, in some ways, of having a safe space to be. I noticed his anxious picking behaviours in the sessions were lessening somewhat, over time. When we had started our work, I had often seen marks on his arms that I thought were the results of self-harming; these faded after some months and no fresh marks appeared. He jumped less frequently if there was any noise outside the room. He also left the sessions less like someone fleeing for their life.

Despite these signs that he felt less anxious in the sessions (which I saw as a sign that he was forming a usefully secure attachment to me and what I stood for), after some months of work with him, I nevertheless found I was aware of some rather unpleasant sensations for me during our sessions. It invariably felt to me as if VJ and I were wandering around together, lost in a greyish maze. We were, at least, walking side by side, by now, rather than him running ahead of me. But it felt a rather fruitless, stale wandering, in which we trod the same gloomy territory repeatedly, getting nowhere. VJ returned again and again to his anguish and sense that he was 'sick' because he still experienced an intense and persistent longing to change his gender. He talked as if he saw this purely as the legacy of Mr X's treatment of him. He longed to be rid of this yearning because it was so 'fucked up', while being utterly convinced he never could be.

I was reluctant to wholly take on VJ's view that he felt the way he did simply because of having been sexually abused. I kept finding the injunction of the same older colleague, whom I had already once quoted to him, come into my mind whenever I thought of VJ. She had once said to me 'We all need to find a story we can live by, rather than a story that limits us.' The story that VJ was currently telling himself (that he had been sexually abused and this had then made him feel he was in the wrong gender, which was sick and wrong) didn't seem to be serving him at all. He was a young, talented, clever, thoughtful, attractive person, spending his time either at his undemanding, boring job or shut away in a room, watching television. I wanted to make more space for the possibility that a different story (a story in which his feelings about his gender were not wholly defined by the abuse, and could be seen not only as dysfunctional and wrong) could serve him better, help to unlock his potential and allow him to live more fully.

But it became apparent, as we worked, how deeply wedded VJ had become to his two limiting 'scripts': first, that his abuse had crucially defined him; and second, that he could not do anything about the fact that he felt more female than male, except hide this from the world, and wish it would go away. When I first attempted to challenge his second 'script' he became angry with me.

Towards the end of one of our hours together VJ sighed deeply after a long silence.

> VJ: I'm scared that I'll never be able to get past all this. I mean, *maybe* I could, as far as the abuse is concerned. But the other stuff. I can't! I mean, what am I supposed to do, knowing that there's something so ... you know ... *out of step* about myself, that can never change, and it's only there because of something that was so wrong in the first place?

There was a pause. I could feel the usual potent swirl of despair and confusion and frustration twisting around inside me that I tended to get in sessions with VJ, which I guessed was the miniature version of VJ's own tornado of inner misery.

Instead of my usual attempts to convey my empathy and understanding of how caught he felt, or mirroring back to him what I was picking up, I found myself saying, with a tiny, but unmistakable hint of frustration, 'Maybe you could cut yourself a tiny bit of slack with this?'

> VJ: [Looking taken aback and not a little put out] How do you mean?
> SARAH: I wonder if you could imagine letting yourself off the hook of having to ...
> [VJ interrupted.]
> VJ: If I *am* on a hook, I didn't put myself there, so how can I be the one who gets me off it?
> SARAH: Right. [Pause.] So, if it can't be you, who do you think *can* you get off?

VJ: Well … No one! If you mean the wanting to be different. I'm never going to get off that hook, because I just can't! I'll never be able to … do anything about that. I've told you how I feel about all that! I can't do anything about it now. Ugh! No! I would just look like a total freak. There's no way I could ever be a believable woman, looking like this.

SARAH: Mmm. [Pause.] I wonder how it would be for you to hear that I have sometimes thought of asking if you would find it helpful in our sessions to explore the more feminine side of …

[VJ interrupted me again, this time with an expression on his face that was part appalled and part scornful.]

VJ: Oh no! You're going to say why don't I come to a session dressed as a woman, aren't you?

SARAH: I'm not sure my invitation was going to be as prescriptive as that. It was more an idea of exploring feminine qualities in a more generalised …

[VJ cut me off again. He put his head in his hands and gave a bitter, short laugh.]

VJ: Oh God! No! That just shows that you really don't get it! After all this time! I can't imagine anything worse than trying to just *play* at being a woman. I don't want to be trying to *fake* it! I need your help trying to make peace with the fact I can never be a woman, and never not have been abused. I don't want you … fanning the flames and making it all worse!

I told him I was sorry that he had found what I had been trying to articulate so unhelpful. I was interested to note that the uncomfortable twist of emotions inside me was changing, and I was feeling strangely refreshed and invigorated, as if a large wave had broken over us, washing through the territory of the session and clearing it of some colourless debris.

[VJ took some swigs of water, and then looked back at me with a scowl.]

VJ: Maybe I haven't been making myself clear. But … I have to say I'm really so disappointed that you would think I might want to come here, sort of … lamely dressed up. That's such a … naff idea. You must think I'm pretty pathetic if you think that that's what my life amounts to is … that I just want to, basically, dress up!

As he spoke these words to me in a tone of deep contempt, I felt a sudden jolt of connection with what VJ had told me about in our very first session: about the joy and delight he had felt when dressing up and dancing with his sisters, and his father's anger and disapproval about this. I looked at his expression, with its drawn, angry brows, tight lips and a piercing gaze that was hard to meet. I wondered if the contempt in his voice, and his way of making it seem as if I was the one who had introduced the idea of him coming to a session dressed as a woman, and then ridiculing and shaming that notion, was an unconscious replay of what had passed between VJ and his father. Only this time, he could be the powerful, critical one, and I could be assigned the role of the hapless child, who had somehow put their foot in it and now could not get out of being in the wrong.

> SARAH: I find myself wondering if *you* were made to feel that it is pathetic to want to play around with different ways of dressing and being. A long time ago. By your father?
>
> [VJ continued to frown at me.]
>
> SARAH: The boy you once were – I think *he* knew that it doesn't have to be sad or weird to play, and wear different costumes and decorations, didn't he? He knew, in a way that his dad didn't seem to, that it can be very potent and liberating to do that. It can be a form of self-discovery that is fun.
>
> [VJ looked down at his fingers as they drummed on his water bottle.]
>
> VJ: [In a sarcastic tone] Well, thanks for that. Thanks for comparing what I just said to you with the way my dad used to speak to me. You're doing a great job of helping me feel better about myself, today. Cheers. So now I'm a bully as well as a freak!
>
> SARAH: Well, look. You *can* be a bit bullying, VJ. Mostly, I experience you as being rather bullying towards yourself. But I'm finding myself on the receiving end of your bullying energy right now, in the way you're speaking. Whose voice *is* that, I wonder – that voice of such critical contempt?
>
> [VJ gave a dismissive snort that was part sneer, part sigh.]
>
> SARAH: I imagine you feel very angry with me right now, just in the way your father seemed to feel so angry with you, whenever you wanted to express aspects of your more feminine energy.
>
> [At that VJ burst out.]

VJ: Of course I'm angry! Why wouldn't I be angry! I'm angry that my parents couldn't get their act together and stop fighting my whole life about everything to do with how I was! I'm angry that I got picked up and then thrown away by that total shit of a human being! I'm angry that my whole life went down the toilet after he finished fucking me. I'm angry that the last ten years of my life have felt like a complete waste of time!

He was shouting by now.

I raised the energy of my voice somewhat, to be able to match some of his force and drive, and meet him in his anger.

SARAH: Right! All valid things to be angry about! And, I guess you are also angry that you live in a time and place where many people don't know how to be around individuals who don't feel they can definitely say 'I'm like this' or 'I'm like that' about all sorts of things. Including how they want to dress, and how they feel about their gender. That would also be a very healthy anger, I think.

VJ: Well, yes. But I still have to live in the world where that's the case!

SARAH: Of course. And there are quite a lot of people in the world who share your way of looking at things, you know! Who are OK with not trying to put things into tidy boxes and categories.

VJ: Oh, here it comes! You're talking about joining some Transgender touchy-feely support group, or going to some half-arsed drop-in event, aren't you? Forget it! I can't imagine anything more tragic!

It was my turn to speak with some asperity.

SARAH: You do seem determined to put words into my mouth today! I'm not talking about anything as specific as that. I'm talking about finding ways to just … seek out and *be around* more people who accept how complex and mysterious any human life is! Prejudice is a horrible reality. But you've read enough great literature, and listened to enough great music, to get that there are plenty of people out there who …

[VJ suddenly sat back in his chair and folded his arms tightly across his chest.]

vj: Do you know what – I cannot bear any more about this right now! Can you just stop talking at me! Please!

I did as he asked, after saying, 'OK'.

And so we sat opposite each other in a fizzy silence for the last few minutes of the session. VJ kept his eyes fixed on the water bottle he held. I imagined his anger as a roiling mass between us. However, I felt there was something hopeful in the fact that he stayed in the room. Also in the fact that, as he left, he mumbled a hurried 'See you next week', which gave me a sense that we had not stirred the pot so much that our connection had been too badly disrupted.

I noticed as I waited for the following session with VJ that I was feeling differently about the prospect of an hour with him. Over the last few months I had begun to feel somewhat dispirited just before he arrived. It was becoming quite draining for me to sit with him and witness his endless self-hatred and disgust. It was painful to hear, every week, how attached he was to the idea that his life had been ruined, and that there was nothing that would ever get him out of his pit of despair. But after his angry outburst at me and our charged exchanges, I was feeling more hopeful and energised. I imagined that if he could contact his anger with me and express it so directly, then he would be trusting, more or less consciously, that our relationship could survive his anger. And if he could trust that, then he would be likely to find more of a capacity to push for what he wanted, and to push back against what he didn't want in sessions. And if he could start to do that with me in a session, then I hoped he could end up taking that capacity out into the world beyond his therapy. VJ had been able, in effect, to practice both feeling and expressing his anger in the session, and we had both survived.

> The patient's thresholds for 'triggering' increase, allowing them to hold onto the ongoing relational experience (the full complexity of the here and now with the therapist) as it is happening … Processing becomes safer and safer, so the patient's tolerance for potential flooding of affect increases. (Bromberg 2006)

When he arrived for the next session, on time, I saw that, very unusually for him, he was not carrying a bottle of water. There was a long pause after he sat down. Eventually, he spoke.

vj: I'm still a bit sore about last week.
SARAH: Are you?

[There was another long pause.]

SARAH: Can you say more?

VJ: I don't know. I … I'm not saying you didn't have a point about some of what you were getting at – about not everyone thinking that I … you know … shouldn't be different or whatever. But … I thought the way you spoke to me was really disrespectful.

[He raised his chin as he said this, so that he was looking down his nose at me.]

SARAH: Did you?

VJ: Yes, I absolutely did! You ended up lecturing me like I was some little kid, or your student or something. And I'm not!

SARAH: I see.

VJ: Why are you pulling that face as if you're trying not to smile?

SARAH: I think it must show on my face that there's something very pleasing to me about seeing you be so clear and direct. I think I am enjoying your assertiveness!

VJ: Huh! Well! OK. Well … good! [Pause.] I didn't mean to be rude to you. I know that you were trying to be helpful, last week. Anyway. Shall we just drop it now? Let's just … let it go and carry on as normal. Forget it happened.

SARAH: Oh, I'm not sure that would be such a good idea.

VJ: [Suddenly looking quite worried] I don't want us to go on rowing.

SARAH: Well, look – I think we did have a heated exchange. And that's because we have a real relationship, and that sometimes happens when two people are being real together. So I don't want us to 'row', either. But I also don't think it's healthy to try and hide the fact that there were some angry feelings in the room last week, and pretend that this was never the case. It makes me wonder … what tended to happen in your family when people disagreed?

VJ: [With a confused air] Uh, I don't know. Just … what happens in any family, I guess. People shout and get upset, stuff gets banged about, doors slammed. Maybe my mum or one of my sisters would storm off in tears. Just the usual.

SARAH: And then … ?

VJ: Then … well, nothing. I mean there'd be a horrible atmosphere for however long. And then it would be back to normal: my mum in the kitchen, probably back to her cooking, and whichever sister was involved – back to whatever she'd been doing, and … that's it. My dad would be just sitting behind the paper somewhere, or watching telly.

The more we explored how his family members dealt with disagreements and times of anger, the more VJ was able to reflect on the impact of growing up in a family where angry disagreements were never fully aired, thrashed out and resolved. From his descriptions of the dynamics he had witnessed, it sounded as if his father and mother both had fiery tempers and stubborn dispositions, and were never really able to reach any kind of compromise with their spouse that felt fair and that could clear the air. VJ's father was immovable on the belief that because he was the man of the house, his word was final. VJ's mother and sisters all chafed under this rule, resented it, and carried out a never-ending war of attrition, aimed at undermining VJ's father in a myriad of subtle ways, which included the encouragement of VJ's fascination with his sisters' make up, clothes, magazines and music, that his father hated so.

Thus VJ had come to unconsciously learn that anger was, at its heart, a toxic, unpleasant emotion, that could only be dealt with by enduring its flare-ups, waiting for it to subside, and then carrying on as if it had never happened. It made me think of a family who have their home next door to a leaking chemical factory and who try to cope with the clouds of poisonous gas that regularly drift over their house by shutting the windows and drawing the curtains until each visible emission passes by. They then open the curtains and windows, as if all is well, and carry on. Until next time.

Over the following weeks, we explored more about anger: VJ's own; the anger he had seen play out in his family; and the meaning he could make of different types of anger and different ways to express it. As we did so, the sessions felt increasingly freer and more hopeful, and VJ appeared more and more at ease when he was in the room with me. To begin with, as he explicitly explored his anger, he tended to make me the target of it. He would let me have it with both barrels when he found something I said unfair or inaccurate, or found something that I did annoying ('You're always repeating some little thing I've said, back to me, with that questioning tone of voice, like you're a bloody little bird, or something!'). For a while, I had to tolerate standing in for the figures he was so angry with, especially his father and Mr X, and I would draw his attention to this way of understanding his outbursts at me when they happened, which he became increasingly able to see.

After some time, he began to be able to use his anger as a force to help him make decisions and to give energy to ideas about projects he wanted to carry through. He decided he wanted to write a symbolic letter to Mr X, bring it to the session, read it aloud and then destroy it, as part of a ritual to represent his wish to transform some of the shame, inhibition and self-doubt that the abuse had left him with.

When the time came, it was very moving to sit as a witness to him reading out this letter – hearing him give voice to what he had never been given the opportunity to say out loud, about what he thought and felt about Mr X and all that had passed between them. VJ ripped up the letter into tiny pieces, dropped them into a large skillet I had provided, and then put a match to them. We watched them burn brightly for a few seconds, and then twist into fine grey ash. The energy and focus with which he spoke, tore up the letter and set the pieces alight were striking. They seemed to me to be the productive 'cousins' of the behaviour that he used to display when he tore and picked at his clothing, or tissues or his nails, with an aggression that had been driven underground by so much shame and prohibition.

VJ then decided he wanted to do something similar and bring a letter to his father. It was also very poignant to be a witness to this second ritual – to hear what VJ wanted so much to say to his father, and to see that, when the point came at which VJ had intended to tear up and burn this second letter, he broke down and sobbed. He became clear that he did not, in fact, want to be more separate from his father, the way he now did from Mr X. He longed, rather, for more closeness, and more meaningful connection with his dad. That session helped VJ decide that he no longer wanted to join in the war against his father that rumbled on within the rest of his family, to do with undermining the father. VJ talked about making an effort when he visited the family home to be more respectful towards his father, and not join in with the subtle jokes and mockery that his mother and sisters constantly aimed at him and his father responded by being a little less prickly, and a little warmer towards VJ.

VJ found that being able to be more conscious of how angry he had been and how much he had had to suppress this anger, seemed to free up something about his creative life. He told me in one session that after work, one evening, he had gone home and instead of doing what he usually did (which was to binge-watch episodes of the latest TV drama he had become addicted to), something had made him go rooting around in some of his old papers instead, in search of the musical piece he had been working on ten years earlier.

> VJ: I was expecting it to be pretty terrible, and that it would make me cringe a bit. But, you know, for a 15-year-old, it wasn't that bad! There was some of it that even impressed me. It made me sort of want to get my guitar out, and go over some of it, to hear it out loud again.

SARAH: 'Sort of want to' or 'want to'?

VJ: A bit of both.

[He did a mock-angry frown at me.]

VJ: It's not that easy, you know: to think about playing the guitar again, when it's so bound up with all that crappy stuff with Mr X!

[There was a silence. A slight grin crept onto his face.]

VJ: But … You can rest easy – I reckon I *am* going to get my guitar out!

As more months passed, VJ decided that he wanted to pick up his education and training again. He was able to share this with his parents, and found that they were both very happy and relieved to hear it. For once, it seemed, he had found something that his mother and father could be in agreement about. They were both willing to get behind supporting VJ with this aim, financially and emotionally. He gave up his job, got onto a music production course at an FE college, moved out of the dreary shared house on the main road in North London, and instead rented a room in a flat in another part of London with friends of one his sisters. He felt able to share some of his story with these flatmates. He found, to his surprise, that they were all very supportive and accepting of who he was and his ambivalence about how he wanted to live.

Although he still talked from time to time about hating to look at his own reflection, or of noticing a beautiful woman in the street or in a café, and wishing that he could change places with her, he tended to dwell less and less in sessions on how terrible it was for him to feel that, and how weird and wrong others would inevitably find it if they knew about his gender fluidity. As time went on, he socialised more, enjoyed his course and, once more, spent time playing his guitar. He showed an increasing self-acceptance and hope. He hardly ever spoke about Mr X in sessions, and if he did, it was in a way that was far less pained and shamed.

In one session, towards the end of the year-and-a-half that he had been coming, VJ had been talking about feeling ambivalent about deciding to change his name, and no longer use a masculine pronoun about himself. He sighed.

VJ: It's not something *you'll* ever have to struggle with. You're lucky.

[I nodded.]

SARAH: Mmm. [Pause.] In one way. But maybe I miss out a bit, as well.

[VJ pulled a 'Oh, come on!' face.]

SARAH: I'm serious. Maybe those of us who 'settle' on one gender miss out on something, in a way. I mean, isn't Tiresias the wisest person in the Oedipus story precisely because he has lived as both a man and a woman?

[VJ sat back and stretched his long legs out before him in their tight black, skinny jeans.]

VJ: It's … it's funny that you mention him. Tiresias is in 'The Wasteland' you know!

SARAH: Oh, yes! Huh! I'd forgotten that.

VJ: Mmm. Well, I'd love to think I've got something from seeing both sides of the … you know … the great divide. But, I'm not sure. I think I've mostly just got a double load of grief.

SARAH: Yes. And maybe that grief has made you wiser than you think. Remember when you first came? Someone gave you some bad advice and sent you the wrong way and then you thought you were lost, but in fact, you weren't. You were just around the corner from where you needed to be all along. Things that happen around a first session often prove to have the seeds of something very symbolic in them, to do with the story of the person who is coming. Maybe that whole incident on the way to your first session tells us that you know much more about where you should be than you think – that you are wiser than you often give yourself credit for …

[VJ gave a crooked smile and tears appeared in his eyes.]

VJ: [Softly] Well. That's a nice thought.

SARAH: Maybe there are things to be enjoyed about understanding how it is to be both male and female …

[VJ shook his head, but also laughed.]

VJ: Maybe. Maybe.

[We sat in silence for another long while. Eventually VJ spoke.]

VJ: I think that the fact I can say 'maybe' probably means I am about ready to stop coming here.

SARAH: Ah. Mmm. Yes, it could. Is that what you're thinking – that you want to draw our sessions to a close?

VJ: Well … Are you going to jump on my case if I say, 'I sort of do and I sort of don't'?

[I smiled and shook my head.]

SARAH: No. I think you should go right ahead and feel ambivalent about it. And I'll join you!

[He laughed.]

vJ: It's been … I am glad I did this. It has helped. And now, I think I'm ready to stop coming here and to have … a bit more fun. Because … like I said, it's been good, but it hasn't been exactly a barrel of laughs.

SARAH: Worthwhile but … hard?

vJ: Yeah. That sounds about right.

After we had agreed a period of time over which we would have more sessions in order to draw the work to a close, we sat in silence to the end of the session. It was a very different silence from the strained one we had endured, some months earlier.

I noticed, during it, how still VJ was able to sit; how easily he could return my gaze when we looked directly at each other.

6

CHRONIC, COMPLEX TRAUMA

THE LEGACY OF SURVIVING ORGANISED
CHILD SEXUAL ABUSE

Stu

No worst, there is none. Pitched past pitch of grief,
More pangs will, schooled at forepangs, wilder wring.
Comforter, where, where is your comforting?
Mary, mother of us, where is your relief?
My cries heave, herds-long; huddle in a main, a chief
Woe, world-sorrow; on an age-old anvil wince and sing -
The lull, then leave off. Fury had shrieked 'No ling-
ering! Let me be fell: force I must be brief.'

O the mind, mind has mountains; cliffs of fall
Frightful, sheer, no-man fathomed. Hold them cheap
May who ne'er hung there. Nor does long our small
Durance deal with that steep or deep. Here! Creep,
Wretch, under a comforter serves in a whirlwind: all
Life death does end and each dies with sleep.
Gerard Manley Hopkins (1844–1889)

An exploration of how certain forms of abuse can leave some clients with symptoms that are too severe to be managed solely by weekly therapy; of the uncomfortable reality of paedophile rings, and large-scale organised abuse, and its consequences for survivors of these. How the issue of being a survivor of sexual abuse is often not picked up in the case of men who have a diagnosis of severe mental illness. This chapter also offers insight as to the emotional and psychological impact on those who work with survivors of organised abuse.

There was very little that felt OK to Stu, about himself or the world. He was in his late forties, but had the build of a slender 16-year-old and the face of an old man. His complexion was sallow with prominent bags under his eyes and broken veins across the tops of his cheeks and nose. He had a jumble of discoloured teeth, and kept his hair closely shaved, so that it was a colourless fuzz over his skull, which seemed to add to the appearance of someone who was not well. He had contacted a community-based service I worked for after he had been picked up by the police following 'an incident'.

He had been arrested for 'shouting abusively' at a man in the entrance to a tube station. Officers had cautioned and released him. It emerged that Stu was well known to his local police team, and this was not the first time he had been involved in such an incident. He had never been violent or broken the law in any other way, apart from this fairly regular occurrence where he would end up shouting angrily at an individual on various streets near to his home.

At the time Stu referred himself for support, I was working as one of the counsellors at a community-based charity in Stu's neighbourhood that offered various sorts of emotional and psychological support. After the Clinical Services Manager met with him for a couple of assessment meetings, they liaised with the community psychiatric services that Stu was supposed to have regular contact with (which in reality did not seem to be happening) and with his GP, to get a sense of whether colleagues in other services thought that some counselling sessions with us would be helpful for Stu, or somewhat destabilising. There was a variety of services involved in Stu's care, and all were in agreement that our counselling service should offer Stu six initial sessions with me, and then there should be a review of how he was finding the process, and what the clinical judgement was, related to how well it was supporting his wellbeing. Stu had a history of chaotic alcohol addiction, self-harm and mental breakdown. He had been given various diagnoses over the years, including 'borderline personality disorder' and 'dissociative identity disorder'.

Stu was the youngest child of seven. His parents, now in their seventies, had always both had various minor physical disabilities, and it seemed likely they both also had some degree of intellectual disability, although there had never been a formal diagnosis of the latter or formal support because of this likelihood. They sounded, from Stu's description of family life, quite child-like. Although they had always been reasonably warm-hearted and kindly to their children, they had also seemed very ineffectual as parents, being utterly caught up and stressed out, as they were, in endless ups and downs with their ill health, money problems and a sense of not quite being able to cope with life. It sounded as if both his parents had had a chronic low-level anxiety throughout his childhood, as well as problems with literacy and numeracy that made any filling-in of forms, paying bills, dealing with anyone in authority, or trying to organise relatively simple things, like arranging repeat prescriptions, seem almost insurmountable to them. They had certainly not been able to ensure that all their children were well looked after, even in various basic ways, such as making sure they each attended school, had the right medical care when it was needed, and were adequately fed, clothed and clean.

By the time Stu was nine or ten, he was missing many days of school. A timid, undersized boy, with poor physical co-ordination, he chose instead to stay at home in the family flat, which his parents allowed. Some days he also drifted rather aimlessly around the large inner-London housing estate that the family home was part of. It was on one of these days of hanging around the estate when someone who he thought had been some kind of youth worker ('someone who was, like, after kids to see why they weren't in school') had approached him. This man had chatted to him, given him a cigarette when he had asked for one, and suggested they go and have a fast food snack together. Stu had been literally hungry, as well as emotionally hungry, for some attention and treats, and had therefore been extremely susceptible to believing this supposed youth worker was a benevolent figure. They met a number of times in the subsequent weeks, and when the man suggested, on the third or fourth time, that Stu could come along to a nice, warm flat nearby and hang out with some other boys whom Stu would probably get on well with, because they were all in the same boat, and they could play some games together and there would be more snacks, Stu had gone along, happy at the prospect of being out of the cold November weather and of having someone to hang out with, and getting to eat more.

He was driven by the man a short way from the estate, into a more wealthy, privileged area of London that was not very far from his neighbourhood. He was then taken into 'a big house with a grey door that was on a grand, wide street' and up several flights of stairs into a 'very nice, very posh flat'. It was in this way that he was groomed for and then delivered up to a group of men who used the Central London flat as a base to sexually use young boys.

A nightmarish existence now began for Stu: he continued to live his usual life at home and on the estate, but every Friday afternoon, for many months, he would be picked up by the man who he believed was a youth worker, and taken to the flat where he spent several hours being witness to sexual abuse or being sexually abused himself. He was often given drinks that he thought later had been drugged as they made him very sick and sleepy and affected his capacity to remember certain things clearly. There were cameras on tripods throughout the flat and Stu thought that the abuse was often filmed. After the men had finished with him, he would then be driven back to a street near his estate to make his own way home, with the reminder that if he did not co-operate or told anyone, his parents would be in big trouble. He was told that the family would be turned out of their council flat if 'the fellers' ever found out he had told anyone, and that then his family would have nowhere to go, and this would be 'on his head'.

Stu could not bring himself to speak much, about what had been done to him or what he had seen, but he was quite clear that the men who had abused him had all been 'posh'. The 'youth worker' assured him that they were men who were high up, in charge, and could make his life and Stu's a misery, if he and Stu didn't do what they wanted. Stu obviously found this threat bleakly funny, in retrospect. He would screw his face into a tight, raging grimace, and say, whenever he mentioned this threat later in the work: 'You tell me, you tell me, Sarah – how much more miserable could my life have got than what they were already making it? The dirty bastards!'

It emerged that the reason that Stu was picked up by the police from time to time was because every now and then he believed he saw one of the men who had abused him. This had happened a number of times when Stu had been due to travel by underground train to visit a friend. On the occasion that had been the catalyst for the most recent arrest, Stu had been walking into the underground station near to his parents' flat, where he still lived, when he saw the man whom he was sure was one of his abusers walking in the opposite direction and coming out through an adjacent barrier.

In our first session Stu tried to convey to me the effect this had had on him: 'I felt like I was going to die, Sarah – my heart started going that hard; I was like, sick to my stomach – seeing him, and I got this terrible bad pain in my guts. Seeing his face and him acting like he hadn't seen me, didn't know me. And he's just strolling out of the tube and down the street, and that. He was probably thinking [and here Stu put on a grotesquely exaggerated posh voice, and twisted his face into a sneering expression that was both superior and gormless] "La di dah. Oh, I'm just going to pop over there to get a coffee" or whatever the fuck he wants. And he gets to live this life where everyone thinks *he's* OK, *he's* a nice old guy … And I'm standing in the tube station, calling out to him, to let him know I seen him. And everyone's thinking *I'm* the nutter, *I'm* the one who's trouble.'

Stu's eyes filled with tears and he wiped them angrily away. His voice rose and cracked, betraying his distress, as well as his anger, 'when it's because of him and his dirty fucking friends that I … And I thought I was having like a fucking heart attack or something, and I'm going to die in this station from the shock of seeing him, right there, again. Like about a year before and I told the police that time and they did fuck all, that time as well. And I feel like, I've got to say to him, "I know you! I see you! Don't think you can pretend!"'

More tears appeared and this time spilled down Stu's cheeks before he could wipe them away. He rolled his head around on his neck miserably, as if simply sitting with me and talking about it was too much to bear. We were ten minutes into our first meeting.

> STU: I've got to go for a smoke, Sarah. I've got to have a break and a bit of a smoke and then I'll be OK to carry on. Is that all right? [He held both hands out in front of him, and we both looked at them as they trembled in the air between us.]
>
> [I explained that it was not usual to take breaks in a counselling session to have a cigarette.]
>
> STU: [Looking crestfallen and extremely anxious] Ah, well. See, Sarah … hmmm … I don't think I'll be able to talk any more, really, without a smoke. Because, Sarah, see, I can't … I'm just that jumpy and …

He closed his eyes and took a deep breath, and then his mouth pulled itself down into a miserable curve, so his face resembled a baby or toddler that is about to bitterly cry. More tears leaked out from under his closed eyelids, and his chest heaved convulsively a few times. He whispered, 'For fuck's sake …' as if to himself, and beat at his own chin with a clenched fist.

> STU: [With eyes still closed] Sorry, Sarah. I can't …
>
> SARAH: You don't think you can stay in the room and talk unless you can go out first for a cigarette?
>
> STU: Yes, that's … Or … no … I'll tell you what …

[He opened his eyes and stared hopefully at me, while rubbing roughly at his face to wipe away the tears.]

STU: I'll just roll one, shall I? Just get one ready, like. That'd be OK, now, wouldn't it?

SARAH: I think that sounds like a really good plan. Why don't we see how that goes?

[Stu began to get tobacco and papers out of his jeans' pocket with shaky fingers, and roll himself a cigarette. He looked at his hands as he spoke.]

STU: The thing is, Sarah, those bastards ... Oh, God. Now. They think they can get away with it, don't they! Jesus. They have up to now! Why is that? You tell me, Sarah, you tell me why! Because ... because you'd think, wouldn't you, if people knew what fucking disgusting things these nonces were doing – and to tiny little kids, mind ... I mean I was like *ten fucking years old*, Sarah! If people knew that these, like, lawyers and politicians ... oh, for *fuck's sake!*

[Stu suddenly shouted these last words and then immediately clapped his hand over his mouth, in an almost pantomime gesture of silencing himself. His wide eyes looking at me from over the top of his hand made him look horror-struck. He lowered his hand.]

STU: Sorry, Sarah. Sorry. See, what gets me is – I see this old feller. I see him walking around, still acting like he owns the fucking shop, and like he's cock of the walk, and he's the ... he was one of them! I know it. I know his face. He knows I know, as well. He acts like he can't hear me shouting and that, but *he* knows.

SARAH: It sounds so very distressing to encounter this man sometimes in day-to-day life ...

STU: It is! It is, Sarah! I swear to God ... And I tell them, each time – the authorities and what not, you know. I tell them, 'It's him! That's the man that was my abuser. That man there is a fucking old pervert! There he goes – he's a kiddy fiddler, that one! It's him, I tell you!' And then they start with the questions, about when and where, and will I make a statement. And I've tried, Sarah. I really have. But then they get into saying, 'And can you describe this, and can you describe that.' And I say, 'Don't ask me any more questions. Don't ask me, because ...'

[Stu's face suddenly spasmed so it was a pure rictus of disgust and outrage, and his voice rose again to what was nearly a shout.]

> STU: ... because I don't fucking remember the address! Sorry, Sarah. Sorry. But I don't fucking remember their names and what not. How can I remember that stuff when I was just a little kid! I never knew names and addresses. All I'm seeing is someone's huge privates in my face, and all I know is some bloke's putting something up my bum and it really fucking hurts. Sorry, Sarah. Sorry to speak like this. But do you understand? Can you see that I wouldn't know the name of some guy who's doing dirty stuff to me from behind.
>
> SARAH: Yes, I do understand that, Stu.

I looked at Stu's face to try and gauge how much he could register that I was hearing him and trying to follow what he was saying. It was hard to pick up what he might be understanding of what I was saying, but what was utterly clear to me was his misery. His face was a mask of archetypal woe, with eyebrows arching up to a miserable point, a deeply furrowed brow, and eyes brimming with tears.

> SARAH: I can see it's so painful and distressing for you to try and talk with me, or anyone, about all this. Perhaps it would be helpful for you to hear from me that we can pace ourselves. I think it's OK to take your time. You don't have to feel you must try and tell me everything that's important, all in one go.

At that, Stu stopped talking. After a muttered, 'OK, thank you, yeah. Thank you, Sarah. Thank you very much', a silence fell over the room. Stu finished rolling himself a cigarette, and then carefully picked up the little shreds of tobacco that he had spilt around him on the floor, put them back in the packet, and tucked his papers and tobacco pouch back in his pocket. I wondered if, rather than experiencing what I had just said as supportive, he had instead heard me as suggesting that he should talk less, that I wanted him to be quiet. Perhaps there had been plenty of people in the past who had wanted Stu to be quiet and not speak of his experiences. There was a slightly more defeated look about him once I had spoken, than the more animated, albeit very angry and upset, demeanour he had had, before I had suggested pacing himself.

I had been somewhat in touch with a stormy whirl of emotions within myself ever since Stu had entered the room, but the sudden silence that fell over the session made it uncomfortably easier for me to be much more open to the affect of that inner storm. I felt a concern and sorrow for the pitiful, broken-down figure of the man before me. As the session had gone on I had also begun to detect an annoyance within me at the fact of his using my name so often, as if he was presuming a kind of friendly intimacy between us which I felt resistant about. And more disconcerting than all these was a strange, muzzy kind of sensation, which made me feel I was somehow sliding down a slope on which there was no purchase – I could feel myself both believing that Stu had been abused, and yet simultaneously doubting the accuracy of some of what he felt so sure about in the present, including that the man he had seen while at the tube station was certainly one of those who had abused him. It felt like a kind of heresy to not feel sure that I wholly believed Stu about this; I imagined that to reveal any hint of my doubt to him would be experienced by him as an awful betrayal.

Part of the feeling of sliding was also to do with the fact of being confronted with, at the very least, the possibility that senior figures of authority and power had indeed sexually violated Stu and other young children and then used their positions to cover this up. Sadly, the fact that powerful, successful, supposedly respectable and trustworthy figures sexually abuse others has been proven to be true on very many occasions, throughout human history. The urge for any member of a society to believe such things are impossible is strong, as it is such a terrible and disorientating thing for most of us to contemplate. The slippery-slope feeling, the sense that not even the actual ground is something that can offer surety or safety, was partly caused by the knowledge that every single thing Stu said could perfectly well be true. I could feel myself sliding, while trying to retain some sense of inner balance, into a place where Stu and I could not cling to anything: where no one can really be trusted or believed – not judges, not politicians, not the police, not youth workers, and also not troubled and traumatised individuals who say they know that for sure that someone is an abuser; nor therapists, who might sit making all the right supportive noises to a client who has been abused, but who internally entertain some doubts about what that client is telling them. In short, a world in which no one can be believed or trusted, including oneself.

I began to feel seriously nauseous and dizzy as we sat in silence. The little room began to feel almost nightmarish, as if Stu and I were trapped in there together – both helpless and at a loss. Perhaps this was what Stu and his small companions had felt in the rooms of the flat years ago? The silence stretched on and on as Stu looked at his cigarette and I looked at him looking at it. It was a silence that felt like an unpleasant strand of glue held between us, being pulled and pulled, and if it were to break, it would only stick to something else and cause more unpleasant stickiness to be dealt with. The only chink of a possibility for some clarity I could feel – the one foothold on the slope – was to hang on to the idea that how I was feeling could be a way of understanding what Stu's inner emotional landscape might be like.

> SARAH: You've told me about such awful and upsetting things that have happened to you in your life. I'm guessing that now you've said some of it, and now I've suggested we can slow things down, you could be allowing yourself the time and space to really feel some difficult emotions, right here and now?

Stu looked up at me and his face crumpled again into a mask of utter woe. He managed a strangled 'Mmm', and then bowed his head and broke down into painful, gulping sobs, which, this time, he did not try to pull himself out of with his anger. He wept bitterly for about a minute.

As he cried, I began to feel myself returning to some kind of state where I knew which way was 'up'. The slope I had been scrabbling to stay on while implacably sliding down seemed to tilt when Stu allowed himself to weep, so that I could feel myself on more of an even keel. I had a place to stand, in as much as I could suddenly feel very clear about some things about the man in front of me: I could feel sure that he had endured some kind of dreadful anguish, and that this anguish still lived inside him as we sat together. I could also feel sure that the feeling in my chest as if something was tugging at my heart, and the prickle behind my eyes that could have been the precursor of tears, both meant that I could feel the relief and release of some compassion for Stu. Compassion could override, for a time, my irritation with him, and my distaste and dislike of some of his habits and ways of presenting himself to the world. This was a huge relief, and I felt the horrible sense of stuckness in the room recede somewhat.

> SARAH: I wonder how you are doing, just being here and talking about things with me, like this?
> STU: [Through his tears] D'you know … it's actually a big strain, Sarah, but it's also, like, a relief. Do you know? I'm feeling like I'd love to run out the door, but I'm just about proud of myself that I'm not doing that, and I'm sticking with it. Do you know what I mean, Sarah?
> SARAH: I think I do. It's not an easy thing: for you to come here and sit and talk with someone about such painful things in your life. But it sounds like you do feel there could be some value, some worth in doing that.

STU: Yeah, I think there is. And do you know, Sarah, in all the times I'm in and out of, like hospitals, and see different key workers, and psychiatrists and that, I never really get any chance to just sit and tell about my life and all that's gone on and stuff.

SARAH: Have people in the services you've been using tended not to ask you about your childhood and what it was like for you growing up?

STU: Not really. It's always been about working out a … a … what-not … a d'you know … *care plan*! That's always the thing. *A care plan* and stuff, and sorting out my medication and whatever, for when I'm self-harming. It's all been about getting my mood up, or getting me down when I'm manic, and giving me different medicines, and that. And one lady, she was trying to get me to go to Keep Fit and stuff. No one's ever just sat and said, 'What's gone on, Stu? What was the abuse like?' D'you know? Funny, that.

SARAH: Mmm. And it could be so important to be able to talk about that.

STU: Well, seems like no one has the time. No one just sits and lets me talk. They always start asking questions, and I can't answer them, I can't tell them the things they want to know. So. It never goes anywhere. But … I do feel better for just … [He sighed and then coughed] … just being able to talk. I do.

[There was a pause.]

STU: I can't wait to go out for this cigarette, mind!

[We both smiled at this.]

It was not an unfamiliar story to hear from someone who used the statutory mental health services. The staff in this field of the NHS, like many others, are hugely over-stretched and under enormous pressure, which has an inevitable impact on the quality of care that can be given. This may be part of why so many private therapy practitioners have requests for help from clients whose first port of call was the NHS, only to find that there usually are long waiting lists, or that there would only be a short course of sessions on offer, and that it is, sadly, rare to be able to have any continuity of personnel over a time period any longer than around six months. People often turn, if they can, to private psychotherapists, counsellors, psychologists, etc. for their help. An enormous 96 per cent of private psychotherapists who responded to a 2016 survey by the UKCP and BPC reported that they had seen clients who had come to them because they had been unhappy with what had been offered by the NHS as psychological support (UKCP and the British Psycho-analytic Council 2015).

Underfunding is certainly one of the reasons why the NHS sometimes badly fails individuals like Stu: people who are chaotic, chronically troubled and struggling with addictions. But another reason is the ongoing taboo of sexual abuse. For the dozens of male clients I have worked with, over many years, who have had severe, chronic mental health problems, and who have also experienced sexual abuse in their childhood, it has been rare to hear from them that they were *ever* asked by their GP, or even by staff in their psychiatric services, about whether something sexually abusive has happened in their history. And even if they are asked, they are seldom given the space and time to then talk about it, in an appropriate setting with someone who is trained and confident to respond. It seems that there is still, sadly, a deep-seated reluctance, even by many in the caring professions, to broach the matter of sexual abuse in a person's history, especially if that person is male, and then to give that man time and space to speak of it.

Stu sat back in the chair and sighed again. He closed his eyes and while one hand went to his cheek and cradled it, the other held his cigarette and I noticed he began to stroke his index finger along the cigarette – a small, rhythmic gesture that was reminiscent of a baby or toddler stroking their own face or hair while they suck their thumb. We sat in silence for a while as I watched Stu soothe himself in this way, still with his eyes closed. I wondered how much Stu had ever been able to feel comforted as a small child. I imagined that if he had, it seemed likely that it would have been because he had found some way to do this for himself. It seemed unlikely that the adults or older children around him would have been able to comfort and soothe him very effectively. And once the abuse had started, his sense of feeling safe in the world would have been even more profoundly damaged. His current poor state of health and wellbeing suggested that he had ongoing problems with basic self-care – he smelled somewhat unwashed, his hair had not been cut in a very long time, his clothes had a patina of grime, his teeth were in a very poor state. He was also underweight and had a rattling smoker's cough. I noticed my irritation with him was diminishing as my cap-acity to imagine what his life had been like when he had been very young increased, and to guess at what stage his development had been more or less arrested by his carers' inability to meet some of his basic needs.

If, as therapists, we have certain expectations of our clients: for example, that they will arrive on time for appointments, or remember to tell us if they cannot make the sessions, or that they will be able to be clear about any payment that needs to be made, or even just stay in the room throughout the session, and then we discover that they struggle with aspects of this, it can be helpful to see this struggle in terms of information about what stage of emotional and psychological development they are, in effect, stuck at. Even though a counsellor or doctor or social worker may be facing someone who looks adult, because they have matured physically, in terms of their skeleton, musculature and so forth, they may also be dealing with an individual who has had their development profoundly interrupted and impaired.

If chronic, long-term neglect, or physical or sexual abuse, is part of someone's story, and there was a lack of either acknowledgement of the pain of such experiences at the time, or support with recovering from the pain, then the people who have survived such life experiences will have had their capacity to regulate their emotions and make meanings out of their sensations profoundly impaired. To expect them to be able to feel and think in the same way as an adult who has not had their development similarly affected can is unreasonable and unrealistic, and will lead almost inevitably to frustration for both parties.

I tried to hold on to the fact that it was a real achievement, in many ways, for Stu to be in the room with me at all.

After four sessions with Stu, in my supervision, I found myself framing what usually happened in our sessions in terms of looking after a very young infant. Typically, Stu would arrive, somewhat late, having been beset with various problems or bits of bad luck, and to begin with he would be preoccupied with these. Then he would often go back over how furious and disgusted he was with the men who had abused him and how let down he felt by authority figures who had failed to do anything about his abusers, since the abuse had come to light. Then there would be a lull, a hiatus in the session, sometimes for many minutes, while we sat in silence. Stu would sit back, appear to relax somewhat, his breathing would deepen and slow, and his eyes would close. He would say something like, 'I'll just have a little sit and think' and appear to semi-doze. I would find myself feeling like a carer being with a baby or toddler, helping it feel calm and relaxed enough to drift off to sleep. I would sit and watch over Stu as he seemed to sleep, aware of a fond, tender, protective feeling towards him, that was mixed in with a semi-exasperated willingness to adapt to him and his rather unusual way he wanted to make use of the therapy session.

My supervisor supported the view that allowing Stu the space and calm to be able to relax and rest, while I watched over him, was likely to be helping him have a vital flavour of how it is to feel safe and protected, if only for a short while. Although it could be argued that there was nothing very visibly productive going on during the time he dozed, in terms of Stu gaining more insight, or feeling clearer about what he could do in life, the sessions were nevertheless giving Stu a deeply significant experience of being in a place where he was seen, where he would not be objectified, and he would have the interest and attention of the authority figure, even if all he wanted to do, or felt capable of, was going to sleep.

It was not always easy for me to keep the faith that *doing* nothing, but simply *being with*, was the essence of the work with Stu. I felt some pressure that our work ought to produce some kind of tangible result, in the block of six sessions – some kind of result that the other services involved in Stu's care would be able to see or measure. However, I was soon left in no doubt as to the impact that simply coming each week was having on Stu.

In the fifth and penultimate session, as we were discussing how he had been finding the process, and what he thought about continuing, he seemed hesitant at first to share his thoughts about this. In the end he was able to let me know that, in some ways, having the counselling had actually been a bit of an ordeal for him.

> STU: Not to be horrible about you, or anything, Sarah. Don't take it personal. But if I'm being honest, it does do my head in a bit, coming here! The travel and the strain of it, you know? And the money each week is not always easy. [Stu paid a very low rate for the sessions, as did all the clients who were unwaged, and yet he struggled to find the few pounds he was charged each time.] Sometimes, I get home after, and I can't do anything except go to bed after I've seen you.
>
> SARAH: It really takes it out of you, somehow?
>
> STU: Yeah, really! But I would like to continue, maybe after a bit of a break?

When the Clinical Services Manager (CSM) and I talked later, about the next step for Stu, we were both mindful of the therapeutic needs of clients who have the profoundly limited ego strength and capacity to regulate their emotions that Stu was showing. Colleagues who have led the field in working therapeutically with those whose intellectual and cognitive capabilities are impaired (Sinason 2010; Alvarez 2012; Corbett 2014) have all made the convincing case for the need for therapy for clients with intellectual disabilities to be offered in ways that allow for more than the usual amount of creative adaptation, in order for it to be effective.

The basic routine of offering Stu weekly sessions was one that didn't seem to be one that wholly suited him, but this was the service's way of working, and we could not radically change that just for him. However, the CSM and I decided we should offer as much flexibility within the basic set up of the service as possible, and offer him the chance of having his sessions in a pattern of attending for six sessions, taking a break for two weeks, and then returning for another block of six.

At our sixth meeting, I proposed this as a way forward, and Stu's reaction was one of instant relief and pleasure.

STU: I think that could do me a lot of good, to be honest. It means I can let the dust settle a bit, in between times, which I think I need. But then, the door's still open, isn't it? So that's good too. Yeah. I can see that working all right, you know, Sarah. And it will be something new to see the same person, like a few months in a row! I don't think that's ever happened before.

SARAH: Is that right? That you haven't been able to keep seeing the same person for support, in any setting, before?

STU: Nope. Never the same person for long, really. And never a chance to just sit and have a bit of quiet time to think with anyone.

SARAH: No?

STU: No. But to be fair, most of the time when someone was seeing me, like the psychiatric people and what not, I was in a right state, and off my head a bit on something, or I'd have had a meltdown on the street again, and been shouting and swearing at that feller, so it wasn't always time for, like, a cosy chat.

SARAH: No, I see that. But I wonder how it was for you each time – often seeing someone new, and it usually being in the context of a bit of a crisis?

STU: I dunno. It was what I was used to, really. It was normal. I reckoned I was lucky to have anyone making a bit of an effort to help me. And I just took my cue from them anyway. They all acted like, 'Of course so and so's moved on, so you'll be seeing this person now', and you'd always have to be going over all the stuff from last time but with a new doctor, or new nurse … thingy … practitioner or whatever.

SARAH: Mmm. I suppose that could get frustrating.

[Stu shrugged. It had obviously been par for the course for a long time.]

SARAH: I wonder how it might feel to come here each week, for a longer period, albeit with breaks, and see the same person each time?

STU: Ha ha! [Stu's chuckle was chesty]. Well, I'm up for it, if you are!

So it was on this basis that we proceeded, and Stu and I had five blocks of six sessions with breaks in between, which took us through a whole year of work together.

Over that year, I noticed a number of very small, very gradual changes in Stu's appearance and behaviour, that were significant. After two blocks of sessions, he began to be more or less on time for his appointment each week. He tended, after a while, to talk less about the man at the tube station whom he was sure was his abuser, in a furiously impotent way, and directed more of his anger at how ignored and invisible survivors of sexual abuse were in our society, in general. He started having his hair cut regularly at a barber's, bought himself a new pair of trainers, and was generally more willing to take better care of his health and wellbeing. He cut down somewhat on his drinking, and made an effort to avoid the people on his estate who were selling soft and hard drugs, who had often targeted him when they knew he had just collected his benefit money. The 'six weeks on/two weeks off' pattern seemed to be suiting him.

I also noticed it was often in the two 'off' weeks that Stu would have done something a little different, as if he had needed a bit of space to experiment and try out things, away from the weekly therapy sessions. After he had been coming for many months, one of his new ideas was that he would set up a group Facebook page as a way of reaching out to other survivors of sexual abuse. He and I talked about this for a number of sessions during our fifth block of work. I wanted to make space for him to imagine the pros and cons of such a project: to help him think about how he would feel and cope if he got posts or messages that he found unpleasant or upsetting; how he would manage his privacy; and how much time and energy he wanted to put into posting things and keeping the page up to date, etc. True to form, while he was coming for sessions, Stu did not do anything to make this idea manifest. Then we had our usual break. And when he arrived for his first appointment of our sixth block, he arrived looking very pleased and energised.

He was grinning broadly as he entered the room, and had barely sat down before he announced, 'You will not be expecting to hear this, Sarah, but I am the happiest man in the world right now!'

SARAH: Are you? Goodness!

STU: Yup. I am! Are you going to ask me why?

SARAH: I certainly am. Why is that?

STU: Because, Sarah, I have found love! I have found a lovely lady who is going to share my life with me. [He beamed at me.]

I could feel myself searching for a fitting response to such a statement, that had a least a modicum of balance, but would not sound dreadfully lukewarm.

SARAH: Wow! Please do tell me about this new development in your life.

STU: So ... You know I was telling you about this Facebook page I was planning – to be a support for other people like me, who've gone through the same sort of stuff?

SARAH: I do.

STU: So I got that up and running, and I did it really properly, you know, like being careful and that, like what we talked about. Looking out for myself and other survivors, you know. And Kev, you know, my eldest brother, he was all saying how I'll just get loads of haters and weirdos posting stuff, and that. But there wasn't one! Not one negative comment, Sarah! Only positive ones. And one of them was Clare – this lady in my life now. Because she had posted a comment, about how she had been abused by, like, her stepdad, and this ring of men that her stepdad knew and had got her all involved in with them when she had just been 13 ...

[Stu's speech was getting faster and faster, and more and more breathless, until he was almost gabbling his account to me.]

STU: ... and we just felt a special connection, you know. And she was sending me messages, and I was getting back to her and we swapped numbers, and in the end, we arranged to meet. So I go up on the train to, like Essex, where she lives with her mum, and we had a very special, lovely time. It's a very special connection, and she feels the same, and basically we know we want to be together, and we're looking at how we can get a place together now, because we have found it, Sarah! Really found it! I have actually found love in my life, which I never really thought would happen. Love in my life.

[He stopped and took a breath, and I noticed his hands were trembling a little more than usual.]

SARAH: Stu! What a lot has happened for you since we last met! You sound so excited and happy.

STU: Well, that's cos I am! And you know, there's the ... I mean, I had given up thinking ... the whole business of ... you know.

[Here Stu began to look a little uncomfortable, and somewhat shy.]

STU: Because, to be honest, Sarah, my ... you know – my bits and pieces and what not ... they were all there and stuff, but after what those bastards did to me, I didn't know if, like, all that would be ... you know. Because I haven't ever been able to, you know ... I couldn't like ... satisfy a woman, really. I mean like, so that she would you know ... come. And I couldn't ever like come, myself, unless I was on my own. So I thought that part of life was just over for me. Is it all right to talk like this, Sarah? To explain this to you?

SARAH: Quite all right. I appreciate you being willing to tell me about such an intimate and important area for you.

STU: OK, yeah, well. So, turns out that Clare is, like, in the same boat. Because she's a survivor, too. And she hasn't ever had a ... you know, good time in bed. And then so, when we ... Well, we have spent the night together, now, and it was ... it was good, Sarah! You know?

SARAH: That's a very important part of a relationship.

STU: Exactly! And in the morning ... this was last week ... in the morning, afterwards, I made her like a cup of coffee and took it to her in bed, and she said ... and [here Stu smiled a most delighted yet bashful smile] ... she said, 'I think I love you, Stu.' So I proposed!

I had been aware of a faint hint of a kind of inner warning bell in my ear about how quickly things had seemed to be moving for Stu. At the news that he had proposed marriage, the inner bell got a bit louder and more urgent.

SARAH: Gosh. Fast work!

STU: [Laughing happily] I don't want to hang around anymore. I haven't got time to kill. I don't want to waste any more of my life!

I wanted to say something that reflected both my wish to affirm and encourage Stu in the idea that he could find happiness and love after so much time being alone and unhappy, and my wish to also make space for some pacing, and for Stu to bring a bit more self-awareness to what he was embarking on. But all I could produce in the moment was an 'Mmm', that I feared sounded rather half-hearted. Stu was too happy to care. He spent the rest of the session talking about Clare, her personality, her appearance, her family, the abuse she had suffered, the house she lived in with her mother, their plans together.

Later, in a supervision session, I reflected on the muddle of feelings I had been experiencing while Stu had been talking, and gave voice to the concern I had that Stu's vulnerability and naivety were leaving him open to getting very hurt and disappointed if he approached this new relationship as if it could be the panacea for all his ills. The main thing I needed some space to talk through and make more sense of was the powerful level of conflict I could feel within myself. One side of me wanted to believe, along with Stu, that he could find happiness, companionship and sexual pleasure with Clare, and that to express doubt or caution about this was me being a cynical old kill-joy; that an overly cautious part of me just wanted to infantilise Stu and take on too much sense of responsibility for how he should lead his life, if I did so. Another side was in touch with how very challenging it can be for anyone to build an enduring, committed sexual partnership, and how much harder this is likely to be if one or both partners have been badly abused and let down in the past. This part felt that the more hopeful side of me was being a mug, a dreamer, someone who was irresponsibly letting Stu go blindly down a path that had pitfalls galore, and it was only a mealy mouthed, sentimental soppiness that was preventing me from getting more robust and real with him about what he was leaving out of the frame. The more I was able, in supervision, to air these two opposing parts of me, and how critical each was of the other's perspective, the more I could become aware of what was playing out from Stu's family history, via my countertransference reactions.

I became more aware as I talked with my supervisor that the dynamic between my two conflicting ways of reacting to Stu's news was a very accurate reflection of how his parents on the one hand, and his siblings on the other, had related to Stu, throughout his life.

His parents' approach had been hopelessly laissez-faire, due to an inadequate grasp of what was needed to effectively parent their children, which was partly due to their intellectual disabilities, and partly due to the social and economic disadvantages they faced, and a lack of ongoing support from the environment. They had often left their children open to harm and neglect by being unable or unwilling to steer their family, and challenge some of their children's inevitably immature decisions. For example, they simply took at face value Stu's reasons for missing days and weeks of school, even when they were as flimsy as, 'The teachers said we didn't have to go in this week.' They missed the disturbing clues in Stu's behaviour and general manner, after the sexual abuse began, that could have alerted them to there being something gravely amiss. Stu had alluded in our sessions to some of the distressing symptoms he had had at the time, including having a very sore bottom, suddenly being sick after meals, having dreadful nightmares, and the development of a stutter and odd facial tics. All of this seemed to have passed his parents by, as they muddled along in their self-absorbed, blinkered way, seeming to be only capable of thinking the best of their kids – that they were all *fine* – even while their kids actually developed health problems and addictions, or got into trouble with authority figures and broke the law, or, in Stu's case, were exposed to sexual abuse.

His siblings' dynamic with Stu, however, had been very different. He had tended to experience their way of relating to him as mostly very intrusive as well as harshly domineering. The oldest brother and oldest sister in particular had seemed to take on parental-type roles in the family, to compensate for the gaps in their parents' capacity, but had done so in ways that were the polar opposite of the helpless and hands-off approach of the mother and father. Instead, Kevin and Maria had been bossy, short-tempered, critical and volatile. They had both continually put Stu down, and teased and mocked him for being the 'retard baby'. He had unhappy memories of them each pouring scorn on his pet projects and hobbies.

He had one particularly bitter memory of bringing home a fox cub, when he was around ten, that someone on the estate had sold him for five pounds, and his parents telling him he could keep it, but Maria insisting that he could not. She pressured Kevin to take the fox cub out and 'kill it' while she marched Stu round to the person who had sold it to him, to demand the five pounds back. Stu had felt utterly grief-stricken at the cub's demise, as well as humiliated at being forced to accompany his sister to the neighbour. He had cringed on the doorstep as Maria and the neighbour had had a stand-up shouting match with each other. When the neighbour had refused to repay the money a furious, tearful Maria had turned on Stu, and, as they walked back home, had smacked him hard around the head a number of times, to 'teach me not to be so bloody soft'. The poignant timing of this tragic little episode was striking – in the year that Stu had begun to be abused, he had wanted to rescue and protect a young creature. The symbolism of the fact that this chance was denied him, and that he was faced instead with the pain of the brutal killing of that animal, and being shamed and criticised for having wanted to help it, was unmistakable.

The more I understood my own inner conflict as to how to respond to Stu's news about planning to get married as a way of getting a felt sense of how the key people in his life had tended to respond to him, the less caught I felt in the urge to split and choose one or other way to address his belief that he and Clare would now get married and live happily ever after. I could find myself more able to imagine a way to respond to him and work with this important new development in his life, in ways that could be both supportive and challenging. After supervision, I felt more hopeful that I could make a space for being both hopeful *and* realistic about Stu's blossoming relationship with Clare, and that we could include the belief that his relationship with Clare would be a positive thing for him, alongside the need to take care of himself in the intense new sea of feelings being stirred up by a romantic, sexual liaison.

Stu began our next session by happily filling me in with various details of what he and Clare had recently been saying to each other via texts, and the plans they now had to meet and go and look together at some bedsits near to her mother's home, with the view to moving in together.

I bit the bullet.

SARAH: I hear how excited and happy you are about this, which is so great to see. And I notice that I also feel a wish for you to carry on looking after yourself, in the midst of all this new excitement. Any new relationship can really stir up powerful stuff, and you and Clare have both been through such a lot. I think I am hoping that the speed of all this won't end up leaving you feeling … a bit overwhelmed. Does that make sense?

[Stu's wide smile remained on his face after I had spoken, but it seemed a little more fixed, as if he was smiling less spontaneously.]

STU: Yeah. Well, I know people think me and her are taking things a bit too quick. My key worker at the drugs place, and Clare's mum, and Kev and Marie, but … But it's not about them, is it? I've never been more sure of anything in my life!

[This last sentence came out in a defiant tone, and his smile had faded a little by the time he said it.]

SARAH: Yes. I see. So … perhaps it seems a bit hurtful if it looks like I'm joining the ranks of the people who are sounding a note of caution about yours and Clare's relationship?

STU: [Shrugging] Doesn't really matter, does it! It's not about anyone else except me and her.

[He was beginning to look annoyed.]

SARAH: It doesn't feel like you're being supported if people express their doubts and concerns for you?

STU: No, because it isn't bloody supportive to do that, is it! But anyway, who cares! How can anyone know what's best for me, unless they've been through what I've been through?

[Stu looked more and more ill at ease and cross.]

STU: When someone else has been abused, week in, week out, all their childhood … when *their* childhood's been took by a bunch of disgusting evil, old perverts. *Then* they can come to me with a load of advice about 'Do this and don't that', or whatever, and maybe *then* I'd listen, cos they'd know what they were talking about. But until then, no one can know what I've been through, and no one can know what's best for me.

[When he finished speaking, he stared angrily at me.]

SARAH: I hear your belief that no one can understand you, or what might be good for you, unless they have experienced similar abuse.

STU: No, they can't!

SARAH: And I'm guessing that in the past, if anyone has tried to advise or guide you to go a certain way, it hasn't always been done in a very understanding way. You have often felt that the people wanting you to do or not do certain things, couldn't really understand what was going on for you. Would that be right?

STU: Yeah, well, I've had enough of it. Sorry, Sarah, but I am going out for a smoke, right now.

[Stu stood up. He had a thunderously angry expression, and his hands were trembling very noticeably.]

SARAH: OK. Do you think you intend to come back, when you've had a smoke?

STU: I don't know. I've just got to clear my head and have a smoke right now.

I judged that the better part of valour was discretion just then, in our work and I simply replied, 'OK, Stu. I'll be here.'

He grunted and went out. I sat, listening to him angrily muttering, while he got some water from the water dispenser in the waiting area. It sounded as if he was having some problem that meant he dropped something as he did so, and he swore angrily. Then the outer door banged shut and I could hear that he had left the building. I stayed sitting and reflected on what had just happened and the different meanings to make of it. There was an obvious kind of mini breakdown in Stu's and my alliance, symbolised by the actual, physical breakdown of the boundary of the session itself, with Stu walking out. I imagined he felt terribly hurt and let down by me, as well as furiously angry with me.

In *Treating the Adult Survivor of Childhood Sexual Abuse: A Psychoanalytic Perspective*, Davies and Frawley have helpfully teased out four recurring patterns of feelings that often play out between clients who have experienced childhood sexual abuse and their therapists, with one person playing one side, and the other playing the opposite side of the following pairings:

the unseeing, uninvolved parent and the unseen, neglected child;
the sadistic abuser and the helpless, impotently outraged victim;
the idealised, omnipotent rescuer and the entitled child;
the seducer and the seduced. (Davies and Frawley 1994)

I imagined that for Stu, he had suddenly found himself re-experiencing the sense of being both the unseen, neglected child and the helpless, furious victim. This would make me the unseeing, neglectful parent as well as the sadistic abuser for him in the session. Coping with this had all felt too much for him.

I pondered on different ways forward, depending on whether he came back to the room or not. The fact that he had actually ended up walking out seemed like a replay of the disastrous ways that lots of basic boundaries in his childhood had been breached and broken down. It did not feel good to sit there, wondering if he would return. I felt as if I had been unskilful, after all, in trying to float the idea that he and Clare might benefit from taking things more slowly. I had made an intervention that now seemed to me clumsily directive, and I was unsure whether I would be able to repair the unmistakable rupture between us well enough. Small breakdowns in the client–therapist alliance are generally an inevitable and healthy part of the work, but for someone like Stu, with a history of such dreadful breakdowns and failure in trust, even a small 'blip' in feeling he could trust the other person would be likely to be felt by him as if it was a catastrophic failure.

After about 15 minutes, I heard the door again and then some footsteps, and I felt a surge of hopeful anticipation. I was glad to be able to detect a faint whiff of stale tobacco, which I was sure heralded Stu's return. He reappeared, looking calmer. He came in, sat down, and promptly started a prolonged and painful coughing fit that rendered him speechless and hardly able to get his breath for quite some time. He coughed for so long, and looked so uncomfortable, that in the end I asked him if I could get him some water. When he nodded with streaming eyes, I walked quickly out to the water cooler, aware that now it was me, albeit on Stu's behalf, that was crossing the usual boundary of the session. I wondered about that later, as a reflection that Stu might believe he could only be properly helped when someone was prepared to step out of the usual guidelines, and make him special and different – the way he had longed to be made to feel in his family, and never had. The only 'special' and 'different' he had ever been allowed to feel as a boy was when he had been targeted for abuse.

Stu took the paper cone of water, drank it, and then did his usual thing of sitting back, closing his eyes and seeming to drift off into a kind of sleep or unconsciousness. We sat in silence for a long while. We sat for so long like this that when I glanced at the clock I saw there were only about ten minutes to go before the end of the session. It was on the tip of my tongue to say, 'Stu, can I ask how you are doing now?' when he suddenly opened his eyes and cleared his throat. He looked a little disorientated for a moment and then his gaze, which had wandered around the room for a few moments, met mine. Different expressions flitted across his face – confusion, embarrassment, annoyance. And then his features settled into one that conveyed some kind of inner pain, and he announced emphatically, 'I can't do this anymore, Sarah.'

SARAH: You can't?

STU: No, I'm sorry. And I don't want to part on bad terms, because you have been a help. I know you have. But it's no good. I'm done with talking about it all now. D'you know what – the past is past. I think you've done what you can and thank you very much, but I'm just done with talking about all of this shit now. I want to move on, and if people can't understand that, and understand that my future is with Clare, then I can't be doing with all that. So I think I'll make this my last session, thanks very much. Thank you for at least trying to understand.

SARAH: Well … I respect that the decision is yours. And … I also want to hold out the possibility that you could find it useful to mull over your thoughts on this, rather than decide right now. From where I'm sitting, I can see that you might find some value in further sessions, so that you can have some ongoing support in this new, more hopeful phase in your life.

Even as I came up with this attempt to get Stu to slow down, I felt I was clutching at straws. He looked unmoved.

STU: No, my mind's made up, Sarah. No one can understand how things are for me right now. Except Clare. But she's been through it too, so she gets it. No one else can.

SARAH: Right. It's your choice, of course, Stu. [A pause.] I don't know if you remembered in our original agreement about the work, that we advise everyone to make the time for an ending session, to draw the work to a close.

STU: Oh. Vaguely, yeah. You mean come to one more? To end?

SARAH: That's right. We suggest that so that the work doesn't finish very abruptly. How would you feel about coming next week to have an ending session?

STU: Fair enough, if that's what I signed up for. Yeah. OK.

I was struck by Stu being so suddenly amenable to my suggestion, after being so opposed to everything I was attempting to put forward. It seemed to me that he would be likely to have both an unconscious yearning for and yet an unconscious dread of containment. Hence his immediate acceptance of the chance for one more session: an ending session would both offer a chance to have a more intimate connection, as well as the relief of that intimate connection coming to an end. I felt unhappily sure that the simultaneous longing for and dread of the containment of an intimate relationship would inevitably be also evoked in his connection with Clare, and that unless he had some time to reflect on what was getting stirred up for him and untangle his past from his present and future (at the heart of the work in so much therapy), then the same tension between longing for and dreading closeness was horribly likely to spoil things between him and his new love.

SARAH: I'm glad you feel able to come next week. And I understand that, at the moment, you are deciding that this will be an ending session. But, if you change your mind, between then and now, please feel free to let me know at the start of the session.

Stu was looking at me, but his focus seemed to be elsewhere. We sat facing each other until his expression subtly changed and his gaze sharpened again, and I felt he was seeing me once more.

STU: Sorry, what was that?

I repeated what I had said, aware that I had probably witnessed a tiny episode of Stu dissociating, which confirmed my sense that he could be finding it very hard to tolerate his feelings of not being understood by me, and know what he could do about that, other than 'check out' and leave.

STU: OK. Fine.

SARAH: So, I'll see you next week.

Stu sighed deeply. We were at the end of the session, and he was about to get up, but I felt a strong impulse to mention again that he didn't *have* to end next week. I may have done so if Stu's mobile phone hadn't gone off just at that moment with a loud blast of upbeat rock music.

> STU: Sorry, Sarah. I've got to take this – it'll be Clare! [He stood up and went to stand near the door to the counselling room.] 'Hello, babes, where are you?'

I sat as Stu took the call, feeling an intense pressure once again on the boundary and containment of our session, and seeing it as another instance of how boundaries in Stu's life were so often undermined or eroded. I stood up myself, with the intention of still wanting to maintain the boundary of the session, and to encourage Stu to leave the room in order to take his call. As he saw me stand, Stu held the phone away from his ear for a moment and said, 'Sorry, Sarah. I gotta go. See you next week.'

He clamped the phone to his ear with his shoulder and struggled to get his wallet out of his jean's pocket and fish out the fee of a few pounds, while he listened to the female voice at the other end of the call, that sounded insistent and emotional.

> STU: All right, babes. Calm down. Try and stay calm. I'm on my way.

He handed me the money, mouthed 'Sorry' again, and opened the door. As he left, still on his phone, I said as calmly and clearly as I could, 'I will see you next week.'

When he had gone and I had taken some deep breaths, I contacted the CSM to fill them in on how things now stood with Stu's sessions. We were in agreement that we would be able to offer Stu the chance of referring himself back to the service at a future date, if he did indeed decide to finish.

During the week that followed I found Stu coming into my mind very often. I wondered whether he would come to the session at all. One minute I could convince myself that he would: that he and I had built a genuine alliance that meant something to him, and that he had the capacity to pre-serve some good and useful things about that, even if he did decide to end. The next minute I would find myself gloomily sure that I would be sitting and waiting in vain at the time of the session: that our work would be ending badly, messily, and that Stu would leave the service feeling once again let down and misunderstood by 'People in Authority' who were supposed to help him, but never could or would.

When the day of the session came, I was on tenterhooks. Stu was the first client I was due to see, and I got the room ready in a state of nervous anticipation that I hadn't felt in many years. I had to restrain the urge I felt (just as I had when newly qualified) to keep checking the waiting area once the time of Stu's appointment had passed, to make sure I hadn't missed him arriving by some weird chance.

About a quarter of an hour after we were due to meet, I heard the buzzer go and a colleague in our reception tell someone to 'Come through'. I would have pricked up my ears if I could, as I listened out for footsteps that I willed to be Stu's. As I heard a chesty cough, and caught the familiar scent of stale tobacco, I breathed a sigh of relief. He had made it. I came to the door of the counselling room and saw him getting himself a drink of water. I held the door open for him, and noticed with a sinking heart that he did not look at me as he came in and took a seat. This did not bode well. He kept his eyes on the carpet as he sat. There was a long silence. After some minutes, I broke it.

SARAH: Well. Here we are.

STU: Yeah. [Pause.] Well. You were right.

SARAH: Oh? Right about … ? [I guessed immediately what he meant, and dreaded hearing it confirmed.]

STU: About Clare. Or, about me and Clare. Whatever.

SARAH: Oh. Oh dear. [I found my face pulling itself out of a fairly neutral expression into the sort of one I might make if I heard from a friend that they'd just broken up with a long-term partner.]

[Stu spoke in a dull, flat tone.]

STU: It's all over. She … took against something I said in a text to her mum. Not even to her. I hadn't meant anything by it, but she and her mum thought I was disrespecting her mum, and … I don't know what they thought really. Anyway, she's … that's it. She unfriended me on Facebook and blocked me on everything, and she's gone back to saying status 'single'. I don't understand it. She won't let me try to explain.

SARAH: I'm really so sorry to hear that, Stu.

STU: Mmm. [He closed his eyes and leant back in the chair in the old pose.]

I sat turning over in my mind the different threads that were before me and which ones I could usefully pick up. The two most pressing seemed to be getting clarity on whether he still wanted to end his counselling, and attending to his distress in the aftermath of his break up. As I pondered on how to broach either, I saw tears trickling out from under Stu's closed eyelids. He placed a hand on his forehead.

SARAH: You're very upset, Stu.

Stu nodded and the tears ran faster. I was about to say something along the lines of asking what I could do to be a support to him in that moment, when Stu spoke through his tears, still with his eyes closed.

STU: I can't do this anymore. I can't stand it anymore. I just can't stand it anymore. No more. No, no, no. Stop it! No more! I don't want it! I can't stand it no more!

Stu's voice rose in pitch as it grew quieter and more forlorn. I watched him regress before me to becoming a small boy giving voice to an agonised protest to the people hurting and mistreating him.

SARAH: Oh, Stu. It was so wrong for the little boy that you were, to be so badly hurt and abused, wasn't it?

Stu nodded with a whimper, and I was glad that he could hear what I had said and agree with it, which suggested he was not wholly caught up in experiencing me as one of the people he needed to protect himself from. He opened his eyes, swiped one palm around his face to get rid of his tears, and then rubbed it on his trousers, in a gesture reminiscent of a very young child.

STU: It's just too much, Sarah. I can't keep coming and doing this. I just can't stand it anymore.
SARAH: Too much pain?
STU: Yeah. That's it. Too much pain.
SARAH: I hear that. And … and I know that this work can be so tough at times. But it can be worth it, in the end. A bit like climbing a mountain: there are some very hard parts of the climb, but it's really worth it, to get to …

STU: [Interrupting] Yeah, but where would I get to? Really, Sarah? Honestly?

SARAH: [Pause.] I think, eventually, you could get to … a place of feeling less unhappy with yourself. More at some kind of peace.

STU: It's not me that I'm not at peace with, though, is it! It's all the fucking paedos and liars and that, that I have a problem with. And coming to counselling isn't going to do anything about them, is it!

SARAH: It's true. There's a definite limit to what therapy can address. It's a bit like the old adage – *'Grant me the courage to change the things I can, the patience to accept the things I can't, and the wisdom to know the difference.'* I don't think coming to counselling can help with ensuring justice can be done with regard to the men who abused you. But in my experience, it certainly *can* help people who have survived abuse in restoring their self-worth, helping them dissolve some of the shame that they might be left with, and …

[Stu cut me off.]

STU: I don't think this is for me. I don't honestly think what you're saying is possible for me, Sarah. Do you know what I'm going to do when I leave here today, now that it's all over with me and Clare?

I felt a prickle of worry at his question, and prepared myself to hear that he had a plan of suicide.

SARAH: No I don't, but I want to hear about that.

STU: I'm going to go back to my mum and dad's. I'm going to have to walk all the way, cos I've lost my Oyster card. And I'm going to go to my room and lie on my bed and smoke, with a million thoughts going through my mind that I can't stop. And none of them is going to be happy thoughts. And then I'm probably going to get some money off my mum, and go down the offie and get some cider. That's what I'm going to do. Because there isn't anything else I can do. Everything is fucked in my life, Sarah. It's all completely fucked. And I don't think sitting here, talking to you, nice as that is, is going to make any difference to my life.

In the next few minutes I found myself trying to teeter along an impossible tightrope, as I tried to both accept and allow Stu's experience of utter despair, whilst also holding out the hope of *some* possibility of change, however small. I pointed out that, until things had gone wrong with Clare, he had been feeling much better about life. That he had met Clare in the first place via his Facebook page and that there were still potential connections to make with new people in life, just as he had made one with Clare so very recently. I let him know that I had seen many significant improvements for him while he had been coming – in his health, how he was coping generally in life, and many aspects of his self-care.

Stu would not, could not, let any of it in. He had been so horribly impacted by Clare's rejection, that he had been sent effectively crashing back to feeling as helpless, let down and despairing as he had when he was a little ten-year-old boy, in the control of a group of abusers, and that was, effect-ively, now his current reality.

> SARAH: I want to check something important with you, Stu. I want to ask you whether you have thoughts at the moment of hurting yourself badly or of ending your life when you leave here?
>
> STU: [With a big sigh] You don't need to worry about that, Sarah. I'm not going to do anything like that. I won't lie to you – I think about it every now and then. But I wouldn't ever do it. Never! One: because I wouldn't give those bastards the satisfaction – they would've won then, wouldn't they? And two: I couldn't do that to my mum and dad. It'd destroy them. I just couldn't.
>
> SARAH: OK. I'm glad I asked, and thanks for your honesty.

Although I was relieved to hear Stu was not suicidal, I was still extremely concerned about what was happening for him. In the session I began to feel the odd muzziness that I had felt in our first meeting, and once again had the sensation of being on ground that was slowly tipping me off balance. I was being not only profoundly *affected* by Stu's pain and despair, but also thoroughly *infected* by it. As I sat with him, I could feel part of me agreeing with everything he said. The odds *were* stacked against him. How on earth could he turn his life round at his stage of life, in the wider social and economic context he lived in? He had very limited support and resources in his family, in his community, in our whole society. Perhaps it was verging on the cruel to keep dangling a carrot of hope that he could have a happier life before him, in the form of these sessions, when that happier life might not actually be possible.

As I felt myself sliding down a slope to join Stu at the bottom of the pit of despair, I was reduced to clutching at straws.

SARAH: If coming here isn't an answer for you, at the moment, perhaps we can think together about things that *could* be a help. (Other than blotting everything out for a bit with booze.) What might you think of that could be a help to you, right now, apart from having a drink? Is there someone you could go and be with, who would be supportive? Could you contact Fran and go and see her? [Fran was the sister closest to Stu in age, with whom he had a reasonably warm connection.] Or is there some little kindness you could do for yourself, right now? Some good place to go and just sit for a while?

[Stu stopped looking at the carpet, lifted his head and turned an agonised face to me.]

STU: All I can think of is being with Clare. Being with her at her mum's place. Sitting with Clare in the kitchen, and her making me a coffee.

[He broke down and sobbed quietly. After a while, through his tears, he spoke.]

STU: Thanks very much for trying to help, Sarah. I appreciate it. I'm afraid I haven't got the money for today. When my benefit money comes through, I'll post it. I've got to go now.

[He stood up and I stood with him, feeling as if I was in a bad dream.]

SARAH: Stu ... I'm so sorry. I don't know what to say to you, except that I wish you would change your mind and come next week.

Stu wiped a hand around his face, rubbed it on his trousers again, and then proffered it to me, before withdrawing it suddenly with a 'Sorry about that. Try this one.' He offered his other, cleaner hand, and we clasped hands for a few seconds in a tight grip.

SARAH: Goodbye, Stu. I really wish you well. I hope ... some good things will come your way soon. You deserve that.

He released my hand and walked to the door. I gathered my scrambled thoughts together enough to be able to repeat that if he changed his mind at any point, he would be welcome to refer himself back to the service. Stu gave no sign that he had heard this, and I watched him walk quickly through the waiting area, and disappear. When he had gone, I sat back in my chair with my head in my hands for a few moments, awash with sorrow and anger for Stu, and riddled with self-doubt as to how I had managed the situation. I hadn't managed to help Stu to an awareness that he was partly caught in experiencing the present as the past: that he had been feeling as if Clare and

I were both abandoning carers and cruel abusers, all rolled into one, but that this feeling could be dissolved, if we could work with it, to help him back to feeling he was an adult, with adult choices and possibilities, not a helpless, furious child. And now he was gone and it seemed too late to help him to greater awareness, and more choice.

I made arrangements to speak with the CSM and my supervisor as soon as I could. The CSM's position was that the service had done all that could be reasonably expected for now, and that they would send a letter to Stu confirming he could re-refer himself, and to clarify he could post the outstanding fee. They also undertook the task of contacting of other services that Stu was using, to make them aware that he had ended with us, and to highlight that it was likely he was particularly vulnerable at this time.

When I talked to my supervisor later that week, I needed to let off steam. They let me rage for a while about the profound damage done to people who have endured the type of abuse and neglect that Stu had undergone, and how little awareness there still seems to be in our society about the agony that so many survivors of childhood sexual violation go through. I happened to have Bessel Van Der Kolk's book, *The Body Keeps the Score*, on working with trauma in my bag, and I pulled it out, in irate frustration, and read out the passage that mentions the US Centre for Disease Control physician, Robert Anda, and his calculation that the overall cost in public health medicine of child abuse (all manner of abuse, not only sexual) exceeds the cost to the US public of treating cancer or heart disease. 'If child abuse was stopped, then depression in the US would be halved, alcoholism reduced by two thirds, and suicide, intravenous drug use and domestic violence would be reduced by three quarters' (Van Der Kolk 2014). When I had railed against everything and everyone that had failed Stu, including myself, and ran out of steam, I was able to contact more of the sadness I felt about the messy, unhelpful ending of Stu's sessions, and I shed a few tears. I told my supervisor that I didn't hold out any hope that Stu would indeed post the few outstanding pounds.

In a clear case of parallel process, whenever my supervisor then named some things that I might feel hopeful about, as regards the work with Stu, I wanted to reject them, just as Stu had rejected my attempts at offering a more hopeful perspective. At the time, I saw them as hopelessly over-optimistic. My supervisor pointed out that we had had many months of good contact, some of which Stu may have internalised more of than either of us could realise at the moment. That there could have been something very powerful and redemptive for Stu in the last session, about both being seen and heard in his profound grief and despair, and about being allowed to make his own decision and feel respected in that.

I heard the supervisor's words, but Stu's despair had got thoroughly into me, and the words washed over me at the time. When they told me that they were willing to bet that Stu *would* post the money, because the work we had done together could still stand for something worthwhile for him (even if it had not been – could not be – perfect), I shook my head with a rather bitter smile. 'Not a chance', I thought.

To my surprise, a few weeks after he ended the counselling, Stu did indeed post something to the service, addressed to me. It was the outstanding fee, and it was wrapped in a small piece of flowery notepaper, on which he had written, 'Dear Sarah, thanks for trying. God bless. Stu.'

I carefully filed it with the rest of the correspondence related to his case, with a heavy heart.

7

TIME-LIMITED WORK WITH A MALE SURVIVOR EXPERIENCING POST-TRAUMATIC SHOCK DISORDER
Neil

The American Psychologist, Silvan Tomkins, explains why shame is one of the most shattering human experiences:

> Though terror speaks of life and death, and distress makes the world a vale of tears, yet shame strikes deepest into the heart of man. While terror and distress hurt, they are wounds inflicted from the outside which penetrate the smooth surface of the ego; but shame is felt as an inner torment, as sickness of the soul. It does not matter whether the humiliated one has been shamed by derisive laughter or whether he mocks himself. In either event he feels himself naked, defeated, alienated, lacking in dignity or worth.
>
> Tomkins (1963)

A description of the challenge of working short-term with a man who had post-trau-matic shock symptoms after a sexual assault by a male colleague. How the work was helped by (1) looking back to understand how he had developed a tendency to feel he could not use his natural aggression in order to defend himself; (2) working in the 'here and now' in order to rework the scene of the trauma; and (3) to make space for the imaginative reconnection with a key attachment figure from childhood, through the use of small symbolic objects in the session.

Neil was referred to me for counselling via an EAP (Employee Assistance Programme). The EAP colleague who gave me some brief assessment details informed me, 'This guy's company offer to pay for six sessions. In exceptional circumstances, they might extend it to ten.'

She then told me that Neil had a middle management position in the IT department for a well-known chain of high street stores. Over the last six months, he had been taking a lot of time off work, calling in sick. When a more senior manager had raised the issue with him, Neil had talked about some private difficulties that he had been trying to cope with, which were getting on top of him. He admitted to this manager that he had been drinking a bit too much at weekends and evenings as a result, and that his hangovers were sometimes so bad that he hadn't felt well enough to make it into work.

On the day that Neil was due to come for his first session he called me in the morning.

NEIL: Hello, Sarah? This is Neil. I'm supposed to be coming to see you later today, but unfortunately something's come up. I've got to wait in for a workman. It's for my boiler – it's a bit of an emergency and the only day he can come is today, but he can't give me a time, so I'm a bit stuck really.

SARAH: Hello, Neil. Sorry to hear that, and thank you for letting me know. Can I just check that you are aware of the arrangement with our sessions – that unfortunately we can't reschedule them. The agreement with your EAP is that you have been offered six sessions with me, and they can't be changed once the first session date was agreed with you. So if you did miss today, that would mean we would only have five remaining.

[There was a silence at the other end that went on for so long, I wasn't sure he was still on the line.]

SARAH: Hello, Neil?

[Neil's tone was one of controlled annoyance when he finally spoke.]

NEIL: Right. I'll find out when the guy's supposed to come, and just … I'll find a way to get there this afternoon.

SARAH: OK, that sounds good. Well, I look forward to … [He had put the phone down on me as I responded].

I was expecting an angry man later that day, and I got one. When Neil's story of sexual violation finally emerged, it was no wonder that he was so bitterly angry, so extremely defensive and on high alert for the least sign of any kind of threat or slight to his person. Nor was it any wonder that he was, underneath his prickly persona, feeling utterly lost and at sea.

When he rang the doorbell that afternoon, I opened the door and saw a serious-faced white man in his early thirties, dressed in a smart shirt, ironed jeans and shiny shoes. He was plumpish, just under six-foot-tall, with dark curly hair that was neatly waxed. He was wearing some stylish, rimless glasses, and had a few days' stubble on his chin. He held a key fob in his hand and after I had said, 'Neil? Hello', he turned away from me so that he could aim the keys at a smart little two-seater Audi parked in front of the house, and locked it from a distance with a beep.

SARAH: I'm glad you could make it in the end. Do come in.

He walked past me, wordlessly, without looking at me, and took a seat opposite me in the consulting space. He had an air that put me in mind of a school boy who has been sent, unjustly, to his head teacher's office – sullen, wary and somewhat aggrieved. Once I too had sat down and looked over at him I found him practically glaring back at me. My usual preamble that was intended to help set people at ease in a first meeting, as well as give them some practical information about the coming session, did not seem to thaw him one bit. There was a stony silence after I had said my opening piece. When it became apparent that Neil was not going to offer anything much to begin with, I tried to get the ball rolling.

SARAH: So. Would you be able to say a bit about what you think might be behind your manager suggesting you come along for some sessions?
[Neil rolled his eyes and a slight flush worked its way up from his neck to his cheeks. He sighed.]
NEIL: Isn't it all down on some form somewhere?
SARAH: There isn't really a form. I was given some brief information about you having missed quite a lot of work recently, and that you've told your manager that you have been having some stress that has led you to using alcohol more than usual. That's pretty much all I know at this stage.
NEIL: Right. [He continued to look annoyed and shifted in his seat. There was another stiff silence.]

When there is a stuck quality in the room it is usually helpful to simply name it, so I ventured to speak about what I saw before me.

SARAH: I'm imagining that you don't really want to be here.
[He raised one sarcastic eyebrow.]

NEIL: You spotted that, then.

SARAH: Mmm. You don't much like the idea of counselling?

NEIL: Uh … not to put too fine a point on it – no. But, it is what it is. I've got to come. So. There we are. We'd better get on with it.

SARAH: Right. Can you explain the bit about 'I've got to come'?

NEIL: [With a small, sour smile] In the contract, isn't it? If the boss says you've got to go to counselling, you've got to counselling.

SARAH: Ah. So it's a three-line whip from work?

NEIL: Yup.

SARAH: And if you *didn't* come?

NEIL: Don't keep to the terms of the contract – no contract. Simples. [He made the clicking noise at the side of his mouth that the meercat character makes in the well-known television advertisements for insurance.]

SARAH: Right. [Pause.] That's tricky. In my experience, sessions don't tend to be of much use if the person who has them feels that they have basically been made to come.

Neil stared at me blankly for a few moments. Then the red flush that had died down reappeared, creeping rapidly back up over his throat and cheeks. His brows drew down and he blinked rapidly for a second or two. A vast number of emotions and impulses seemed to me to be surging around inside him, with no easy way for any of them to be expressed to me.

NEIL: Right. Well. Thanks. Thanks for your time. [He stood up abruptly and made towards the door.]

A very small, muted sound of surprise escaped my lips at this. I tried to gather my thoughts, and was glad to suddenly catch hold of the old, simple advice for therapists of 'Never collapse, never retaliate.'

SARAH: Do you think you might be able to stay a little longer while we think together about how to work things out so they can feel a bit better for you?

[Neil was at the door of the room. He did not turn around, but stood in front of it with his back to me.]

NEIL: You've made your feelings about me coming pretty clear. Goodbye. [He put his hand on the doorknob.]

SARAH: Neil, I'm sorry if I didn't express my concern very well about you getting the best support possible. I would really like it if you could sit with me now, and explain a little bit about what's going on for you at the moment. That could help us work out what *would* be the best help for you.

Neil kept his hand on the doorknob, but turned his body a little so that I could see his face. He did not actually look at me, but at the floor. He seemed furious, but also now hurt and upset: his eyes were shiny with tears; his mouth was being pulled down at both corners, his chin was trembling; and the flush on his throat and cheeks had blotches of a particularly intense red throughout. He looked desperately uncomfortable, and his voice quivered as he spoke, even though he tried to disguise this by clearing his throat.

NEIL: Look – I didn't want to come here. But the boss says I've got to, so I do. I get here, ready for whatever it is I'm supposed to do, and you say, 'Oh no, this is no good: you can't come here unless you want to come.' So … Fine! Either way, I'm … It's like … *What on earth do you people want? Blood?* Forget it. I'll just go back to my boss, shall I, and tell him that I came, but you sent me away with a flea in my ear?
[He yanked the door open.]
SARAH: Neil, I really am very sorry that what I said came across to you as meaning that you shouldn't be here. I think coming here *might* be exactly what you need right now, but I wanted to be sure that you wouldn't prefer some other kind of support. I do hope that can you find it in you not to leave, just yet.
[He stood still, at the open door, with his back to me.]
SARAH: If you would be willing to give up just ten more minutes of your time now, to come and sit and talk with me, we can try and clear the air and think what's best for you. If you still want to leave after those ten minutes, then that's fair enough, and I will contact the EAP to explain that we agreed there wasn't a good 'fit' and that you may do better with a different practitioner.

I watched Neil's back. A horribly long pause ensued, during which he continued to stand at the open door, and I waited in my chair.

Short of pleading with him not to go, I felt I had done all I could. I had never had a client walk out in disgust after less than a minute of a first meeting, in nearly 20 years of working! I tried to reach through the white noise of anxiety and confusion inside me that was making my thinking so foggy, in order to try to pay better attention to my feelings, and reflect on them. Out of the fog emerged the fact that my predominant emotion in the moment was that I felt … a fool. I had mucked up the beginning of trying to offer support to Neil, the session had got badly derailed, and not only had that made Neil feel worse, but others would have to know about this and it would probably get talked about – by colleagues at the EAP, perhaps by personnel at Neil's workplace. So as well as foolish, I felt somehow nastily exposed as lacking, inadequate.

As painful as it was to admit to myself that I felt somewhat ashamed and humiliated, this was of course invaluable information in terms of the countertransference. Those feelings in me were, in effect, the trail of white stones that could lead me, and thereby Neil, out of the dreadful dark wood of shame that he and I had suddenly found ourselves in. They gave me a vital clue as to what was causing Neil such distress: I was able to wonder if *he* had been dreadfully humiliated in some way.

After what seemed like an age, and to my immense relief, Neil turned round. He stayed at the door, but did not let go of the handle. I realised as he did so that I had been actually holding my breath. I ensured that I then gently exhaled and slowly breathed in, and continued with some slow, regular breaths to help better regulate myself and restore my own equilibrium, trusting that Neil would detect this modelling, and that it might help him to do likewise.

Calm, slow breathing is such a simple way to help the frontal cortex to come back 'on line' after it has been 'switched off' in order for a flight/fight/freeze/flop reaction to be activated, when someone's nervous system is dealing with what has been perceived as a dire threat to their safety. Slow breathing is so simple, so basic, that it can get neglected as a resource in a session, available at any moment, and in any situation. If a therapist is able to calm themselves this way in a session when a client is distraught, it both soothes that therapist, and acts as a powerful aid to the client feeling that they might be able to do the same.

> Not only is the therapist being unconsciously influenced by a series of slight and, in some cases, subliminal signals, so also is the patient. Details of the therapist's posture, gaze, tone of voice, *even respiration* are recorded and processed. A … therapist may use this processing in a beneficial way, potentiating a change in the patient's state without, or in addition to, the use of words. (Meares 2005; my italics)

Neil walked back to his chair, sat down and folded his arms emphatically across his chest. He directed a marble-eyed stare not quite at me, but at a spot on the wall that was behind and slightly to one side of me.

> NEIL: OK. Ten minutes, then.
>
> SARAH: Great. I appreciate you being willing to give us that. [Pause.] I'd like to offer you an idea I have: I'm imagining that you could be dealing with something that has been difficult for you … traumatic, even. And that your starting to drink more heavily than usual might be related to this.

I saw Neil's eyes make a very brief flick towards my gaze and immediately, in much less than a second, go back to fasten on the wall. Encouraged by this tiny sign that he could bear to make at least some visual contact with me, I continued.

> SARAH: It is this fact of wondering if there has been something seriously painful that you are dealing with, that was making me think that perhaps six counselling sessions isn't really going to be enough to address the … the depth of pain that you might be coping with.

There was a very long silence. Neil continued to stare fixedly ahead for some time. Then all of a sudden he dropped his gaze so that he seemed to be studying his own lap. After a few seconds he lifted one hand and put it over his face, which pushed his glasses slightly askew. His other hand clenched into a fist as it rested on the arm of the chair and he began to cry. His sobs were long and loud, each one a painful cross between a gasp and a kind of suppressed yelp. He cried and cried for nearly a minute, in a way that was agonising to hear. The sound he made put me in mind of some animal trapped in a hunter's snare: it had a desperate, keening quality. I found myself feeling the urge to clench my own fists to somehow help me hang on to my own capacity to maintain some calm as Neil gave voice to such abject suffering.

I was also aware of a sudden strong impulse to look away as he wept. This could have been explained as a respectful wish not to increase Neil's shame by continuing to observe him at a time when he so obviously wished to be hidden away from a feeling of exposure. However, I noticed a kind of frozen, horrified quality to my wish to look away, which suggested that, rather than it being about feeling sensitive to what Neil needed, my urge to turn my gaze away was more to do with a countertransference reaction of longing to protect myself from feeling his overwhelming pain.

Porges' idea of a polyvagal system (1997) proposes that there are different levels of becoming affected by what is distressing for us – and one is the level of dissociation. A classic manifestation that someone has been plunged into this dissociated state (in which 'the stressed individual passively disengages in order to conserve energies … and allow restitution of depleted resources by immobility' (Schore 2012)) is to behave in a way that aims to stop the input of any more stimuli, even stimuli that is visual.

The person who is attempting to protect themselves from any further visual stimuli will usually do so by either turning away their head and/or eyes completely (which Neil had often been doing during our meeting), or by still seeming to look, but with a gaze that is simply a vacant, glazed stare, which does not truly connect with what is looked at (which he had also done during the session). I could now feel myself at the affect of these same urges to cut off from Neil's suffering by not looking. My wish not to see him as he wept seemed likely to be a mirroring of Neil's own response to a trauma – an urge to protect himself from feeling the full force of a horror by becoming numb to it; and was also, perhaps, a mirroring of how others in his life may have wanted to look away from or ignore the depth of his suffering at crucial times.

This sensation of not wanting to witness Neil's distress was extremely unpleasant to focus on within myself. How tempting it can be for a therapist to distance themselves from their dark, complex responses to a client's suffering by either disowning them completely, or by ticking themselves off in a shaming way for their lack of compassion! But the fact of recognising that my urge to look away could be countertransference (i.e. Neil's unconscious communication to me, non-verbally, about his trauma and also about other people's response to his pain) meant that something shifted inside me. I stopped feeling ashamed that I wanted to look away, and I also stopped feeling it might be wrong to look at him as he cried so bitterly.

I was able instead to connect with the idea of how it need not be cruel or wrong for a caregiver to continue to look at their baby if the baby is crying. Indeed, how vital it could be for a caring adult to continue to gaze at a distressed child, precisely in order to help them gauge what the child needs in order to be comforted.

> The most significant relevant basic interactions between mother and child usually lie in the visual area: the child's bodily display is responded to by the … mother's eye. (Kohut 1971)

I found a way back from my initial urge to cut off from Neil as he cried and instead was able to think that to look at him as he wept was not intrusive or inappropriate, but that it might be, in fact, exactly what he needed, as it would be part of my capacity to still care, to still stay connected with and sensitive to him, in the midst of such distress. I was able to unclench my own fists and jaw muscles, go on with my slow, deep breaths, and continue to watch Neil. After about a minute, his sobs began to slow and then subside. He plucked his glasses off with the hand that was not in front of his face, put them on the low table at his side and reached inside his jeans for a large, ironed, cloth handkerchief. He wiped his face with this. Then he spoke into the palm of the hand covering his face. His voice was a little muffled, but I could hear him.

> NEIL: Last year I got a promotion. And my boss ... He was really pleased with my work and he said he was going to send me to this important weekend conference.

Neil put the hand in front of his face cautiously down at this point and glanced at the glass of water near him. He took it and drank all the water in a few huge gulps, and then sighed deeply. The water and the sigh both seemed to help him feel a little more together, and he was able to continue speaking without needing to actually cover his face with his hand. He lent forward instead, clasped both hands together and told the story of his assault to the floor between us.

The following account weaves in some of the details that Neil included later in subsequent sessions.

He was the only child of parents who were both secondary school teachers, and fairly quiet, steady people. They had given Neil a calm, stable home and upbringing, which had been secure, but had not had much excitement or passion in it, nor much chance to mix socially with people his own age. He had been somewhat shy and unassuming at school, and found the beginning of each new academic year difficult, as he seemed to be a target for bullying each time a new year started. His brightness, especially at maths and sciences, saved him from being very low status at school, and he did well academically in all his subjects. He left to do an economics degree, and then did an MBA at an American university. Throughout his twenties he felt he was increasingly finding his feet and enjoying life. When he came back from America he got a well-paid job in IT straightaway, and, with his parents' help, bought a studio flat in what was then a rather run-down part of London, but which, over the following few years, became fashionably cool.

Neil looked for an even better job and got one. He was then headhunted by his current boss, and began work at the job he was in when he came to see me. All was going well for him, apart from the fact that he was rather at a loose end at evenings and weekends. He had never been very socially outgoing, and this, added to the fact that he had been so focused on his career for a number of years, meant that he didn't have much of a network of friends, or many opportunities to meet people of his own age, outside his work environment. He was straight and tended to find it hard to strike up conversations with women he found attractive. He'd had a couple of flings over the last few years, but nothing that turned into anything more.

In a later session, when he was telling me about some of his background, he fixed me with an intense look that I found almost accusatory.

NEIL: I'm not gay, you know.
SARAH: Right.
NEIL: It's just that I'm … not great at asking women out.
SARAH: Yes. I can understand that.

On the whole, however, Neil felt quite happy. He loved his flat and his job. He splashed out on the little sporty Audi that was his pride and joy. He had a plan to save some money and then take six months out, in a few years' time, to travel around Australia. Maybe there he would bump into his soulmate.

On the day that his boss told him about sending him to a weekend conference, Neil had felt particularly buoyed up and happy; he could tell this was a real vote of confidence in him from his managers and he was determined to ensure that this would be justified.

NEIL: The hotel where the conference was, was in Kent. A really nice place, out in the countryside.

When he arrived on the Friday afternoon, Neil was suddenly struck with a bit of anxiety, rather as he had used to feel whenever a new school year began. Once he had checked in and received his delegate badge and pack, and joined the throng of people waiting around in the tea/coffee and registration area, he began to feel a bit shy. It was, therefore, a pleasant surprise and relief when a man about his own age approached him and began to chat. The man introduced himself as Dave and asked Neil about his journey, what car he drove, where he was based, and before he knew it, Neil was talking with Dave as if they were old friends. Dave was the sort of person

Neil usually found rather intimidating: self-assured, stylish, taller than average, muscular, and conventionally rather handsome. But in this setting, Neil found that he and Dave seemed to hit it off and become friendly quite quickly. After the first seminar in the early evening, they continued chatting over supper and then in the hotel bar afterwards. They were joined by a few others, and Neil spent an enjoyable few hours drinking and socialising with a half dozen or so other young men who gathered around Dave and himself. Dave was funny and loud and confident, and he told stories that made everyone laugh about his work, his girlfriend, the golf club he was a member of. Neil liked Dave, and felt flattered at being singled out by him. He remembered the little surge of pride and pleasure he felt at one point in the evening when, after three or four pints, Dave gave Neil's shoulder a playful punch and announced, 'Top man, Neil! We should have a round of golf, sometime!'

Eventually the others in the group finished their drinks and headed back to their rooms. Dave suggested one last drink when Neil announced he too ought to turn in, as he wanted to be ready for the next day with its full schedule of seminars and presentations. They both had a last pint in the bar, and then headed for the lift. Dave had asked, 'What floor are you on, mate?' and when Neil had told him, had said, 'Coincidence! Same as me.' They rode the lift together, and walked along the corridor until they reached the door of Neil's room. Neil had said 'This is me. See you tomorrow.'

Dave had said, 'Shall we be devils and have a night cap before we get our beauty sleep?'

At this point in the story, Neil made a fist with one hand and pressed it hard against his forehead.

> NEIL: I knew I should say 'no'. I was definitely drunk. I could tell, once we were in the lift, I'd had more than I realised when we were in the bar. And I had this … this feeling deep down, as soon as he said that, like … I suddenly thought that maybe his room wasn't on this floor really, that he'd just said that to come along to my room and that … something wasn't right. But I ignored it. Why! Why didn't I listen to that feeling! Why did I let him in?

Neil and Dave went into Neil's room and Dave went to the mini bar and got out a small bottle of vodka and one of whisky. He asked Neil which one he preferred and when Neil said 'whisky', Dave suddenly threw the little whisky bottle at him, quite hard. When Neil dropped it, Dave laughed long and hard and called him 'butterfingers'. Somehow the friendly, companionable feeling that Neil had been enjoying between them seemed to be dissipating and turning somewhat sour. As they drank, Dave speculated as to whether or not they would be able to access pornography on the room's television set. Neil did not want to watch porn, he wanted to go to bed and get some sleep. He protested slightly but Dave was already flicking through the different channels.

Again, Neil reproached himself as he recounted the events that led up to his attack.

NEIL: Why didn't I just say, 'No. Turn it off. If you want to watch porn, go to your room and watch it!'?

A few sessions later, once we had more of an alliance, I challenged some of his self-blame. I pointed out, for instance, that having had a lot of alcohol would have impaired his capacity to think and speak clearly and assertively, and that it was likely Dave had counted on this fact. But challenges to Neil's narrative were not for this session. When he first told his story, I simply listened.

Dave turned the TV off and, at this point, Neil's memory of precisely what happened and in what order became hazy.

NEIL: I think I said something like, 'Oh, look, mate. I'm really quite pissed, and I've got to get to bed', meaning, you know, that I needed to get to bed to go to sleep. And he … it seemed like he just flipped and he got this really nasty look on his face and said something like, 'You dirty fucker. Who do you think you are – talking to me like that?' And I was … I didn't really get what he was so annoyed about. I just said something like, 'Don't misunderstand me – Sorry. I'm just drunk and tired and need to go to bed.' And he said …

Neil's voice became higher, more breathy and broken, as he described what happened next.

All of a sudden Dave had become unmistakably aggressive. He walked over to Neil and stood right in front of him, with his face close to Neil's and jabbed him sharply in the chest, saying, 'What the fuck are you suggesting?' When Dave stood so close, Neil became very aware of how much taller and more powerfully built Dave was than he. His own drunken state was making it hard to think straight or read the situation for his own safety.

When Dave suddenly punched him hard in the stomach, it seemed to come out of nowhere and utterly disorientated Neil. He doubled over in pain, feeling instantly dreadfully winded and nauseous. He was vaguely aware that Dave seemed to be undoing his own trousers but couldn't quite believe he would be doing such an odd thing. The next thing he knew, Dave had shoved him face down on the bed, put a knee on Neil's back and was roughly undoing Neil's trousers.

When Dave took his knee off Neil's back, he then took hold of the back of Neil's neck in a powerful grip, pinning his head flat to the bed. Dave then yanked down Neil's underwear and pushed his erect penis between Neil's buttocks, and rubbed it vigorously there for some time, all the while speaking in a frightening and abusive way to Neil, saying things like, 'This is what all you benders like, isn't – a real man to give you a seeing to? I'm not going to do it right up the arse the way you're gagging for, though. I don't want to take some dirty poofters' disease home to my missus.'

Neil lay and endured it. He closed his eyes and pretended to be asleep. He remembered thinking that perhaps if Dave thought he had passed out or gone into a drunken sleep, he would leave him alone quicker and the torment would be over sooner. After some time, Neil could not tell how long it was, Dave ejaculated onto Neil's back and buttocks. Neil heard sounds of Dave moving away, a rustling of tissues being taken from a box and of Dave doing his trousers back up.

Neil recounted every word that Dave then said to him, as if they were something he had bitterly learned off by heart and repeated often in his memory.

> NEIL: Then he said, 'All right there. Neil? Enjoyed that did you? Now you can go back to all your shirt-lifter pals and tell them you did it with a real man.'

Neil had continued to lie motionless with eyes closed.

Suddenly he became aware that Dave was standing very close to the bed again; he could smell Dave's aftershave as he bent down to put his face very close to Neil's and whispered in his ear. 'I know you're listening, you soppy twat. If you ever breathe a word of this to anyone, I'll have your bollocks for breakfast. You get me?'

He gave Neil a vicious dig in the shoulder, and then added in a jeering tone, 'Cheerio, then, bro. Nice shagging you!' He laughed and smacked Neil hard on the backside before walking away from the bed.

Neil heard some footsteps and then the sound of the door to his hotel room open and close. He continued to lie still and silent. He had a dreadful fear that Dave was continuing to torment him – that he was tricking Neil and making him believe Dave had left, but was in fact still in the room, and would renew the humiliation the moment Neil made a move. He didn't know how long he lay there, with all his senses straining to try and detect if Dave really had gone or not. Eventually, he risked just turning his head slightly to one side to breathe a little more easily. Nothing. He raised one hand to bring it to his face. Still nothing. He began to believe Dave had indeed left the room.

Suddenly the terrifying thought came to him that Dave had gone, but if the door was unlocked he could be back at any moment. He tried to get off the bed to go to the door and lock it, but found that his legs had no strength in them, and his knees simply buckled. He crawled on his hand and knees, with his trousers still around his ankles, across the floor to the door and with trembling hands that couldn't move fast enough, he locked it. He had then sat by the door, on the floor, for a few moments, waiting until some strength returned to his knees before he made his way to the bathroom. He threw up violently in the sink, turned the shower on to its hottest setting, undressed, got in and stood in the water for a long time. Even though he was standing in water that was practically scalding, he found that he soon began to shake uncontrollably and could not stop for some time.

He remembered knocking his forehead repeatedly against the shower cubicle tiles, clenching his teeth and whispering 'Why, why, why, why, why, why'. Why had he let Dave into his room? He had never regretted any-thing more in his entire life. He found himself replaying what had just happened, and each moment of humiliation felt as if it was scorching itself more and more deeply into his memory, becoming more and more of a solid, ghastly reality. He got out, dried himself, put on his pyjamas, got into the bed and lay there wide awake until the beginnings of daylight showed through the curtains.

He was then faced with a grotesque dilemma: leave the conference immediately and protect himself from having any kind of further interaction with Dave, but then have to explain his absence to his boss; or stay at the conference and run the risk of having to encounter Dave somewhere. At no point did Neil ever consider ever speaking a word of what had happened to anyone, or reporting what had happened to the police or hotel staff.

His loyalty to his boss and job won out, and Neil made himself get up, get dressed and go down to the first seminar. He passed the day in what could be called a 'fugue state' – one of almost total dissociation that still allows the dissociated person to perform usual day-to-day functions, apparently normally, with almost no consciousness on their part, as if they are sleepwalking. He could not quite remember how he got through the day or what happened in it. He could not even remember if he ever saw Dave during that day or not. He did remember the last part of his car journey home, in the evening of that day, once he was nearing his home, and his dissociated state began to lift.

But once Neil was back in his own flat, he found that something had radically shifted in his sense of himself and of the world. He no longer felt safe. The attack continued to haunt and affect him. He described symptoms that are common in post-traumatic stress disorder. He became hypervigilant, and would start at the slightest sound. He also became compelled to check that his front door was secure many times over, whenever he was in his flat alone. He found he had no appetite and yet grazed continually on foods that provide a short burst of comfort – those high in salt, sugar, fats and carbohydrates. He had distressing intrusive thoughts, and flashback-type images would come unbidden into his mind throughout the day, of Dave's face, his voice, the smell of his aftershave, the feeling of being in Dave's power, and the annihilating sense that went with this of being utterly demeaned and humiliated.

A day spent at work would not be so bad, as he was able to lose himself in intense busyness, tasks and problem-solving. The worst times were those he spent alone in his flat. Neil began to suffer from insomnia, and found that when he went to bed he would lie for many hours, unable to stop thinking about the events of that dreadful evening. Once he was in bed, he would feel eaten up by intense shame and regret, mixed with a murderous hatred for Dave and an unbearable sense of his own powerlessness to do anything about what had happened. To try and deal with the ghastly feelings that he felt burning around inside him more or less constantly, Neil began to drink alcohol more heavily than usual, when he was at home. He found that alcohol was the only thing that took the edge off the intolerable misery which he found was waiting for him, as soon as his front door closed. He began to drink a particularly large amount just before he went to bed, to try and ensure he could blot things out, for at least a short while, in order to try and fall asleep and have a few hours' respite from his inner torment.

In our first session, after he had recounted what had happened, and given me a flavour of what his life now felt like, he paused. There was a long silence. Then he said in a very low, very quiet voice, 'I wish he had killed me that night. I would honestly rather he had attacked me and killed me. Then at least I'd be dead, and this would be over. I remember realising in that room, in bed, that night: "My life is over now. My life is ruined now. This will never have not happened to me. It's over – the life I had." And there's times now that I just wish I was dead.'

There was a silence once he had finished speaking that seemed sombre. Fittingly, the weather outside had been changing gradually as he had been telling his story. Heavy clouds had rolled across the sun and the light coming through the windows into the room had waned and become a watery grey. I was acutely aware of the immense harm that had been done to Neil and to his sense of self, and also of the stringent time restraints we had in order to deal with some of the effects of that damage.

> SARAH: You've been through such a terrible experience. It sounds just so shocking and overwhelming to have been attacked in this dreadful way. I see that it took a great deal of courage to speak about it here.
>
> NEIL: [Frowning] I don't know about courage. More like, it just came out.

There was a long silence. To begin with, Neil continued to look down. Although he had apparently rejected my naming the courage that he had shown, I wondered whether my comment had gone in, under the radar, which might be playing a part in him feeling a little less collapsed, because after some moments he sat back, and took some deeper breaths, his spine straightened somewhat, his shoulders dropped a fraction, and he lifted his head and looked me in the face. I looked back at him, wanting my expression to be one in which he could read that, although it had been shocking to hear of Dave's cruelly aggressive behaviour and the awful consequences for Neil, I wanted to meet his gaze and see beyond the horror of what had happened, in order to meet someone who was more than only the survivor of abuse. We held each other's gaze for a few moments before he dropped his eyes once more.

> SARAH: I'd like to ask how you are feeling – now that you've been able to tell me about all you endured, and have been going through ever since?
>
> NEIL: [Shrugging] I don't know. Nothing. I … It's …What good's it going to do, anyway – talking about it all? I mean … I can't …
> [He sighed.]

NEIL: The only thing that would help is if someone could make it never have happened. But that's not possible. So. I ... What's the point?

SARAH: No, that's right. There's no way to make it so that this never happened. [Pause.] And that's so hard to bear.

There was a silence, during which Neil turned his face slightly to one side and I saw some tears trickle down his face. I felt encouraged that he did not seem to need to hide his face as he wept, to the same extent that he had when he had bowed his head or completely covered his face with a handkerchief.

SARAH: It's so tough. And counselling can't magic the horror away. But it *could* help with giving you some more tools to deal with the dreadful fact of it having happened.

[Neil wiped his face and looked up.]

SARAH: I mean, you have found some coping tools already – working harder, and drinking more. But those strategies tend to bring their own difficulties in the long run.

[Neil gave a very tiny, tight lipped smile and raised his eyebrows a fraction in a wry acknowledgement.]

NEIL: You could say that.

SARAH: I am very glad that you were able to tell me the reason behind your using a lot of alcohol since the attack. [Pause.] I am struck by the fact that you don't seem to have told anyone else about the underlying reason for your drinking ...

[Neil broke in angrily at this point.]

NEIL: Do *not* tell me that I ought to report this guy! There is *no way* I'm going to put myself through that. I'm not a complete mug. I've seen enough police shows to know what that would be like. I am not going sit in some police station and be told it's his word against mine, and get dragged through the mud all over again. Forget it!

SARAH: Right. I hear that the thought of reporting Dave to the police makes you feel very angry and uncomfortable. Perhaps it would be helpful to know that my position is that I will support you in whatever decision you make around reporting or not reporting.

[Neil grunted an acknowledgement.]

NEIL: Right. OK. Well. Now you know.

[There was a silence again.]

NEIL: So if you're not going to give me advice, what *are* you going to do?

By now I had formed an impression of Neil as someone who would be most receptive, to begin with, to the practical, solution-focused type of support that sessions could offer. This, added to the fact that we had, at the most, nine more appointments, and perhaps even less, meant that I decided that the most useful tack to take for us would be a focus on basic damage limitation, as far as the trauma of his recent violation was concerned.

> SARAH: Well, I think we could look at ways to help your body process a bit more of what happened to you when Dave behaved in such a shocking and abusive way to you. It sounds like some of that experience had to go into a sort of deep freeze, to get you through the next night and day. I imagine some of his attack on you has remained pretty much frozen. But every now and then, bits of it get suddenly defrosted, so it feels almost as if it's all still happening. That might be why you are getting the post-traumatic shock symptoms you have described.
>
> NEIL: Is that what you think? That I've got that? Post-traumatic shock-whatsit?
>
> SARAH: Yes. I would say so. The horrible symptoms are there: hypervigilance, the intrusive thoughts, the insomnia. They're all typical of someone attempting to process and digest something catastrophic, but the original event was so shocking and overwhelming, that the attempts just don't really work and the feelings simply go round and round, without changing.
>
> NEIL: And counselling can help with that?
>
> SARAH: In my experience – yes.

I began to experience a subtle change in the way Neil was behaving: he was looking directly at me more, his body posture seemed a little more relaxed without actually being collapsed, his facial expressions were softer and more open. I imagined that he was tentatively allowing himself some hope that I might know what I was talking about, that I might be able to offer him some helpful strategies, and that being in the session was not only something that was required by his boss, but could possibly be of benefit to him.

We spent the rest of the session looking at some simple techniques that Neil could take away with him and begin putting in place, that would help with two essential things: first, with giving more of a conscious place to his feelings, so that they did not have to stay stuck in the deep freeze; and second, with providing a structure for containing those feelings so that he could dip in and out of them, and they would not become so overwhelming as they unfroze.

I showed him how to get into a rhythm of breathing, where he inhaled for a count of five, held it for three, and then breathed out for a count of seven, which helps to imitate the breathing rhythm of someone in a calm relaxed state, to encourage the healthier regulation of his 'on/off' system, and allow Neil to, in effect, coax his body down from being permanently on high alert.

I talked him through a way of combating dissociation and fostering a greater sense of being safe and sure that he was really 'in' his own body, which entailed 'mapping' his own body whenever he had a warm shower or bath, by simply putting his own hands firmly on parts of his body and naming them: *this is my right ankle, this is my left calf, this is my right bicep,* etc. I also let him know that shaking and crying were both very normal ways that the mammalian body deals with having been through something enormously stressful, and that to shake or cry in the shower was not a bad or foolish thing, but was, rather, a very useful and healthy way of recovering from stress.

Lastly, I suggested he get hold of a blank notebook and begin keeping a daily record of his feelings, at certain points throughout the day, and to include in his notes how much he was drinking, at what times and, in particular, what his feelings and thoughts were just before and just after he took each alcoholic drink.

Having some concrete suggestions of things he could be proactive with and focus on actually doing seemed to give Neil a further boost. By the time we came to the last ten minutes of the session, he was much more engaged, less rigidly defended, and had decided that he would like to come back and have the remaining five sessions. As we walked to the front door, the contrast between the crackly frostiness between us when he had arrived, and the softer, warmer feeling between us as he left was striking. He turned on the doorstep and held out a hand which, when I shook it, surprised me by being both very warm and very firm. We shook hands and Neil gave me a hint of a smile as he said, 'I shall see you next week, then.'

SARAH: You will indeed.

In the following two sessions we spent a lot of time making space to review Neil's week, and allowing him to fill me in on the minutiae of how each day had gone for him, which was helped by Neil referring to his journal in the session. He was surprised to find how comforting it had been to simply have a structure in place that required him to notice and make a note of his thoughts and feelings, in the belief that someone else would be interested to hear about both. He had tried to do some of the calming breathing every day, and found that when he was driving in to work was a good time for this. He hadn't 'got on' with the body mapping, finding it 'just a bit too weird'. So we refined this and he found that the idea of just looking at parts of his body and saying, silently, to himself 'This is my right hand', etc. felt more manageable, and still seemed to have a calming, helpful effect.

Once we had more of a working alliance and Neil was beginning to feel more hopeful about finding ways to process his traumatic attack, and to calm himself when alone, I wanted to also open up the area of Neil's family background and childhood experiences, to make some links between how he had been trying to cope with his dreadful attack, and how he had been taught to cope with difficulty as a child. Neil was unreceptive to my gentle invitations to open up the subject of his childhood. As far he could see, his problems were wholly to do with Dave's attack on him and there was no earthly reason to look at anything else. I, however, wondered about the issue of Neil's difficulty in feeling he deserved support with his awful pain and shame; also his lack of confidence and his wish to always fit in and please others, which was often at such a cost to himself. It sounded like a powerful negative pattern in his life, and I thought it may even have played a part in being singled out and targeted for such gross bullying by Dave in the first instance.

In the third session I asked Neil if he would be able to give me a snapshot of the important people in his life, and to do so by using some of the small objects and figures I kept in the consulting space. He agreed but started to look vaguely uneasy when I brought out a wooden box in which I kept some toy figures, ornaments, stones, shells and so on. I invited him to choose one object for each important person in his childhood. He leaned forward in his chair to shoot a brief glance into the box. He quickly selected three large stones. He put these down on to the carpet between us, and then sat back.

We established that the three stones stood for his mother, father and his maternal grandmother, to whom he had been very close as a boy.

He explained that this grandmother had looked after him every week, from the time he was about two until he started at school, once his mother was back at her teaching job. And once he started school, his grandmother was the person who collected him every weekday. Throughout his whole time in primary school, she had picked him up from school and taken him back to her house. He had stayed with her there for a few hours, until he went home with his parents at five o'clock. She was now very elderly and frail, and lived in a care home many miles from London, and Neil did not see much of her any more.

When I asked him to include himself and also choose an object that stood for him, he leant forward again, and, in a perfunctory way, selected a small ball of woollen thread, that was a soft greyish blue, and dropped this near the stones. He did all this with the air of a man who is humouring someone and doing something that they think is a waste of time, in order to be polite. However, the more I invited Neil to look at how the objects that he had chosen might reveal qualities about the people they stood for, the more our exchanges opened up and deepened a connection to Neil's childhood experiences and some important memories.

I invited Neil to tell me first about what struck him about the large, smooth, pale stone that he had chosen to represent his grandmother. He talked about the patch of quartz crystals on its surface, and how this had made him think of his nan. He talked about the sparkly brooches she often wore on the lapels of her jackets and coats, and how her hair had also seemed magically silvery to him when he was little. He described being in her house when he had been small, and the special little glass and china ornaments she had kept in a lighted cabinet which had glittered and shone and been enchanting to his young eyes.

One memory led to another and Neil talked more and more. He talked about his time spent with Nan; about what they did together; what their relationship had meant to him; how she made sure she always had the foods he liked, ready in her kitchen for him; and how her little mongrel dog, Topsy, would patiently let Neil march his toy people up and down her back when he played with his Lego on the floor. Topsy would also do tricks like offer a paw or play dead for Neil, and best of all, cuddle up next to him on the sofa when he watched children's television programmes, while Nan was making him his tea in the kitchen, to eat before he went home to his parents. He teared up at one point when he recalled how upset she had been when she had allowed him to get some of her precious china ornaments out to play with and he had accidentally snapped off one of the antlers of a little porcelain deer.

NEIL: She didn't get cross, but I could tell she was heartbroken. I felt terrible, but I couldn't say anything. And then, she would always say, when she got them out after that, for me, 'Will you please be *very* careful, because we know what happened last time ...' and I couldn't really enjoy playing with them after that. [He sighed.]

We turned our attention to the other objects he had chosen, and they each unlocked more about Neil's childhood memories and some of the family dynamics he had been at the affect of, as he was growing up.

He had chosen a large, heavy reddish stone, that was full of iron ore, to represent his father. As he talked about why the stone might have reminded him of his dad, a picture emerged of a solid, softly spoken and patient man who had worked hard as a teacher and head of chemistry in the same secondary school that Neil attended as a pupil. Neil remembered an incident involving his father that seemed to sum up the emotional repression that ran like a thread through Neil's upbringing. When he was around 16, he had asked to borrow his father's camera to take photos for a school project, and had somehow damaged it. When he told his father about this mishap, Neil was stricken by the disappointment and dismay his father obviously felt, which was clear to see on his face, even though he said nothing.

> NEIL: I hated seeing that look on his face. It was worse than having to pay for the camera to get repaired out of my allowance, even though that meant I was broke for two months after that. He never lent it to me again. Well … I never asked again.

I noted that two key memories Neil had shared were to do with his having accidentally broken something and the acute feelings of shame and regret that he had been left with, as a consequence, and the painful disturbance his mistake had brought about in the connection between himself and two of his important attachment figures.

The stone that Neil had chosen to represent his mother was a kind of slate, with smooth flat planes and sharp edges. As Neil described what struck him about this stone's appearance, he went on to make links between the stone he had picked to represent his mother, albeit in such a desultory way, and the resonances his choice had with some qualities he saw in her.

> NEIL: She's like everyone's idea of a perfect mum, really. She's a great cook. She does all the decorating and gardening. She likes everything 'just so'. She's a music teacher – the violin. And she's very … precise. She likes her hospital corners, does Mum. Know what I mean?
>
> SARAH: House proud?
>
> NEIL: Oh yeah. Everything spick and span. And she runs a local kids choir. [Pause.] And she volunteers once a week for the Samaritans.

SARAH: Gosh.

NEIL: Yeah. She was a busy lady all the time I was growing up.

Neil said less about the ball of wool he had chosen to represent himself than he did about the other three objects. That in itself seemed symbolic of how he tended to put himself and his needs last in many situations. He did mention feeling that there was something soft about the ball of wool that reflected the fact that he felt there was something soft about himself, and that he did not like this quality, feeling it made him somehow 'less than' other men who would probably be able to see themselves as 'tough' or 'hard'.

The more Neil talked and reminisced and filled me in, the more I was seeing a picture of a quiet, sensitive little boy, growing up with adults who liked things to be neat and ordered, and who expected people to be polite and punctual and reliable and hard-working, in the same way that they were. It seemed to me that Neil had loved these adults and felt loved by them and that he had intuited that if he also displayed the qualities that they held dear and embodied, he would gain their approval and esteem. But he also learned that if he fell short, and was not tidy and careful and considerate, they would be bitterly disappointed and displeased with him. So he learned to try and avoid failures and mess-ups and muddle at all costs.

However, once he reached adolescence, he bumped up against the limits of what being quiet, polite and self-effacing could get him in the world. Whenever what was needed was for him to be a little more potent, a little more energised and to stand up more definitively for his own needs and wellbeing, Neil tended to flounder. He was, on the whole, not good at sticking up for himself, and this had been dreadfully highlighted by Dave's outrageous exploitation of his mild manner and lack of self-confidence. I judged that what might be needed in our remaining time was to find something that would both help Neil with continuing to find ways to gradually incorporate the horror of what had happened to him as a bearable reality, and to practise some of the skills he would need if he was going to be able to be more assertive, and a little more 'tough', on occasion, when appropriate.

In our fourth session I asked him how he would feel about working in an imaginative way with the scene of his traumatic attack, with a view to reworking it so that it did not remain in his mind as a purely toxic and humiliating encounter, but one that could be altered and modified in his mind's eye. That way, it could begin to lose some of its hold on him because of the feelings of unbearable shame and powerlessness that it currently conjured up whenever he thought of it.

My aim was to gently work with the feelings that had been so overwhelming at the time that they had to go 'on hold' in the deep freeze of Neil's being, occasionally flooding him when they thawed out every now and then, and washed him away in an internal agony. I hoped he could be supported in gradually experiencing little bits of what had to go into the deep freeze, without defrosting the entire mass of horror and terror for his life, as long as it was within what Ogden *et al.* (2006) describe as: 'the relational context under which the client can safely contact, describe and eventually regulate their inner experience'.

We spent some time building up his connection to a scene he identified as one that made him feel happy and safe when he thought of it. This was related to a memory he had of sitting with Nan on the sofa at her house, watching a film together, eating bacon and eggs from trays on their laps, while Topsy snoozed on the floor by Neil's feet.

Once we had anchored this scene as a resource for Neil to recall and reconnect to if he began to feel too stressed during the replay, I invited him to imagine the hotel room where he had been attacked. I got him to describe the room to me as if he was currently in it – what he could see, hear, smell in the moment. Then I invited him to shift back to imagining his happy, secure scene once more, and to describe the smells, sights and sounds there too. Once he had had the experience of shifting his focus from one to the other, so that they were both places he knew that he could vividly imagine, and he had had the experience of knowing he could choose to imaginatively inhabit one or the other, I suggested that we begin the replay.

I emphasised again, just before we began the replay, that he could stop imagining the hotel room at any point during the exercise, and instead come back to the room with me, or imagine that he was in his nan's sitting room – whichever he preferred. I also explained again that we were going to work with reimagining the scene of his trauma, not in order for him to relive it, but to have the opportunity for him to imaginatively *reshape* the scene so that it could play out in a way that would help him feel he could regain some power and control whenever he thought of that room, or of Dave and their encounter. To that end, I suggested that we keep speaking about what he was seeing in his mind's eye in the present: that way, we were not describing and working with what *had* happened; instead, we were describing and working with what was happening in the here and now, as he had the chance to imagine himself doing and saying whatever he needed to do, in order to look after himself. I invited to him close his eyes, but to open them at any time he felt he wanted to, and also to let me know if wanted to pause or stop the process at any point.

> SARAH: So. Let's start to play the scene through, with the chance to make things go differently. Can you imagine you are standing in the hotel room now?
>
> NEIL: Mmm.
>
> SARAH: OK. Good. I invite you to imagine that Dave is there with you. It is around the time that he first does something that you feel really clear is not OK. When is that?
>
> NEIL: When he threw the whisky at me.
>
> SARAH: OK. So now you have the chance to respond to him when he does that, in a way that lets him know that this is not OK for you.
>
> NEIL: Mmm.
>
> SARAH: Can you picture him throwing it?
>
> NEIL: [Flinching ever so slightly, and in a dubious tone of voice] Mmm.
>
> SARAH: And, knowing you have every right to stick up for yourself, can you imagine what you might say to let him know that this was not OK?
>
> NEIL: I … I dunno. I should have said …
>
> SARAH: I would keep it in the present. You say to him … ?
>
> NEIL: I say … Uh … I don't know. I …

I decided to add a little extra support here, and give an example, to help model for Neil what a statement that was more assertive could sound like.

> SARAH: Could it be something like … 'Hey! Don't just chuck it straight at me!'?
>
> NEIL: [With a renewed energy in his voice] Yeah. And … maybe … 'Excuse me! What … what … Why the hell did you do that?'
>
> SARAH: Good! And I've got a feeling that statements are going to be more powerful than questions for now. What other statement might you make to Dave?
>
> NEIL: I … Just … 'I don't want any more to drink right now, actually. I'd like you to go.'
>
> SARAH: Great. That's so clear and direct. But let's imagine he doesn't go. OK to work with that?
>
> [Neil cleared his throat and sat up straighter.]
>
> NEIL: Yeah.

SARAH: Now he comes over to where you're standing and he's definitely looking aggressive. He says something like 'Who the fuck do you think you are, talking to me like that!' And you can stand up to him now, so you … what do you get to do this time round?

NEIL: I wish I'd said, 'Why don't you …'

SARAH: Keep it in the present.

NEIL: [In a mildly testy tone of voice] 'Why don't you just go away and fuck off.'

SARAH: Right! And if you made that even more forceful – made it a statement?

NEIL: [With a sudden rush of angry energy] 'I didn't ask you in here – you invited yourself. So why don't you just … piss off back to your own room!'

SARAH: Mmm. And notice how you feel as you say this to him.

NEIL: I'm … I … I just feel furious!

SARAH: Right. And now … he looks like he's going to try and punch you in the stomach, so you … ?

NEIL: I … I don't know … I can't …

[Neil's voice faltered and he opened his eyes and looked into my face. He shook his head.]

NEIL: Can I … I just … I would like … something, but it might sound a bit … Can I just see that stone again? The one that reminded me of my nan? I think it would help.

SARAH: Absolutely.

As I looked it out from the box of objects, Neil said, 'Does that sound mad?'

SARAH: Not at all. I think it sounds very sane indeed. The stone stands for a very good thing in your life. That's so helpful to connect to!

[I held out the crystal-coated stone.]

SARAH: Where would you like it?

Neil took it from me, held it tightly in one hand for a moment and then said, 'I'll just keep it here', and placed it on the end of his chair's arm.

NEIL: OK. I'm ready now.

[He closed his eyes again and took a deep breath in.]

NEIL: If he does try to punch me, I'll … Oh, I don't know …

SARAH: OK. Well, I invite you to imagine that he is about to. He's going to try. How do you stop …

NEIL: [Breaking in] I block his fist as it's coming at me, and knock it away. I say, 'Hey! Keep your hands to yourself! Just get away from me!'

SARAH: Yes. You really stand up for yourself again.

NEIL: And I'm making him leave. I'm …

There was a brief pause. Neil's expression changed subtly in the short silence from one of determination to one of being mildly discomfited. He seemed to be struggling internally.

SARAH: You can picture anything you want in order to play the scene so it goes the way you want it to go.

NEIL: I know. I'm pushing him towards the door.

SARAH: OK. What could you tell him as you push him?

NEIL: I …

[Neil's breathing became louder and faster.]

NEIL: [Raising his voice] 'Get out! Get out! Get out! Get out! Get the fuck away from me! Get out!'

[I could see a slight sheen of sweat suddenly break out on his forehead.]

SARAH: And is there a movement your body needs to make as you picture this?

[Neil clenched both hands into fists and then flung both arms straight out in front of him, as if he was repelling a heavy weight. He shouted with renewed vigour, as he did so.]

NEIL: 'Get out! Get out! I'm going to call the police and have you arrested, you disgusting, stupid … bastard!'

SARAH: Yes. And what do you picture now?

NEIL: I've pushed him to the door, and I … I …

[He faltered again. His breathing came in little gasps for a few moments.]

SARAH: What help do you need right now, Neil?

NEIL: I can't get him out of the door! He's fighting back. I need …

SARAH: Help can come in any form. You can have anyone or anything you like to help you in this room. Whose help would you like?

NEIL: I want a wolf. No – a dog, a massive dog. An Alsatian. It's my dog. I call it from the bathroom, and it comes out, growling. And I … 'Right. You have ten seconds to get out before I set my dog on you and get him to rip your bollocks off!'

SARAH: OK. And now?

NEIL: Yes! He's out of the door. And I'm locking it, and I get my phone out to call Reception to tell them I've been assaulted in my room. [Neil's voice cracked as he spoke, and he began trembling slightly.]

SARAH: OK. And your dog?

NEIL: Yes. He's still here, near me. 'Good boy. Good lad. Well done.'

[A tear ran down Neil's cheek and his trembling grew more pronounced.]

SARAH: What a great dog to have. Can you imagine how he feels to the touch?

NEIL: Yes. I'm stroking him. He's come to sit right up close, sitting on my feet.

SARAH: Has he? How's that feel?

NEIL: Warm. Soft. A bit heavy. I can hear his tail thumping on the floor because he's wagging it.

SARAH: Such a good, loyal companion! He's helped keep you safe.

NEIL: I think I want to stop now.

SARAH: Of course. Any time is fine.

[Neil opened his eyes and blew out a huge sigh.]

NEIL: Bloody hell. [He cleared his throat and pushed his glasses up his nose.]

SARAH: Mmm. That was quite a reworking!

NEIL: It was really … real! And really good to make it go another way. Good to make that … [He clenched one hand into a fist and tightened his lips].

SARAH: That … ?

[Neil frowned and smiled at the same time, then picked up the quartz-covered stone from the arm of the chair.]

NEIL: I'm just going to give you this back, to put away.

[He held the stone out to me and I did as he asked. When I sat back and looked at him he finally finished his sentence.]

NEIL: … that stupid, evil *cunt*! [He spoke this last epithet with a force and venom that made it seem as if he was spitting out the word.]

SARAH: Yes.

[There was a moment's pause and then a sheepish smile appeared on his face, and Neil laughed rather uneasily.]

NEIL: I don't really like that word. It's pretty offensive to women, really. I hope it didn't seem … That's why I had to get you to put that stone away, almost like … I had to make sure Nan wouldn't hear me say such a thing.

[He laughed again and shook his head.]

SARAH: Mmm. Maybe we could say that there was something about how you felt which could only be expressed by using a word that is extraordinarily powerful. And not at all nice. But that's what was needed?

NEIL: Yes! Because that's the only thing to call him really. [Pause.] God. I hate him! I really fucking hate him for what he did. I wish he was dead! I'd dance on his fucking grave if he died!

SARAH: I hear that. You'd be glad if he was dead, and you could even *wish* he was dead. I notice that's quite different from wishing *you* were dead. Which you have expressed here.

NEIL: Mmm. [Pause.] I wouldn't actually do anything about either of those, you know? You do know that I'm not going to try and kill myself? Or him?

SARAH: Yes, Neil. I know that.

NEIL: I just wanted to be clear that you didn't think ... [His voice tapered away].

SARAH: Perhaps it's not about something as concrete as you actually wanting to kill Dave or yourself. Maybe you're expressing something that's more to do with two very different responses to being ... under attack.

NEIL: I'm not following you.

SARAH: Well ... Suppose someone breaks into my home and scribbles abusive graffiti on the walls and smashes up my furniture and walks out with some of my valuable possessions. One response would be for me to be furiously angry about that, and maybe I would feel some hatred and rage towards the person who had done it. Another response would be for me to get all filled up with self-hatred and self-blame for ... I don't know ... for not having installed a burglar alarm. And then to wish I was dead.

[Neil gave a short, surprised laugh. Then he frowned.]

NEIL: Is that what you think I've been doing? The second thing?

SARAH: What do you think?

NEIL: Maybe. In a way. Blaming myself when ...

SARAH: When ... ?

NEIL: [In a voice that was suddenly much softer and lower in tone] When there's nothing to blame myself for.

The atmosphere in the room seemed to me to have suddenly changed once Neil had said this. It was paradoxically both lighter, as if there was a clarity suddenly for Neil, which was a relief; but there was also a new heaviness that I could feel in my chest, as if a weight was pressing suddenly on my heart with a dark melancholy. There was a long silence during which I felt unpleasantly at the affect of this oppressive sensation even in the midst of a new clarity, and I wondered what the clarity and the melancholy might mean in relation to Neil's story.

After a pause he spoke, as if to do so was painful, but vital.

NEIL: When I was getting bullied at the start of each year at school, I know that it was … difficult … for my parents. They were teachers at the same school, and … there was a limit to how much they could keep raising with their own colleagues that … the situation wasn't getting dealt with properly. I know they did their best. But … there was a definite feeling at home that …

[Neil's gaze drifted away from my face to the spot on the wall that he had stared at so intently, without ever seeming to truly see it, in our first session.]

NEIL: … they never said so, but it was always as if they were thinking, 'oh, what's he done *this* year that's made everyone gang up on him again? Why can't he …'

[He sighed and looked down.]

SARAH: What did you imagine they wanted of you?

NEIL: I … suppose just … Just be the sort of person that didn't get bullied, somehow.

SARAH: And that sort of person would be … ?

NEIL: I don't know. It wasn't possible! They … I mean, I just was a quiet, shy person, I mean – boy! A shy boy. That's just who I was. That's how they were too, really, deep down. If they'd wanted someone who was a bit of a fighter or something, they'd have had to raise me differently!

SARAH: That sounds like quite an insight. So the message from them was something like, 'Never be rude and pushy, but also make sure you can throw your weight around a bit, if needed'?

NEIL: Yes! But like, I said, that was just not possible. Not for me.

SARAH: So, what if you could let yourself feel that you really had nothing to blame yourself for about getting bullied at school?

NEIL: Well, I don't think I ever actually blamed myself really, deep down. But what hurt me and what I never really wanted to let myself … really admit, was that somehow … I felt like my own parents were kind of blaming me for making life all difficult for *them* when I got bullied. I mean, they were sorry, too, that it was happening to me, and they would never have said it out loud, but … [He sighed deeply] I think they did sort of resent me for … being unhappy at school and it all being so difficult, at the start of each year.

He blinked a few times and returned his gaze to my face. At the same time, I felt the weight in my chest begin to ease. Perhaps I had just had a brief taste of the heartache that Neil had lived with as a boy, when he had felt unsupported and even subtly blamed by his parents, as he tried to cope with the bullying he had endured. It seemed that he had never felt able to admit this heartache to them, or even to himself. But as he felt able to name it in the session, this meant that a dreadful sense of being let down by them could be spoken of, acknowledged, and thereby become not quite so burdensome.

SARAH: I hear that. Another important, but not an easy, insight.

Towards the end of this session, I checked with Neil if he was aware that we were at the fourth of the six initial sessions he had been allocated. He confirmed that he knew this was the case. He also mentioned that he was aware he could ask for a total of ten sessions if he wished to extend the counselling, and I let him know I would be happy to see him if he decided this was what he wanted. We talked about making sure he continued with the things he had been doing to help ground himself, in the coming week, and to continue with his journal.

As he left, he seemed to me to have a different air about him. He walked to the door with something like a firmer step, and as if he felt more OK about the space in the room that he took up.

At the start of the next session he did something that took me by surprise. He sat down and announced with a pleased grin, 'I brought you a present!'

SARAH: Oh?
[He put his hand in his trouser pocket and drew out a squash ball.]
NEIL: I'm donating it to your collection of objects. I thought … if I don't really want to be that fluffy thing any more, and you don't seem to have anything that is halfway between a hard stone and a cuddly kind of ball, then I'd better find something for myself that would be about right. So, I thought this could go in the collection, to be me! I mean, it can be for future people too – the ones who need something a little bit hard, but not too hard.

[He tossed the ball up slightly and caught it again, and then cocked a mischievous eye at me.]

NEIL: Catch?

I smiled back and opened my hands.

He lobbed the squash ball gently at me, and I did manage to catch it. As I did so I felt aware of the way that this was a redemptive re-enactment of a similar activity of throwing and catching, which had passed between Dave and Neil on that awful evening. That had not been pleasantly playful, but had been part of a cruel game that Dave had been playing in order to humiliate Neil. This tossing of an object between two people today, could, I imagined, be feeling very different for Neil now, in the session with me. It was as if throwing and catching could be reinstated as something mutual, fun and that did not involve one or other of a dyad having the upper hand.

I gently squeezed the ball.

SARAH: It's really quite tough, isn't it? But it has some 'give' in it, too. What an interesting donation!

NEIL: Are you allowed to accept things like that? It's not like I'll be seen as trying to bribe you, or anything like that, is it?

SARAH: I'm not seeing it as you trying to bribe me.

A number of thoughts about possible interpretations to do with male potency, sexuality and 'balls' popped into my mind. Although there may have been a place in the session for some kind of unpacking of the possible erotic symbolism of Neil (a straight male client) giving me (his straight female therapist) a ball as a gift, I decided not to foreground any such unpacking. There was not going to be time to helpfully explore various undercurrents of our relationship, and therefore a kind of 'benign neglect', which is needed in short-term work, seemed the wisest way to respond to this area of my countertransference.

Instead I chose to offer another suggestion as to what his gift might represent.

SARAH: I guess there's a way of thinking about it that suggests you've brought something that stands for you, and you want to give it to me to keep, so that a part of you will stay here, even after your sessions are over.

NEIL: Well, funny you should say that, because when you said about there only being two more sessions last week, I thought … that I'm not ready to just leave it at six sessions, really. So … I went back to

my boss and asked for the extra four meetings and they've agreed
that. So it won't just be the ball that's here, for a bit longer, at least.
I'll actually be here in person. Because …

[Here Neil put on the rather breathy, cloying tone used in the voiceover
catchphrase for a famous cosmetics company's commercial.]

NEIL: … *because I'm worth it.*

I gave a surprised smile and short laugh at his accurate imitation, and he
laughed too. I noted the contrast between the small, rather sour smile that
Neil had worn after he had imitated a television advertisement in our first
meeting, and the softer, more good-humoured expression he wore this time,
as he made his ironic and slightly self-deprecating joke.

Throughout our remaining sessions Neil continued to extend his capacity to be a bit kinder and softer with himself, whilst being able to be a bit
firmer and more assertive with others when needed. He decided he would
cut back slightly on his working hours once he had finished a particular
project he was working on. He booked himself some holiday. He also told
his mother he would like to come up with her the next time she went to visit
her mother, which seemed to have both delighted and astonished her. Neil
and his mother had not been close in the last few years, and he was beginning to realise it was partly because he did feel some hurt and resentment
about the way she had dealt with his being bullied, and how she had seemed
to have time for everyone else, except him, when he had been a teenager.
He talked about the fact that driving his mother to visit his nan would be
an opportunity to have a talk with her about some of what he had been left
with, emotionally, as a consequence of this, and mend some bridges.

He was especially pleased to tell me, one week, about an incident in a
coffee shop when someone at the table next to him (a rather loud, brash,
confident young man, from Neil's description) had irritated Neil by leaving
his mobile phone on the table with its volume on high, so that its jokey
ringtones and text alerts blared out continually while Neil was on his lunch
break, trying to read the paper and enjoy a sandwich and drink. After about
ten minutes of pings and whistles and Samba dance riffs, Neil had lent over
and asked the other man if he could please turn his phone on to 'silent', to
prevent it from disturbing others sitting nearby, which the man had immediately done. He had even apologised to Neil for the disruption.

NEIL: I would never have done that, before.

SARAH: Wouldn't you?

NEIL: No. I'd have just … fumed and simmered in private.

SARAH: Right. But this time, you felt more able to stand up for yourself?

NEIL: I suppose that's what you could say. Yes.

By the time we came to our tenth and final session, it was clear that Neil was in a much better state than when he had first arrived. We talked for a while about this, as we looked back over the sessions and how he had experienced the ten-week process.

NEIL: It *has* helped. But it's hard to say how, exactly.

SARAH: Hmm. Maybe there's something about being listened to by someone else that helps us listen properly to ourselves.

NEIL: [With a slightly provocative smile] Huh! That's it? That's the secret of counselling?

SARAH: [Returning the smile] Well, that's a lot!

[There was a pause.]

SARAH: Have you ever heard the story of the Goose Girl?

NEIL: [Still with a smile] Nope. I've got a feeling I'm about to.

SARAH: It's a bit long to tell it all now. But towards the end, there's a part of the story that seems really relevant to what you've found helpful here. Early in the tale, an innocent princess has been horribly betrayed by her servant. This means she has lost everything, is under a curse and has to live as a servant and goose girl for a king whose son she was actually supposed to marry. Her wicked servant has tricked everyone, taken her place and even persuaded the king to cut off the head of the true princess's faithful talking horse. But another servant has told the king how extraordinarily beautiful and charming, even magical, the new goose girl is. So the king calls for her to come and speak with him at the castle, and he asks her to tell him all about herself. She miserably tells the king that she is under an oath never to tell another person the truth of her story.

Neil appeared utterly absorbed by what I was saying. His eyes had opened slightly wider than usual and he had an unusually calm and open expression that could almost be described as rapt.

SARAH: The king, who was a wily old man, was sure that this young woman was not all she appeared to be, but he did not press her further. He told her that if she could not tell him her truth, that was fair enough, and he would leave her now, but although she could not tell a living soul, she could at least tell her real story to the old iron stove in the corner of the room.

NEIL: And that lifted the curse?

SARAH: Not quite. But it didn't need to. Because the wily old king went to another part of the castle and put his ear against an old pipe that led all the way from the stove to the very top of his palace and this allowed him to hear every word of how she had been betrayed and had her place taken by her treacherous serving maid.

[Neil's eyebrows shot up in delighted surprise.]

SARAH: Once the king had heard the whole story, he called the false servant to him and asked her how she thought that someone who had betrayed their mistress should be punished. When the false servant described the horrible punishment that she thought would be fitting, the king replied, 'So shall it be', and ordered her to be taken out and punished in that very same way. Meanwhile the true princess (or goose girl) was summoned, and the king announced that she would now marry his son.

[Neil tutted, gave a little nod and smiled slightly.]

NEIL: And they all lived happily ever after. [A slight frown appeared on his face and his smile faded.] Which, let's face it, is bollocks.

SARAH: In concrete, literal terms, of course. But if fairy tales don't have to be taken as the literal truth, then they can be understood in another way: as stories that offer us important insight into basic truths about human psychology and emotions. In those terms, perhaps 'happy ever after' simply means something like, 'happy within oneself' or 'on an even keel, and able to live normally again'.

NEIL: Mmm. So … You're saying that *you*, sort of, represent the king in this scenario – and you help me out, because … *I'm* like the goose girl?

SARAH: Umm. No, I don't think so. I don't think I'm the king. I think it's more like – you are both the goose girl *and* the king. And I think the sessions are (or I am, if you like) the iron stove and the pipe. I just need to sit there and receive what one part of you says. And that allows another part of you to hear it properly for the first time. I don't really *do* anything. The counselling is just the means by which the part of you that is The King Of Your Life – a part that can rule and be in charge – gets to hear the true story of another part of you, which is a betrayed and hurt part. Just allowing one part of you to really communicate with another part enables something to happen deep within you: something that is healing and restores equilibrium.

NEIL: [With a pleased laugh] Heh heh. So my company has been paying for me to talk to an old stove!

[We both laughed.]

SARAH: What would your boss make of that?

NEIL: I don't think he would care, as long as it worked.

SARAH: Right. He's probably a wise man!

[Pause.]

NEIL: Do you think the counselling *has* worked?

SARAH: What would you say?

NEIL: I … I'm not feeling as bad as I did when I came the first time. So, maybe. Probably, yes. I'm not drinking as much, for sure.

SARAH: Right. You seem to me less stressed and on edge.

NEIL: Mmm.

SARAH: I would say you have been pretty successful in learning some new ways of coping with your traumatic attack. And you're feeling more able to be … for yourself in the world.

NEIL: Mmm.

[Pause.]

NEIL: But … Do you think that stuff might come back? The insomnia and other PTSD stuff?

SARAH: I think recovery takes time, and you probably need to keep going with some of the calming techniques you've learned to do, for a while. And there could be times the symptoms flare up again, if they get triggered by new stressful things. But in my experience, it is possible to keep bringing ourselves back to an even keel, even if we get upset again, once we've learned how to. We're bound to get knocked off course in life, from time to time, but once we have some good coping strategies, we can more easily and quickly get ourselves back on track once more.

NEIL: Yeah. Good. But …

SARAH: But … ?

NEIL: There's something I wanted to ask. You probably won't say what you think about it, but …

[There was a long pause. Neil looked down.]

NEIL: Do you think he'll do it again?

SARAH: Do you mean Dave?

NEIL: Yeah.

SARAH: Hmm. Can I ask what's behind your question?

NEIL: [Looking up] Well, I want to know your opinion.

SARAH: And if I said, 'No, I don't think he will'?

NEIL: I wouldn't believe you.

SARAH: Ah. And if I said, 'Yes, I think he probably will'?

NEIL: I would believe you.

SARAH: So. It seems like asking me what *I* think is a way of you working out what *you* think about that. And y*ou* seem to think he might attack someone again?

NEIL: [With a heavy sigh] I keep thinking that if I don't report him – don't report what happened – even if they say they can't do anything about it, then he's just ... free. And that ... I mean, that includes being free to ... do it again. And I'd ... I feel like I have that on my conscience somehow.

SARAH: That sounds a heavy thought.

[Neil sighed heavily and shifted restlessly in his seat.]

NEIL: You're not going to tell me what to do, are you?

SARAH: No.

[There was a short silence.]

SARAH: But I would want to support you with whichever choice you make about this. Would you want to spend some time here, thinking with me about the different meanings for you of reporting and of not reporting his attack?

[Neil frowned.]

NEIL: But, but ... there aren't any *meanings* to it! There's ... either I report it, which is the right thing to do; or I don't, which is ... the ... I mean, if I believe that he's out there and he could do it again to someone else, then what is there to explore? I'm a coward if I don't report it. But I ... I can't put myself through it! I just can't.

SARAH: I hear that. [Pause.] I wonder what you would say to a guy who was, say, the same age as you, from the same sort of background, who had been assaulted in the same way that you have, and who was struggling with the same dilemma?

NEIL: What would I say to them? I don't know what I *could* say. I mean ...

SARAH: Would it include something like, 'You really must report the guy who did this to you'?

[Neil pulled a face as if he was being forced to choose between two unpleasant foods.]

NEIL: Well ... Obviously ... no. But ...

SARAH: But … ?

NEIL: I don't see what you're driving at.

SARAH: You seem to find it hard to offer yourself the same understanding that you would be able to offer someone else.

NEIL: Oh I don't know, Sarah! Is it about understanding myself, or is it more to do with being a bloody coward!

SARAH: What's going on inside you as you say that?

[Neil's characteristic flushing began to reappear on his throat, a sign that he was once again getting flooded with some shame.]

NEIL: I … I … I just feel like shit. Because he's won, hasn't he, really? If I don't report him. But … I …

SARAH: And when you say you feel 'like shit' can you describe that? Is it here?

[I placed my hand on my front, around the level of my diaphragm.

Neil mirrored me and placed his hand on his own solar plexus. There was a pause.]

NEIL: Yeah. It's churning. A bit hot … like, I could be sick, but … just, totally … Oh God!

[He lent forward and put his face in his hands and half groaned, half sighed. Then he said something into his hands that I didn't properly hear. There was a silence and he continued to sit forward.]

SARAH: I didn't quite catch what you said, then.

[Neil sighed again, rubbed his face roughly and sat back once more.]

NEIL: I said, 'I'm scared.'

[I nodded.]

SARAH: Ah. I can understand that. [Pause.] Although a reality check could be good here – you're not in any danger here, right now.

NEIL: [Sadly] I know.

[Neil glanced at his wristwatch and then turned around to look at my clock on a nearby shelf.]

NEIL: How long til the end?

SARAH: About 20 minutes.

[Neil sighed again.]

I felt the pressure of time once more in our work. The work in the rest of this last session needed to be more to do with ensuring some seeds were planted at this point, some of which might grow and flourish after Neil left, and which I would be unlikely to ever see flower, than it was to do with trying to reap an immediate harvest.

SARAH: Can I offer a thought?

NEIL: I wish you would.

SARAH: Maybe the question of whether or not you will report Dave is going to be something that you are simply going to have to mull over for a while. How would it be if you just allowed that this can't be fully resolved by us right now?

[Neil continued to look pained.]

NEIL: Mmm.

SARAH: What might help you with that mulling is to at least *imagine* that there isn't a wrong or a right thing to do about it. What if there are only different choices, each with their own pluses and minuses?

[Neil shook his head and said nothing for a while. Then he cleared his throat and clasped his hands together.]

NEIL: Do you ever … I mean are you ever able to come and, sort of accompany someone, if they did decide to go to somewhere … to a police station or a court or something? Do you … can your work include that?

SARAH: I'm very pleased to hear that you are imagining you might need support, if reporting *was* what you decided. The answer is that it couldn't be me offering that support, as your counsellor – it steps too far out of the counselling role. (I think that iron stoves just have to stay being stoves in the castle.) But I have colleagues in this field who can do exactly that. Their role is that of an 'ISVA' – an Independent Sexual Violence Adviser. I can give you the details of how to contact my male ISVA colleague who is based in a specialist service in London that supports any man who has been sexually violated.

NEIL: Right. OK. And they can do things like go with someone to a police station?

SARAH: Absolutely. And they are also happy to meet with someone and talk all that stuff through, and they can still offer support even if someone decides they don't want to or can't report something at present.

NEIL: OK. Great. I'd like to follow that up. Thanks.

[I wrote some contact details down for him and handed him the paper.]

NEIL: Thanks. I … I hope you didn't think it was inappropriate to ask you?

SARAH: Not at all. I'm really glad you thought of reaching out for extra help around this. It makes such a big difference – not feeling alone in it all.

NEIL: Mmm.

There followed a long silence. In the minute or so that elapsed, I noticed a creeping sadness within me at the prospect of saying goodbye, shortly, to Neil. There was something poignant about closing our relationship down just as it was getting going. I thought back to the bitterly angry man, fighting to conceal his hurt, rage and shame behind a mask of contempt and superiority, who had arrived for a first meeting a few months ago. There was a striking contrast between that man, and the one who now sat before me, ten weeks on, who was much warmer, more open, more able to trust another and be spontaneous.

I was reaching around inside me to try and find a way to name and affirm the changes I could see in Neil, when he spoke first.

NEIL: I know we're coming to the end now, so I wanted to thank you for your help. It's been good to … erm … well, I was going to say 'meet you' but that's not quite right. It's been good to have a stove to come and talk to each week!

SARAH: Well, it's been a pleasure to witness one part of you be able to communicate with and come to understand another part so much better.

[Neil gave a short, shy laugh.]

SARAH: I hope those two sides of you will carry on being in touch with each other, once the sessions are over.

NEIL: Yup. I hope so too. I'll try to keep, you know, keep the journal going and the breathing and grounding stuff.

SARAH: Great.

[There was another pause while we looked at each other.]

NEIL: Well. It's weird, in a way, being sorry to leave now. Because obviously, it would have been better really, not to have needed to meet you – better not to have ever needed to talk to an old stove in the first place!

SARAH: Quite.

NEIL: But once I needed to get it all out, it was good to at least have found a stove to do that with!

SARAH: Long may you continue to find old stoves whenever you need them, in the future.

[Neil nodded with a hint of a smile.]

NEIL: I can live with that.

REFERENCES

Allen, G. and Dempsey, N. (2016) House of Commons briefing paper. SN/5G/04334.

Alvarez, A. (2012) *The Thinking Heart: Three Levels of Psychoanalytic Therapy with Disturbed Children.* London: Routledge.

Arnold, M. (1993) *Selected Poems and Prose.* London: Everyman's Library.

Bishop, E. (2004) *Complete Poems.* London: Chatto & Windus.

Bromberg, P.M. (2006) *Awakening the Dreamer: Clinical Journeys.* New Jersey: Analytic Press.

Corbett, A. (2014) *Disabling Perversions: Forensic Psychotherapy with People With Intellectual Disabilities.* London: Karnac.

Corbett, A. (2016) *Psychotherapy with Male Survivors of Sexual Abuse: The Invisible Men.* London: Karnac.

Davies, J.M. and Frawley, M.G. (1994) *Treating the Adult Survivors of Childhood Sexual Abuse: A Psychoanalytic Perspective.* New York: Basic Books.

Freud, S. (1938) *Splitting of the Ego in the Defensive Process.* Standard Edition, Vol. 23. London: Hogarth Press.

Haught, K. (1995) *In the Palm of Your Hand.* Ed. S. Kowat. Thomaston: Tilbury House Publishers.

Hopkins, G.M. (1986) *The Major Works.* Oxford: Oxford University Press.

Jung, C.G. (1963a) *Collected Works of C.G. Jung,* 20 vols. Ed. Herbert Read, Michael Fordham and Gerhard Adler. Trans. R.F.C. Hull. London and Princeton: Routledge and Princeton University Press.

Jung, C.G. (1963b). *Memories, Dreams, Reflections.* London: Routledge.

Kohut, H. (1971) *The Analysis of the Self.* New York: International Universities Press.

Levine, P. (2010) *In an Unspoken Voice.* California: North Atlantic Books.

Levine, P. and Frederick, A. (1997) *Waking the Tiger: Healing Trauma – the Innate Capacity to Transform Overwhelming Experiences.* California: North Atlantic Books.

Meares, R. (2005) *The Metaphor of Play: Origin and Breakdown of Personal Being.* London: Routledge.

Miller, A. (1987) *The Drama of Being a Child.* London: Virago Press.

Mitchell, P. (2017) 'Boys can be victims too'. *Therapy Today 28(8),* 34–7.

Ogden, P., Pain, C., Minton, K. and Fisher, J. (2006) 'Including the body in mainstream psychotherapy for traumatised individuals'. *Psychologist-Psychoanalyst XXV,* 19–24.

Porges, S.W. (1997) 'Emotion: An evolutionary by-product of the neural regulation of the autonomic nervous system'. *Annals of the New York Academy of Sciences 807,* 62–77.

Read, J., Harper, D., Tucker, I. and Kennedy, A. (2017) 'Do adult mental health services identify child abuse and neglect? A systematic review'. *International Journal of Mental Health Nursing 27(1),* 7–19.

Rhodes, J. (2015) *Instrumental.* Edinburgh: Canongate Books.

Rilke, R.M. (2012 [1907]) *Letters to a Young Poet.* Trans. Soren Filipski. London: Snowball Publishing.

Rothschild, B. (2000) *The Body Remembers: The Psychopathology of Trauma and Trauma Treatment.* New York: Norton.

Schore, A.N. (2012) *The Science of the Art of Psychotherapy*. New York: Norton.

Sinason, V. (2010) *Mental Handicap and the Human Condition: An Analytic Approach to Intellectual Disability*. London: Free Association Books.

Stevenson, R.L. (1948 [1885]) *Child's Garden of Verses*. London: Puffin Books.

Tomkins, S. (1963) *Affect/Imagery/Consciousness: Vol 2. The Negative Affects*. New York: Springer.

UKCP and the British Psychoanalytic Council (2015) Public psychotherapy provision. (Online) www.psychotherapy.org.uk/UKCP_Documents/Reports/PublicPscyhotherapyProvision-FINAL-WEBsmallpdf (accessed July 2015).

Van Der Kolk, B. (2014) *The Body Keeps the Score: Mind, Brain and Body in the Transformation of Trauma*. New York: Penguin Books.

Winnicott, D.W. (1956) *Collected Papers*. London: Tavistock Publications.

FURTHER READING

TRAUMA

Chu, J.A. (2011) *Rebuilding Shattered Lives: Treating Complex PTSD and Dissociative Disorders*. New York: Wiley.

Haines, S. and Standing, S. (2016) *Trauma is Really Strange*. London: Singing Dragon/Jessica Kingsley.

Kalsched, D. (1996) *The Inner World of Trauma: Archetypal Defenses of the Personal Spirit*. New York: Routledge.

Kalsched, D. (2013) *Trauma and the Soul: A Psycho-spiritual Approach to Human Development and Its Interruption*. New York: Routledge.

Sanderson, C. (2013) *Counselling Skills for Working With Trauma: Healing From Child Sexual Abuse, Sexual Violence and Domestic Abuse*. London: Jessica Kingsley.

Spring, C. (2016) *Recovery is My Best Revenge: My Experience of Trauma, Abuse and Dissociative Identity Disorder*. Huntingdon: CSP.

UNDERSTANDING THE DEVELOPMENT OF PATHOLOGY AFTER EARLY WOUNDING

Balint, M. (1979) *The Basic Fault: Therapeutic Aspects of Regression*. Hove: Northwestern University Press.

De Zuleta, F. (2006) *From Pain to Violence: The Traumatic Roots of Destructiveness*. London: Whurr Publishers Ltd.

Gerhardt, S. (2004) *Why Love Matters: How Affection Shapes a Baby's Brain*. Hove: Brunner Routledge.

Jacobs, M. (1998) *The Presenting Past*. Buckingham: Open University Press.

Johnson, S.M. (1994) *Character Styles*. New York: Norton.

Klein, J. (1987) *Our Need for Others and its Roots in Infancy*. London: Routledge.

INTERPERSONAL NEUROBIOLOGY

Music, G. (2014) *The Good Life: Wellbeing and the New Science of Altruism, Selfishness and Immorality*. Hove: Routledge.

Schore, A.N. (2003) *Affect Dysregulation and Disorder of the Self*. New York: Norton.

Schore, A.N. (2003) *Affect Regulation and Repair of the Self*. New York: Norton.

Siegel, D.J. and Solomon, M. (2013) *Healing Moments in Psychotherapy*. New York: Norton.

Wilkinson, M. (2006) *Coming Into Mind. The Mind-Brain Relationship: A Jungian Clinical Perspective*. Hove: Routledge.

EMBODIED PSYCHOTHERAPY

Judith, A. (2004) *Eastern Body, Western Mind: Psychology and the Chakra System as a Path to the Self*. New York: Random House.

Kepner, J.I. (1987) *Body Process: A Gestalt Approach to Working with the Body in Psychotherapy*. New Jersey: Gestalt Press.

Lowen, A. (1975) *Bio Energetics: The Revolutionary Therapy That Uses the Language of the Body to Heal the Problems of the Mind*. New York: Penguin Books.

Sletvold, J. (2014) *The Embodied Analyst: From Freud and Reich to Relationality*. Hove: Routledge.

Totton, N. and Edmondson, E. (2009) *Reichian Growth Work: Melting the Blocks to Life*. Monmouth: PCCS Books.

A TRANSPERSONAL PARADIGM

Assagioli, R. (1974) *The Act of Will*. Wellingborough: Turnstone Press Ltd.

Fordham, M. (1978) *Jungian Psychotherapy: A Study in Analytic Psychology*. London: Karnac.

Hillman, J. and Ventura, M. (1992) *We've Had a Hundred Years of Psychotherapy and the World's Getting Worse*. New York: HarperCollins.

Kopp, S. (1972) *If You Meet the Buddha on the Road, Kill Him! A Modern Pilgrimage Through Myth, Legend, Zen and Psychotherapy*. California: Science and Behaviour Books Inc.

Macy, J. (1991) *World as Lover, World as Self*. California: Parallax.

Moore, T. (ed.) (1990) *A Blue Fire: The Essential James Hillman*. London: Routledge.

Moore, T. (1994) *Care of the Soul: A Guide for Cultivating Depth and Sacredness in Everyday Life*. London: Harper Perennial Paperback.

Patrice, S.M. (1995) *Of Water and the Spirit: Ritual, Magic and Initiation in the Life of an African Shaman*. London: Arkana.

Plotkin, B. (2003) *Soulcraft: Crossing into the Mysteries of Nature and Psyche*. Novato: New World Library.

Rohr, R. (2004) *Adam's Return: The Five Promises of Male Initiation*. New York: Crossroad Publishing Co.

Samuels, A. (ed.) (1985) *Jung and the Post-Jungians*. London: Routledge.

Somers, B. and Marshall, H. (ed.) (2004) *The Fires of Alchemy*. Dorset: Archive Publishing.

Totton, N. (2011) *Wild Therapy: Undomesticating Inner and Outer Worlds*. Monmouth: PCCS Books.

Weller, F. (2015) *The Wild Edge of Sorrow: Rituals of Renewal and the Sacred Work of Grief*. California: North Atlantic Books.

SEXUAL VIOLATION

Ainscough, C. and Toon, K. (1993) *Breaking Free: Help for Survivors of Child Sexual Abuse*. London: Sheldon Press.

Draucker, C.B. (1992) *Counselling Survivors of Childhood Sexual Abuse*. London: Sage.

Parks, P. (1990) *Rescuing the 'Inner Child': Therapy for Adults Sexually Abused as Children*. London: Souvenir Press.

St Aubyn, E. (1992) *Bad News*. London: William Heinemann.

St Aubyn, E. (1992) *Never Mind*. London: William Heinemann.

St Aubyn, E. (1994) *Some Hope*. London: William Heinemann.

St Aubyn, E. (2006) *Mother's Milk*. London: Picador.

St Aubyn, E. (2011) *At Last*. London: Picador.

SHAME

Akhtar, S. (ed.) (2016) *Shame: Developmental, Cultural and Clinical Realms*. London: Karnac.

Bradshaw, J. (1988) *Healing the Shame that Binds You*. Florida: Health Communications Inc.

Brown, B. (2015) *Rising Strong.* London: Vermilion, Ebury Publishing.

De Young, P.A. (2015) *Understanding and Treating Chronic Shame: A Relational/Neurobiological Approach.* London: Routledge.

Jacoby, M. (1994) *Shame and the Origins of Self-esteem: A Jungian Approach.* London: Routledge.

Kaufman, G. (1980) *Shame: The Power of Caring.* Vermont: Schenkman Books Inc.

ISSUES FOR MEN AND BOYS

Bly, R. (1990) *Iron John: A Book About Men.* Shaftesbury: Element Books.

Lee, J. (1991) *At My Father's Wedding: Reclaiming Our True Masculinity.* London: Piatkus Publishing.

Lew, M. (2004) *Victims No Longer: The Classic Guide for Men Recovering from Sexual Child Abuse.* New York: Quill.

Woods, J. (ed.) (2003) *Boys Who Have Abused: Psychoanalytic Psychotherapy with Victim/Perpetrators of Sexual Abuse.* London: Jessica Kingsley.

CONSCIOUSNESS OF ISSUES OF DIFFERENCE AND DIVERSITY

Barker, M. (2013) *Rewriting the Rules: An Integrative Guide to Love, Sex and Relationships.* London: Routledge.

Davies, D. (ed.) (1996) *Pink Therapy: A Guide for Counsellors and Therapists Working with Lesbian, Gay and Bisexual Clients.* Buckingham: Open University Press.

Lowe, F. (ed.) (2014) *Thinking Space: Promoting Thinking About Race, Culture, and Diversity in Psychotherapy and Beyond.* London: Karnac.

Marshall, S. (2004) *Difference and Discrimination in Psychotherapy and Counselling.* London: Sage Publications.

McKenzie-Mavinga, I. (2009) *Black Issues in the Therapeutic Process.* Basingstoke: Palgrave Macmillan.

THE THERAPEUTIC RELATIONSHIP

Clarkson, P. (1995) *The Therapeutic Relationship in Psychoanalysis, Counselling Psychology and Psychotherapy.* London: Whurr Publishers.

Hycner, R. (1991) *Between Person and Person: Towards a Dialogical Psychotherapy.* New York: Gestalt Press.

Kahn, M. (1997) *Between Therapist and Client: The New Relationship.* New York: Henry Holt.

IMAGINATION, CREATIVE LANGUAGE AND POETRY

Astley, N. and Robertson-Pearce, P. (2007) *Soulfood: Nourishing Poems for Starved Minds.* Northumberland: Bloodaxe Books Ltd.

Bettelheim, B. (1975) *The Uses of Enchantment: The Meaning and Importance of Fairy Tales.* New York: Penguin Books.

Holmes, J. (2016) *The Therapeutic Imagination: Using Literature to Deepen Psychodynamic Understanding and Enhance Empathy.* London: Routledge.

Lakoff, G. and Johnson, M. (1980) *Metaphors We Live By.* Chicago: University of Chicago Press.

VARIOUS

Amen, D.G. and Smith, D.C. (2010) *Unchain Your Brain: 10 Steps to Breaking the Addictions That Steal Your Life.* California: Mindworks Press.

Coren, A. (2001) *Short Term Psychotherapy: A Psychodynamic Approach*. Basingstoke: Palgrave Macmillan.

Freshwater, D. and Robertson, C. (2002) *Emotions and Needs: Core Concepts in Therapy*. Buckingham: Open University Press.

Gomez, L. (1997) *An Introduction to Object Relations*. London: Free Association Books.

Greenspan, M. (2003) *Healing Through the Dark Emotions: The Wisdom of Grief, Fear and Despair*. Boston: Shambala Publications Inc.

Kottler, J.A. and Carlson, J. (2003) *Bad Therapy: Master Therapists Share Their Worst Failures*. Hove: Brunner-Routledge.

Laing, R.D. (1971) *The Politics of the Family and Other Essays*. London: Tavistock Publications.

McGilchrist, I. (2009) *The Master and His Emissary: The Divided Brain and the Making of the Western World*. London: Yale University Press.

Mitchell, J. (ed.) (1986) *The Selected Melanie Klein*. New York: Penguin Books.

Mitchell, S.A. and Black, J.M. (1995) *Freud and Beyond: A History of Psychoanalytic Thought*. London: HarperCollins.

Winnicott, D.W. (1964) *The Child, the Family and the Outside World*. London: Pelican Books.

Winnicott, D.W. (1965) *The Family and Individual Development*. London: Tavistock Publications.

Winnicott, D.W. (1971) *Playing and Reality*. London: Tavistock Publications.

Winnicott, D.W. (1975) *Through Paediatrics to Psycho-analysis*. London: Hogarth Press & the Insitute of Psycho-analysis.

INDEX

aggressive behaviour
    see angry behaviour
        case study
ambivalence, benefits from
        145–147
Anda, Robert 178
anger, re-experiencing as
        positive 139–145
angry behaviour case study
    assertiveness without anger,
        modelling 33–34
    discharging stress
        hormones 42–43
    family background 17–18
    helping men with 16
    narratives told
        through 15–16
    non-violent expression of
        anger 37–42
    psychoanalytic theory/
        practice 36
    recalling in session 34–36
    risk assessment for
        sessions 17
    sexual abuse by mother 18
    writing used to deal with
        angry feelings 43–46
antisocial behaviour see angry
        behaviour case study
anxiety of therapist for client
        105–109
Arnold, Matthew 70
assertiveness
    and family background
        199–202
    without anger,
        modelling 33–34
attachment-based work
    attachment to carers,
        lack of 100

past, addressing the 12
primary maternal
    preoccupation 107
attentiveness to bodily
    sensations 66
autonomic nervous system
    (ANS) 19–22
    discharging stress
        hormones 42–43
    on/off system 19–22
    reliving trauma during
        session 111
    see also bodies

being, focus on 13
beyond, the, in integrative
        therapy approach 11, 13
bodies
    attentiveness to bodily
        sensations 30–32,
        66
    autonomic nervous system
        (ANS) 19–22, 42–43,
        111
    body-focused trauma
        work 13
    body language of client 99
    changes in during session
        195, 197
    dissociation, benefits of
        explaining 60–61
    empathy, learning 62–63
    mapping the body 198, 199
    on/off system 19–22
    past, addressing the 12
    physical contact during
        crisis in session
        110–111
    picking behaviour 120,
        121, 125

positive feelings, physical
    sensations of 66
teddy bear, positive
    memories of
        109–118
vulnerability, cutting off
    from 78–79
Body Keeps the Score, The (Van
    Der Kolk) 178
body language of client 99
boundaries, yearning for/
    dreading 171, 172
brain
    triune 112
    watching others and 62–63
breathing, slow 185, 198,
    199

case studies
    use of in book 10–11
    see also angry behaviour
        case study;
        dissociation case
        study; mental illness,
        severe, case study;
        music; paedophile
        ring case study; safety,
        psychological and
        emotional, case study;
        vulnerability, cutting
        off from, case study
chaotic life of client 99–101
child abuse
    costs of 178
    see also sexual abuse
childhood
    suppression of emotions 81
    see also families; safety,
        psychological and
        emotional, case study

children, contact with in later
    life 79–80
choices, difficulties making
    23, 24–25, 26–27
Ciaghero, L. 62
confidentiality of sessions
    26–28, 33–34
containment, yearning
    for/dreading 171,
    172
Corbett, Alan 53, 64–65
countertransference 165,
    186–187, 211
    defined 14
    present, addressing the 13
creativity
    attentiveness to bodily
        sensations 66
    drawing 88–90, 94–95
    making room for 13
    music 61–68, 144–145
    songwriting 68
    tattoos 45
    teddy bear as talking to
        client 116–117
    writing used to deal
        with angry
        feelings 43–46
crying client, connecting with
    186–188

Davies, J.M. 168–169
decision-making, difficulties
    with 23, 24–25,
    26–27
dissociation case study
    crying client, connecting
        with 186–188
    episodes of in session
        54–60, 171–172
    explaining, benefits
        of 60–61
    fugue state after assault
        193–194
    grounding strategies 68,
        198
    recollection of triggering
        event 54–60

distrust
    clients' desire to open
        up and 52
    clients' initial 48
drawing 88–90, 94–95

ego defences 71
    breaking through in
        session 84–91
    dismantling 78
    making light of
        trauma 75–78
    needs of others, focus on
        71–75, 82–83
embodied reactions see bodies,
    physiology of
emotions
    children, contact with in
        later life 79–80
    see also safety, psychological
        and emotional;
        suppression of
        emotions
empathy, learning 62–63

families
    background of clients
        17–18, 48–49,
        81, 97, 122, 123,
        165–166, 188–189,
        199–202
    difficulties in 72–75
    divisions in families 18–19
    fathers, lack of connection
        with 128
    letter to father 144
    past, addressing the 12
    reconnection with
        son 91–93
fathers see families
feelings
    attentiveness to bodily
        sensations 30–32
    lost, feeling of being 136
    patterns of feelings
        between clients and
        therapists 168–169
    positive feelings, physical
        sensations of 66

recording 198
    writing used to deal with
        anger 43–46
first impressions of clients 48
Flint, F.S 119
Frawley, M.G. 168–169
freezing when reminded of
    trauma 24, 25

gender identity case study
    ambivalence, benefits from
        145–147
    anger, re-experiencing as
        positive 139–144
    changing, thoughts about
        132–140
    current background
        situation 121–122
    difficulties revealing issues
        123–126
    family background 122, 123
    first session 120–125
    grooming and abuse
        by guitar teacher
        126–132
    incident from past recalled
        in session 122–123
    lateness of client to first
        session 120, 146
    letter to abuser 144
    letter to father 144
    lost, feeling of being 136
    music, returning
        to 144–145
    newspaper coverage of
        abuser 129
    pain and self-doubt as
        recurring after abuse
        129–130
    picking behaviour 120,
        121, 125
    secrets, revealing of by
        clients 125–126
gestalt therapy
    attentiveness to bodily
        sensations 30–32
    present, addressing the 13
Goose Girl story 213–215

hero, being the *see* vulnerability,
    cutting off from
Hopkins, Gerard Manley 148

imagination
    drawing 88–90, 94–95
    making room for 13
    reimagining of assault
        scene 202–209
    songwriting 68
    tattoos 45
    teddy bear as talking to
        client 116–117
    writing used to deal with
        angry feelings 43–46
imperfection, accepting 93
infecting the therapist, clients
    as 107–108
inhibition, capacity for 49–50
integrative therapy
    approach 11–13
internal splitting 88–90

Jung, C.G. 105, 107–108

larger stories, reflection on 13
Levine, Peter 53
lost, feeling of being 136

mapping the body 198, 199
maternal preoccupation 107
mental illness, severe,
        case study
    adapting therapy services
        160–162
    angry behaviour towards
        suspected abuser 149,
        151–154
    boundaries, yearning for/
        dreading 171, 172
    breakdown of client/
        therapist alliance
        167–172
    conflict, therapist's,
        at client's new
        relationship 162–167
    dissociation episode in
        session 171–172

end of client's relationship,
    impact of 173–177
ending therapy, client as
    174–177
family background
    149–150, 165–166
first impression of
    client 149
gradual changes in
    client 162
NHS mental health
    services 153–154,
    156–158
paedophile ring, client's
    experience of
    150–151
patterns of feelings
    between clients and
    therapists 168–169
referral to therapy,
    background to 149
safe place,
    sessions as 159–160
self-soothing
    behaviour 158
therapists, emotional
    and psychological
    impact on 154–156,
    177–179
military metaphors 77–78
Miller, Alice 82
mirror neurons 62
Mitchell, Phil 9
mothers
    primary maternal
        preoccupation 107
    sexual abuse by 18
    see also families
music
    as resource for traumatised
        clients 53–54
    returning to 144–145
    sharing in sessions 61–68
    songwriting 68
mystical aspects to
    existence 13

narratives *see* case studies
nauseous, clients feeling,
    during sessions 109
needs of others, focus on
    70–71, 75, 82–83
nervous system
    discharging stress
        hormones 42–43
    on/off system 19–22
    past, addressing the 12
    reliving trauma during
        session 111
    see also bodies
NHS mental health services
    153–154, 156–158

observation of others 62–63
Ogden, P. 203
on/off system 19–22
organised abuse case study
    see paedophile ring
    case study

paedophile ring case study
    adapting therapy services
        160–162
    angry behaviour towards
        suspected abuser 149,
        151–154
    boundaries, yearning for/
        dreading 171, 172
    breakdown of client/
        therapist alliance
        167–172
    conflict, therapist's,
        at client's new
        relationship 162–167
    dissociation episode in
        session 171–172
    end of client's relationship,
        impact of 173–177
    ending therapy, client as
        174–177
    experience of, client's
        150–151
    family background
        149–150, 165–166

first impression of
    client 149
gradual changes in
    client 162
NHS mental health
    services 153–154,
    156–158
patterns of feelings
    between clients and
    therapists 168–169
referral to therapy,
    background to 149
safe place,
    sessions as 159–160
self-soothing
    behaviour 158
therapists, emotional
    and psychological
    impact on 154–156,
    177–179
parasympathetic nervous
    system 19–22
past, addressing the
    approaches used 12
    difficulties linking
        past/present
        experiences 100
    integrative therapy
        approach 11, 12
    recalling of angry
        behaviour in
        session 34–36
    see also families
physiology
    attentiveness to bodily
        sensations 30–32, 66
    autonomic nervous system
        (ANS) 19–22, 42–43,
        111
    body language of client 99
    changes in during session
        195, 197
    dissociation, benefits of
        explaining 60–61
    empathy, learning 62–63
    mapping the body 198, 199
    on/off system 19–22
    past, addressing the 12

physical contact during
    crisis in session
    110–111
picking behaviour 120,
    121, 125
positive feelings, physical
    sensations of 66
teddy bear, positive
    memories of
    109–118
vulnerability, cutting off
    from 78–79
picking behaviour 120, 121,
    125
polyvagal system 187
Porges, S.W. 187
pornography, early
    exposure to 18–19
positive feelings, physical
    sensations of 66
post-traumatic stress disorder
    case study
    assertiveness and family
        background
        199–202
    avoidance of first session
        181
    bodily changes during
        sessions 195, 197
    breathing, slow 185, 198
    bullied child, parents'
        reaction to 209–210
    conflict, improved ability to
        deal with 212–213
    crying client, connecting
        with 186–188
    dissociation 193–194, 198
    family background
        188–189, 199–202
    feelings, recording 198
    fugue state after
        assault 193–194
    Goose Girl story 213–215
    kindness to self,
        improvement in 212
    mapping the body 198,
        199

not wanting to be there,
    client as 182–185
present of ball to therapist
    210–211
referral to therapy
    180–181
reimagining of assault
    scene 202–209
reporting assault 196,
    215–218
sexual assault, client's
    account of 189–193
shaking and crying as part
    of recovery 198
shame and humiliation,
    clues towards
    184–185
symptoms, client's 194
techniques to help with
    197–198, 215
time-limited work 180,
    181, 197, 210, 217
work background 188–189
see also trauma
present, addressing the
    approaches used 12–13
    attentiveness to bodily
        sensations 30–32
    difficulties linking past/
        present experiences
        100
    integrative therapy
        approach 11, 12–13
    recalling of angry
        behaviour in
        session 34–36
primary maternal
    preoccupation 107
psychoanalytic theory/
    practice
    angry behaviour 36
    past, addressing the 12, 36
    primary maternal
        preoccupation 107

rape 50–52
reassurance from therapists
    135

recreation of abuse dynamics
    with others 22–24
resourcing
    music 53–54
    of traumatised
        clients 52–53
Rilke, Rainer Maria 15
risk assessment 17
Rizzollatti, G. 62

safety, psychological and
        emotional, case study
    anxiety of therapist for
        client 105–109
    attachment to carers,
        lack of 100
    babies, lack of for 97
    body language of client 99
    chaotic life of
        client 99–101
    children, impact on of lack
        of safety 98
    experience of
        therapy 97–98
    family background 97
    infecting the therapist,
        clients as 107–108
    past/present experiences,
        difficulties
        linking 100
    physical contact during
        crisis in session
        110–111
    positive memories 104–105
    primary maternal
        preoccupation 107
    revisiting trauma/
        retraumatising, fine
        line between 103–104
    safe place,
        sessions as 159–160
    sexual abuse at residential
        school 102–103
    teddy bear, positive
        memories of
        104–105, 109–118
    value of sessions for
        client 101–102

secrets, revealing of by clients
    125–126
self-regulation, capacity
    for 49–50
self-soothing behaviour 158
severe symptoms see mental
    illness, severe, case study
sexual abuse
    children, contact with in
        later life 79–80
    and gender identity,
        thoughts about
        changing 132–140
    grooming and abuse
        by guitar teacher
        126–132
    letter to abuser 144
    by mother 18
    pain and self-doubt as
        recurring 129–130
    patterns of feelings
        between clients and
        therapists 168–169
    pornography, early
        exposure to 18–19
    rape 50–52
    recreation of abuse
        dynamics with
        others 22–24
    at residential school
        102–103
    susceptibility to and fathers,
        lack of connection
        with 128
    taboo subject, male sexual
        violation seen as 9,
        158
    see also angry behaviour;
        dissociation; gender
        identity; paedophile
        ring case study;
        post-traumatic stress
        disorder case study;
        safety, psychological
        and emotional;
        vulnerability, cutting
        off from

slow breathing 185, 198,
    199
soldier metaphors 77–78
solution-focused work 13
soulful aspects to existence 13
spiritual aspects to
    existence 13
splitting 88–90
Stevenson, Robert Louis 96
stories see case studies
stress hormones
    discharging 42–43
    see also autonomic nervous
        system (ANS); bodies
stuck, being 25
suicide, risk of 64–66
superficial interaction during
        sessions 80–81, 83–84
    breaking through 84–91
supervision
    conflict, therapist's,
        at client's new
        relationship 162–167
    emotional and
        psychological impact
        on therapists 177–179
    positive aspects of client's
        life 53, 61
    secrets, revealing of by
        clients 125–126
    usefulness of session
        for client,
        checking 101–102
    worry of therapist for client
        106–108
suppression of emotions case
        study 70–71
    breaking through in
        session 84–91
    childhood 81
    children, contact with in
        later life 79–80
    dark parts of life,
        drawing 94–95
    dismantling ego
        defences 78
    drawing 88–90, 94–95
    ego defences 71–78

imperfection, accepting 93
making light of trauma 75–78, 82
needs of others, focus on 70–71, 75, 82–83
physical signs of 78–79
prep school, going away to 81–82
reconnection with son 91–93
son as prompt to examine 83
splitting 88–90
superficial interaction during sessions 80–81, 83–84
sympathetic nervous system 19–22

taboo subject, male sexual violation seen as 9, 158
tattoos 45
teddy bear, positive memories of 104–105
crisis during session, use during 109–118
theoretical models
countertransference 14
integrative therapy approach 11–13
transference 14
therapy practices
issues brought to 73
therapy/therapists
adaptation of therapy services to clients' needs 160–162
anger, clients, positive impact on therapist 141
anxiety of therapist for client 105–109
breakdown of alliance with client 167–172
conflict at client's new relationship 162–167

emotional and psychological impact on 154–156, 177–179
expectations of clients 158–159
helpful factors in therapy 9–10
infecting the therapist, clients as 107–108
lost, feeling of being 136
as modelling infant care 97–98
nauseous, clients feeling, during sessions 109
patterns of feelings between clients and therapists 168–169
reassurance from therapists 135
safe place, sessions as 159–160
value of sessions for client 101–102
time-limited work
present, addressing the 13
see also post-traumatic stress disorder case study
timing of insights by therapists 39
toys, positive memories of 104–105
crisis during session, use during 109–118
transference
defined 14
present, addressing the 13
trauma
body-focused trauma work 13
dissociation, benefits of explaining 60–61
freezing when reminded of 24, 25
making light of 75–78, 82
nervous system and reliving trauma during session 111

past, addressing the 12
resourcing of traumatised clients 52–53
revisiting/retraumatising, fine line between 103–104
teddy bear, positive memories of 104–105
see also post-traumatic stress disorder case study
Treating the Adult Survivor of Childhood Sexual Abuse: A Psychoanalytic Perspective (Davies and Frawley) 168–169
triune brain 112
trust
distrust, clients' initial 48
open up, clients' desire to 52

value of sessions for client 101–102
Van Der Kolk, Bessel 178
vignettes see case studies
violent behaviour
narratives told through 15–16
non-violent expression of anger 37–42
recalling in session 29–30, 34–36
see also angry behaviour case study
vulnerability, cutting off from, case study
breaking through in session 84–91
childhood 81
children, contact with in later life 79–80
dark parts of life, drawing 94–95
dismantling ego defences 78
drawing 88–90, 94–95
ego defences 71–78

vulnerability, cutting off
from, case study
(*cont.*)
imperfection, accepting 93
making light of trauma
75–78, 82
needs of others, focus
on 70–71, 75, 82–83
physical signs of 78–79
prep school, going away
to 81–82
reconnection with
son 91–93
son as prompt to
examine 83
splitting 88–90
superficial interaction
during sessions
80–81, 83–84
suppression of emotions
70–71
watching others 62–63
Whitman, Walt 47
worry of therapist for client
105–109
writing used to deal with angry
feelings 43–46, 144